ART HERITAGE OF ASSAM

ART HERITAGE OF ASSAM

BY

R.D. CHOUDHURY

ARYAN BOOKS INTERNATIONAL
NEW DELHI

Art Heritage of Assam

Published in 1998 by:
ARYAN BOOKS INTERNATIONAL
4378/4B, Pooja Apartments
4, Ansari Road, Darya Ganj
New Delhi-110002 (India)

ISBN-81-7305-147-X

Computer Typeset at Aryan Books International, New Delhi.
Printed in India at Print Perfect, New Delhi.

Presented
to
Monoj and Mubin

Contents

Preface

The study of art history in Assam began as early as 1902. Dr. T. Bloch, the British scholar-administrator of the Archaeological Survey of India took the initiative to visit some sites of archaeological interest. During the winter season in 1902, he visited Hayagria Mādhava temple at Hajo, a temple of the Koch King of 1505 śaka (1583-84 A.D.) Kārengghar, multistoreyed royal building of Āhom king, at Gargāon, and Dimapur, the capital of the Kachārī kings (ARASI, 102, 1903, reprint 1990, p. 22). During the course of his visit for conservation he studied the architectural and sculptural aspect of the ruins and monuments at the places. In 1904-05 report of ARASI, (reprint, 1990), Dr. Bloch has mentioned about the ruined temple at Śadiyā (Tāmreśwarī temple), which are completely eroded by the Brahmaputra leaving no trace of the temple now, the terracotta plaques depicting birds, men, animals, flowers and geometrical pattern, Dimapur ruins, especially the 'Chessman' pillars and bifurcated columns, wooden pillars of Garo hills of "Chessman" type, as he visited these places or area during the course of his exploration and conservation.

No report has been made in the report of ARASI 1905-6. Only a casual reference of the work of the conservation in Assam is made. In the report of 1906-07, Bloch has made a detailed description of the sites he visited. He has quoted the letter of Mr. Manahan, dated 18th January, 1906 and gave a description of the sculptured stone blocks and architectural members of the old temple, discovered while digging for the construction of the Deputy Commissioner's additional building at Tezpur. He also mentions about ruins of Bāmunīpāhār at Dimāpur, ruins at Kāsomārī, ruined temple at Śadiyā (Tāmreśwarī temple) and Biṣmak nagar, to the east of Śadiyā. He visited all these sites of ruined temple in 1905 and published a long report along with photographs of a number of terracotta plaques, architectural pieces, sculptural pieces of the old temple structure of the pre-Āhom age. Thus, it is Dr. Bloch, who opened our eyes through his illustrated reports on the study on the art heritage of Assam.

These reports on exploration and conservation were on the ruined temples, stones sculptures and icons, which are the basic elements of art heritage. But these reports deal with the art and architecture of Assam and not the pre- or proto-History. R.M. Nath, and B.K. Barua, in their works made discussion with illustrations. K.L. Barua and P.C. Choudhury, like Nath and Barua, referred to the Annual Reports of the Archaeological Survey of India, while writing their books. Nath did a lot of field work and contributed a series of articles in the *Journal of the Assam Research Society*.

After a gap of some years, in the last twenty five years, R.D. Choudhury (the humble self), N.P. Choudhury, P. Sharma and Manoranjan Datta has made systematic studies on art and architecture of Assam. Presently H.N. Datta is working on the subject. A.K. Sharma has also published his report on the excavation at Bhāitbārī in the form of a book.

The earliest evidence of the art history of Assam can be seen at Śrī Sūrya Pāhār in the Western part of Assam on the South bank of the Brahmaputra. Here two votive *stūpas* bearing the early characteristic feature prove the architectural artistic activities of the 100 A.D. This is discussed in one or two papers included in this book. The sculptural art reached its zenith by 12th century A.D. as in the neighbouring Bengal and Bihar region. The icons or sculptures of Assam belonging to the period ranging from 6th to 12th century, can be grouped in the eastern Indian medieval school, having very close relation to art of Bengal and Bihar.

The sculptures belonging to the Āhom period, are executed with folk elements and not in classical style. So, there is a marked difference between the sculptures of the Āhom period and pre-Āhom period in the matter of style. Though the pre-Āhom sculptures are included in eastern Indian mediaeval school, or they bear post Gupta style, some regional variations can be noticed in some sculptures, particularly, from Deopānī-Sarupathār region.

All types of materials, such as, rock, stone, wood, bronze, brass, and clay, were used for making sculptures or icons. H.N. Datta has noticed a wooden image of Vishnu of c. 8th century style at Sarupathār region. However, to confirm that c. 14 test is necessary. The illustrated manuscript of Assam portray some aspects of the medieval Assamese Society. We do not get any manuscript belonging to the pre-Āhom period, though we get reference to the existence of the paintings in the pre-Āhom period. The manuscript paintings of Assam can be treated as a separate school in All India basis, because of its distinctive style. However, in this book no article on paintings have been included. Regarding the style of temple architecture belonging to pre-Āhom period, though not a single temple of that period is extant today in standing positions, due to fury of the powerful earthquakes, yet we can have a fair idea about its style from the fragmentary architectural parts. The style of the temple have a close relation with that of Central India of Indo Aryan style with variation. But the temples of the Āhom periods were constructed in Indo Aryan formula under heavy influence of Bengal sultan style of late mediaeval period.

The present book contains research papers on the sculpture, iconography and architectural remains in the state of Assam.

I apologize for any mistake, that may have crept into the book while making my observation or otherwise.

I am thankful to Mr. Vikas Arya of Aryan Books International, for taking up the work of publication of the book. My thanks are also due to Shri R.C. Das, Curator, Assam State Museum, Sri Gautam Kr. Sarma, Photographer and Sri Sarat Goswami, Darkroom Attendent, A.S.M. for supplying the photographs of the book.

I shall be failing on my duty, if I do not express my thanks to Miss Cabini Kakati, of the Directorate of Museum, who does all the typing works of my letters and papers etc.

R.D. Choudhury

List Of Illustrations

1

Antiquities of Śrī Sūrya Pāhār: A Source of Early History of Kāmarūpa

Śrī Sūrya Pāhār, located at a distance of about 14 km East from Goalpara town, can be reached by the Goalpara Dudhnoi-via-Mornoi road. The exact site of the antiquities is about a mile West of the Sainik School, Mornoi, on the slope of the Śrī Sūrya Pāhār.

There is a modern tin-shed sanctuary and an ordinary Assam-type house of the Śrī Sūrya Pāhār committee. Now-a-days in good weather any vehicle can reach this place. Towards a little north on the slope of the hill a row of rock-cut sculptures, a few rock-cut caverns and a few votive *stūpas* are seen. The site is full of huge boulders under which a small spring flows. Reaching the site one first faces the row of rock-cut sculptures, which are as many as eight images, in *samapādasthānaka* attitude. The first image of the row (from left to right) is a four-armed male figure representing Śiva. The upper hands hold a *sarpa* and a *triśulā* while the lower ones appear to show *varadamudrā*, and an *āyudha*, i.e., weapon. Below the god Nandī is shown in crude form. The next two-armed image represents Viṣṇu holding *gadā* and *cakra* and bedecked, with a long *varadamudrā*. The third image represents four-handed Śiva holding the same object as the other Śiva image.

To the left of the third image there is a little blank space, where traces of an almost erased image are noticed. This was an image of a Ṛiṣi holding a *kamaṇḍalu*. This figure may clearly be observed in the photography published by P.D. Choudhury along with his article in 1960.[1] Towards further right are seen the other five rock-cut images. Among them the first three two-armed imaged represent Viṣṇu. Each of them holds *gadā* and *cakra* in the hands. The fourth image possibly represents Hari-Hara, holding in its upper right hand a *triśulā,* and in the upper left a *cakra*. The lower right hand is in *varadamudrā*, while the lower left holds an indistinct object. The god wears a *vanamālā*. No *vāhana* is shown. The last image of the row possibly represents Viṣṇu. All the images have suffered badly from weathering effect, and hence, the details of the sculptures have been fairly damaged.

To the right of this row of sculpture across the streamline there are two rock-cut miniature caves, inside of one of which is seen (not very clearly) a small *Śiva liṅga*. The lower portion of one of these caves is under the sand. The *Śiva liṅga*, which is also partially under sand accumulation, possibly was placed later as the stone quality of the exposed *liṅga* differs from that of the caves.

Just above the rock which carries the row of icons described above three *Śiva liṅgas* are seen. The *liṅga* portions of these objects however, are almost broken off. Above these broken *Śiva liṅgas* is seen a twelve-armed *sthānaka* icon of some deity on a separate rock facing to the east. The deity wears a *kirītamukuṭa* (?) and above the head is seen a seven-hooded snake canopying the deity. The *kaṭivastra* worn by the deity almost reaches the ankles. A *vanamālā* is also seen on the body of the deity. It is difficult to know about the precise identity of the icon. P.D. Choudhury, who visited this site in 1960, identifies it with Manasā. From the photograph published by Choudhury[2] along with his paper, it becomes clear that the icon in question represents some female deity with raised breasts. But G.N. Bhuyān[3] is of the opinion that since Choudhury white-washed the icons of the site before taking the photograph, in order to bring the prominence of the sculptures, it is highly possible that there must have been some wrong. But in the photograph of the same image published by R.M. Nāth[4] in 1948, the female breasts can be traced. Nāth has also identified it with Manasā. Bhuyān, however, thinks the present image is nothing but the representation of Ananta, a form of Viṣṇu. The image in question can be compared with the twelve-armed male figure[5] from Sonarang district Dacca, Bangladesh. As not a single *āyudha* held in the hands of the deity is identifiable and as there is a controversy with regard to the sex of the divinity, the problem should be kept open at this stage.

P.D. Choudhury[6] has said that the five rock-cut sculptures chiselled just below on a separate rock, which have been already described along with other three images, one representing Viṣṇu and the other Śiva in the same row, should be regarded as female figure and he has identified them with Durgā, wife of Śiva. He has further commented that some scholars have wrongly identified a few images as those of Bodhisattvas. Possibly, Choudhury made this comment in regard to a remark of S. Kataki.[7] It appears that the identifications of both the scholars are totally wrong. Bhuyān[8] has rightly pointed out their mistakes.

Stylistically, this group of rock-cut sculptures may be assigned to *c.* 8ht or 8th century A.D. and as such, we are in agreement with Bhuyān who has placed them in *c.* 8th century.[9] This row of sculptures can be compared with rock-cut sculptures from Bengal illustrated by R.D. Banerji.[10]

Above these sculptures behind the controversial twelve-handed deity, a few rock-cut images representing Viṣṇu and Gaṇeśa are noticed. Stylistically, they may be placed in the same period, i.e., *c.* 8th-9th century A.D.

Further, above at the top on a separate huge rock two miniature votive *stūpas* are seen. Each of them is about 3' high. At the base of one of these three circles are noticed. The other has possibly two such circles at its base. On the tapering portion of each *stūpa* is seen a raised square based hole, which, it appears, is partially damaged. Towards a little north a half done similar miniature votive *stūpa* is noticed.

One can visit a natural cave towards a little south of this site where two Jaina images can be seen. The site is about ten minutes walk. On the way, a rock-cut monolithic miniature votive *stūpa* is found. It is bigger in size than the two others described earlier. At the top of this *stūpa* there is no trace of raised based-hole, etc. It is in a better state of preservation.

A little south of this *stūpa* is located the natural cave formed by two huge boulders. Inside is seen three rock-cut sculptures on the northern wall of the cave. Of these three images two represent Ādinatha or Ṛaṣabhānatha in *Kāyotsarga* attitude. The first image (135 cms high) has a *dharma-cakra* symbol below the feet of the deity, while the second figure (93 cms in height) shows a Ṛṣabha symbol at the feet. In both the cases the deity is made to stand naked in *samapādasthānaka* attitude with hands banging down below the knee level (Katyabilambita). Kataki[11] and Choudhury[12] have wrongly identified them as *dvārapāla* and Śiva respectively. Recently, a seated rock-cut image of Ṛṣabhanātha have been discovered at the place[13a].

The figures are in relief (not very high) and stylistically they may belong to *c.* 8th-9th century. Bhuyān[13] has also offered the same views with regard to the identifications of the images and their dates. The third image represents Gaṇeśa which may be dated on stylistic ground about the same period, if not later. On the eastern wall of this natural cave is seen an inscribed line of letters. P.D. Choudhury[14] and D.C. Sircar who made repeated attempts to read these obliterated letters have suggested that "the writings contain only some names of devotees or pilgrims and nothing else". They conjecture that these pilgrims visited this rock place which looks like a cave and offered worship invoking the blessings of Lord Śiva. On palaeographical ground, Choudhury says the inscribed letters may be dated in 8th-9th century.

Proceeding a little south-east from the house of the Śrī Sūrya Pāhār Temple Committee, a tank can be reached. To the right bank of the tank there is a tree under which is a small modern shrine with C.I. sheet roof. In this shrine an *Āditya-cakra* sculptured on a block of stone is noticed. Here Kāsyapa is shown seated in a cross-legged posture in the middle and around him are seen miniature figures of twelve Ādityas, sons of Aditi, wife of Kāsyapa.[15] The details of the images cannot be recognized owing to their smallness. On the other hand, all the images are under a thick layer of vermilion. However, a close observation reveals that the centrally seated male figure representing Kāsyapa is four-faced and four-armed. The *āyudhas* held in the hands cannot be recognized. The fourth face is not shown and it is supposed to be hidden. Below the seat of the god is depicted something. Possibly, it is his *vāhana* representing a swan. Each of the twelve miniature figures seated cross-legged is depicted one-faced and two-armed holding some object, possibly lotuses. This *Āditya-cakra* is sculptured in the same way as the *Navagraha-cakra* from Khiching, illustrated by J.N. Banerjea.[16]

However, the theme of our sculpture is quite different from Khiching *Navagraha-cakra*. As it appears, the *Āditya-cakra* in question was possibly used as a ceiling slab of a temple.[17] It may be noted that in that site old bricks and brickbats of the pre-Āhom style are lying scattered. In many ruined temple sites, in the pre-Āhom age, a *Viśva-padma,* i.e., a huge lotus inside a circle on a huge slab of stone used as ceiling slab of the original temple is noticed. It cannot be ruled out that the present slab containing the *Āditya-cakra* was used ceiling slab of such a temple in lieu of the common *Viśva-padma* motif. In that case it may be inferred that this piece of *Āditya-cakra*, on stylistic consideration (which can be placed in a period not earlier than 9th-10th century A.D.) was used as a ceiling slab of Sūrya temple after which the Śrī Sūrya Pāhār might have been designated.

In the pre-Āhom period Sūrya cult was popular in this locality. We find a stone *dvāra-śirapatti* showing some solar deities, a *dvāra-sākhā* showing some *avatāras* of Viṣṇu and a *dehalī.* All these three architectural pieces belong to a *dvāra* of a temple. These three pieces were dug out from a temple site, except one *dvāra-sākhā* at the site itself, by the local people of Choudhurīpārā of Marnoi, about a mile east of Śrī Sūrya Pāhār. Now all these pieces have been lying neglected in front of the Choudhurīpārā *nāmghar.* The middle seated cross-legged figures on the *śirapatti* is sadly mutilated. However, traces of lotus on either side of the figure shows that it possibly represents Sūrya. On either side of this middle figure, are seen eight seated figures in a row. All these miniature figures are shown as two-handed and as holding lotuses. The last two figures on either side of the row possibly represent female divinities, of which the extreme right and extreme left figures represent some four-armed ones, holding something in the hands. The *dvāra-sākha* shows the figure (from lower level upwards) of Kūrma, Matsya, Parśurāma, Balarāma and Rāma, *avatāras* of Viṣṇu, and a standing male figure holding lotuses in his two hands which is evidently the figure of Sūrya. The precise identities of the figures shown in the *śirapatti* are not clear. However, it is sure that the *dvāra* belonged to some ruined temple in the same locality dedicated to some solar deity. Stylistically, these architectural pieces may belong to *c.* 10th century or so.

The medium-size black basalt image of Sūrya of beautiful execution, preserved in another *nāmghar* of the locality proves the popularity of Sūrya worship in this region in the pre-Āhom period. Stylistically, the image may belong to *c.* 11th century. The image was discovered during the erosion of the southern bank of a canal of the Brahmaputra. In the past, it is learnt, the main course of the Brahmaputra used to touch Marnoi. Now this canal is dead and the main current of the Brahmaputra flows a little north of Marnoi. Hence, the place is named after the dead canal, i.e., Marnoi.

On the other side of the Śrī Sūrya Pāhār, on the right side of the P.W.D. road from Śrī Sūrya Pāhār archaeological site to Goalpara town, two votive *stūpas* are noticed. They are also sculptured in the same way. In the vicinity of Śrī Sūrya Pāhār at Dek-dhowā, Nandeśvar Devālaya, Bāmun Pāhār, etc,. remains can be noticed. From the nature of the finds, it appears that they may belong to a later period than the Sūrya Pāhār relics.[18] However, the ruins of the añcharatna temple near the Pañcharatnaghāt of the Brahmaputra may belong almost to the same period to which the Sūrya Pāhār relics belong. At this place at the foot of the hill at present there is a modern temple. Around it remains of pre-Āhom period are noticed. A huge Gaurīpīṭha of a damaged *Śiva liṅga* cut out from a rock can still be seen in site. Possibly, it was the main icon of the temple, which is in complete ruins now. The *Chāitya* type dotted design on stone employed in the temple lying at the site recalls architectural motifs of 6th century, or even earlier period.

Just above the temple on the slope of the hill another votive *stūpa* is seen. Towards a little north-west at a lower level, in the same site, a peculiar monolithic design representing possibly the base of a *dvajastambha* is seen. All these show that Brahmanical and Buddhist faiths did exist there as in Śrī Sūrya Pāhār.

Two small rock-cut caverns are seen on a rock facing the river Brahmāputra about half a km east of Pañcharatna-ghāt on the right side of the national highway. A flight of steps also can be traced linking the entrance of one of the caverns. A similar cavern is seen in a rock on the same bank of the river just near the Pāglātak modern temple. Across the Brahmāputra just opposite to this site similar rock-cut caverns numbering about four with a flight of steps can be seen on the Jogīghopā hill. A few of them are facing the river. All these miniature caves are almost similar to the ones at Śrī Sūrya Pāhār noticed above.

Recently a terracotta plaque (13½ x 7½ cms) was discovered at Sūrya Pāhār, which is now in the Assam State Museum.

The above description of the remains at *Śrī Sūrya Pāhār* amply proves that in the pre-Āhom period there were also some pockets of Buddhism and Jainism. The sculptural style shows that the pocket of Jainism and the popular Brahmanical faith existed in the locality in 8th-9th century A.D. and the latter continued also in subsequent periods. The votive *stūpas,* particularly those chiselled above the row of the images of Śiva, Viṣnu, etc., and the twelve-armed deity, possibly may be placed in the early Christian centuries on stylistic consideration. These votive *stūpas* cannot be placed be placed in the period to which the images of the site belong. For, the votive *stūpas* of 8th-9th century or 10th-11th century bears relief of the images of Buddha normally. As for example, a stone votive *stūpa* from Bihar, now being preserved in the Assam State Museum, belonging to 8th-9th century A.D. bears on all the four sides a Buddha image in relief. Another two piece of sculptured stone show votive *stūpa* design on the body of which are seen Buddha images. In both the cases, unlike Śrī Sūrya Pāhār votive stūpas, the upper portions of the *stūpa* are pointed and the first one bears a chitra design, which can very well be seen in some of the Pāla sculptures. On the other hand, the upper portion of the votive *stūpa* of our discussion is tapering. It appears, therefore, that S.K. Saraswati[19] has rightly placed them (the first two) in *c.* 100 A.D. or 100 B.C. Even if they do not belong to the period assigned by Saraswati, they should be placed in early Christian centuries and certainly they bear the message of the Hinayana doctrine of Buddhism.[20] The existence of a pocket of Mahāyana Buddhism at the place in the Pāla period is proved by the terracotta plaque bearing two rows of stamped images of Bodhisatta, which can be compared with two plaques of terracotta showing stamped Bodhisatta images in two rows from Sabhār in the Dacca district of Bangladesh, illustrated by Bhattasali.[21]

The rock-cut caverns at Śrī Sūrya-Pāhār, Pañcharatna and Jogīghopā hill should not be of later date. S.K. Saraswati thinks that they should be assigned to an early period.[21a] The name Jogīghopā, as the local tradition goes, is derived from the caverns of the Jogīghopā hill. Jogi means a monk and ghopā means *gomphā* or *guhā,* i.e., cave. The local tradition says that in the past momks used to do their penance in these small caves. Although these look very small from below, possibly somehow one could sit inside these cave. Someone may say that these caves might be used by the spies to watch the movement of enemies through the river Brahmāputra. But, this is a wrong idea as proved by the existence of similar small caverns at the site of the rock-cut sculptures and votive *stūpas* at Śrī Sūrya Pāhār, about thirty miles off from Pañcharatna and Jogīghopā cave sites.

Similar small caves in Malabar hills near Cochin in Kerala are noticed by Y.D. Sharma[22] and others. These rock-cut caves are also very small in size like ours. In his *Vedic Antiquities* G.J. Dubreuil pleads for a Vedic origin for these rock-cut cave of the Malabar hills. He further states that the Buddhist *stūpa* is a reproduction of an earlier hollow Vedic-*stūpa,* which originally was probably a domical hut built of bamboo and wooden ribs, imitating hemispherical wooden huts of Aryan chiefs.[23] The local tradition has ascribed a Buddhist origin to the rock-cut caves. They have sometime been regarded as the abodes of hemits, who flourished in these parts when Buddhism and Jainism were popular in Kerala.[24] Sharma on the basis of pcesnce of some pots and a few other things, opines that these small rock-cut caves were used as burial tombs by the Megalithic people and he has dated these caves in a period between 300 or 200 B.C. and 100 A.D.[25] However, it is surprising that no skeletal remains have been discovered in these small caves and so it is doubtful, as it appears, to say that these caves were burial tombs. Whatever may be the case, these caves, though located far off from Śrī Sūrya Pāhār, are as small as ours and quite old as the caves in question, though no relation between these two groups is possible.

Thus, the votive *stūpas* at Śrī Sūrya Pāhār should be the earliest archaeological evidence of the historical period of Assam and also the rock-cut caverns in the locality belong almost to the same period. The remains of Śrī Sūrya Pāhār prove that Buddhism and Jainism had some pockets in that region. The Brahmanical religion, which was accepted by all the Kāmarūpa Kings of the pre-Āhom period had also influence on the Śrī Sūrya Pāhār region.

The name of the hill must have been derived from some Sūrya temple or Sūrya cult that existed in the locality. The existence of Buddhism, Jainism and Hinduism at the same site at Śrī Sūrya Pāhār and the remains of Buddhism and of Brahmanical icons at Pañcharatna ruined temple site prove tolerance and harmony amongst the followers of different faiths in the past. As such, Śrī Sūrya Pāhār relics furnish the earliest and one of the most important sources of the socio-religious history of Assam.[26]

Notes and References

1. 'Some Ancient Site in Assam', *Journal of the Assam Research Society (JARS),* Vol. XIV, 1960, pp. 110 ff.
2. *Ibid.*
3. 'Śrī Sūrya Pāhār', *Assam Sāhitya Sabhjā Patrika (ASSP),* June 1976, pp. 38-39.
4. *The Background of Assamese Culture,* 1st edition, see plates.
5. R.D. Banerji, *Medieval School of Eastern Indian Sculpture,* 1933, Pl. XXXVIII.
6. *Op.cit.*, p. 110
7. *JARS,* Vol. II, No. 1.
8. A.S.S.P, p. 39.
9. *Ibid.*, p. 40.
10. *Op.cit.*, Pl. I, Door lintel of Dharmapāla (1 M No. B482).
11. *Op.cit.*,
12. *Op.cit.*, pp. 111.
13. *Op.cit.*, pp.38-39.

13a. *Kṛṣṇa Smṛti (Prof. K.D. Bajpai comm. Vol.)*, 1995, p. 233.

14. *Op.cit.*, p. 112.
15. *Ibid.*, p. 111.
16. *The Development of Hindu Iconography*, 1st edition, see plates.
17. For this suggestion I am grateful to Dr. P. Sharma, Guwahati.
18. Bhuyān, *op.cit.*, p. 40.

19. Choudhury, 'Adhyāpak Saraswatidevar lagat *ek* Saptāh, Prakāsh, Assamese magazine, Guwahati April 1977, pp. 45-46.
20. Professor B.N. Mukherji after visiting the place in my company expressed the same opinion.
21. *Iconography of Buddhist and Brahmanical Sculpture in the Dacca museum,* Pl. X (1) and (b).

21a. R.D. Choudhury, *op.cit.*, pp. 45-46.

22. 'Rock-cut Caves in Cochin', *Ancient India,* no. 12, 1956. pp. 93ff.
23. *Ibid.*, p. 107.
24. *Ibid.*, p. 109.
25. *Ibid.*, p. 114.
26. Also please see my paper "Assam's Earliest Archaeological Evidence at Śrī Sūrya Pāhār" *Facets of Indian History, Culture and Archaeology,* Ed. S.P. Gupta or K.S. Rāma Chandran, Indian History and culture Society, New Delhi, 1991. pp. 62-64. Also see, *The Assam Tribune*, a daily, Guwahati, 27th January, 90 (included in this book).

2

Gupta Influence in Kāmarūpa as Known from Archaeological Evidence

It is known from archaeological evidences that, like other parts of India, Kāmarūpa also came under Gupta influence directly or indirectly. The ancient name of Kāmarūpa was Prāgjyotisa as is mentioned in the *Rāmayaṇa* and the *Mahābhārata*.[1] After that, for the first time, we know this country as Kāmarūpa' from the Allahabad pillar inscription of Samudragupta. The mention of Kāmarūpa in this inscription of 4th century is an important fact. In this famous epigraph it is written as follows: "Samatata-Davāka-Kāmarūpa-Nepāla-Kartripura ādipratyanta mṛatīb hir...".[2] It is learnt from this epigraph that although Kāmarūpa did not form a part of the Gupta dominion, the king of Kāmarūpa obeyed the orders of the Gupta emperor, paid taxes and honoured him.[3]

The Nilāchal rock-cut inscription incised on a rock at the slope of Nilāchal hill, Guwahati, is also an important document. It was caused to be incised by king Surendravarman, who has been identified with Mahendravarman. It does not bear any date. However, on the basis of the character of the script, D.C. Sircar has placed it in 5th century A.D.[4] The character of the script of this inscription bears Gupta style or atleast it is similar to the script that was used in North India, which is derived from Brāhmī. The second inscription of the same style belong to the same period *i.e.* 5th century. It is known as Khanikar gāon-Nagājari lipi.

The Doobi copper plate inscription of Kumār Bhāskarvarman,[5] the most important ruler of Kāmarūpa in the 7th century A.D., also reflects Gupta tradition. The character of the script used in this inscription is quite similar to the script of the Gupta period that was popular in North India in that time. From this copper plate inscription it is learnt that King Bhutivarman of Kāmarūpa used the epithet *'Mahārājādhirāja'* and performed a horse sacrifice[6] which were nothing but borrowed traditions from the neighbouring Gupta dominion. Probably, taking advantage of the decay of the Gupta might in the 6th century, Bhutivarman threw up the yokes of the Gupta emperor and used the epithet *'Mahārājādhirāja'*.

Davāka, a place in the district of Nowgong, is identifiable with 'Davāka' of the Allahabad Pillar Inscription. In the Gupta period, as N.K. Bhattasali thinks, Davāka was most probably a small but independent kingdom. He further says, "there is evidence to show that Davāka, in the present district of Nowgong, was originally a separate kingdom and in a way independent of Kāmarūpa.[7] Sylhet and Nowākhāli districts of Bangladesh and Tripura State (Tiperā) were included in the Samātata kingdom and the Kapilī, Yamunā and the Kollong valleys were most probably included in the Davāka kingdom.[8] It is possible that this small kingdom could exist at least up to 5th century A.D. Afterwards, when the rulers of Kāmarūpa became more powerful, it could not, it is likely, continue its independence. It is learnt from a Chinese account *Shung Shu* that an envoy of the King from Kapilī valley was sent to China in 428 A.D.[9] In any case, it can be rightly supposed that the Kingdom of Davāka was to the east of Kalang, Kapilī and Yamuṇā valleys and the eastern limit of Kāmarūpa stood there.

In addition to the Allahabad pillar inscription, the Nilāchal rock-cut inscription, Doobi plates, and the Bargaṅgā rock-cut inscription of King Bhutivarman of Kāmarūpa inform us that the king performed a horse sacrifice and he used the epithet *'Mahārājādhirājā'*. The inscription is incised in well cut Gupta Characters, and it bears date in Gupta era which corresponds to 554 A.D., according to N.K. Battasali.[10] The ruins at Mikirāti, a village near Davāka, also bear semi Gupta characteristic features. Here we find two types of sculptures—the first having Gupta trait and the second bearing Pāla features of the 10th-12th centuries. The remains of brick built *garbhagṛha* of a temple at the site are noticed and the *Śiva liṅga* installed in it is in *situ*. In addition to three broken pieces of three different stone images, two female figures and the other a male figure—bearing Gupta modelling bespeak of the influence of the great school of art that flourished in that golden age. The two broken pieces of images do not provide any clue to their identities. It is possible that they were damaged by some iconoclasts. The first broken piece has already been removed to the Assam State Museum. In addition to all these there is a Viṣṇu image (stone) in the tin shed where a few other stone images also have been kept. This image is also sculptured in Gupta style possibly in early Pāla period. From the scattered ruins at Mikirāti, one can very well conclude that there were about four or five small temples. But whether these small temples or shrines of pre-Ahom age belong to the Gupta period is not known. It deserves a thorough examination.[11] Recently in a small excavation taken up by the Department of Archaeology and Assam State Museum, a few earthen pots were revealed. All the pots are full with some substances. After their examination in the Assam Forensic Laboratory, it was found that the substance in pots represent paste of rice. It is possible that carbon-14 test may give some clues to the antiquity of the pots.

Just near the Bargaṅgā rock-cut inscription near Hawrāghāt, mentioned above, there are two rock-cut big sculptures representing a Dvārapāla. The style of the headgear and the anatomy of the figure reflect Gupta traits. Behind the rock-cut inscription in the same site remains of a plinth of a temple could be noticed. It is possible that the temple was constructed in the same period to which the sculpture and the inscription belong.

R.D. Banerji has placed the famous ruined temple *dvāra* of Daparvatiā in the 5th/6th centuries A.D.[12] P. Sarma has made a study on the *garbhagṛha, maṇḍapa* etc., the plan of the original temple and placed this ruined temple in the 5th century A.D. He also has opined that this is the first brick built temple in Gupta period.[13] Sarma has, no doubt, rightly drawn the plan of the temple, but we beg to differ in point of the antiquity of the temple. After the comparison of the present temple *dvāra* with the *dvāras* of the temples found at other places belonging to the Gupta period, we are inclined to place the *dvāra* in the 6th century A.D., and so, in our opinion, the present ruined temples cannot be the oldest brick built temple of the Gupta period.[14] S.K. Sarasvati has revised his opinion and would like to place it in the 5th century A.D.[15] While clearing the jungle at the site, R.D. Banerji found a few terracotta plaques which, on stylistic grounds, may be placed in the 6th century A.D.[16] On the whole, it can be safely concluded that the ruined temple with the beautifully sculptured figures of Gaṅgā and Yamunā bears Gupta features both in architecture and art as well.

Recently, an image of Viṣṇu was discovered at Khārāmedhipārā near Dudhnoi in the Goalpārā district. We could see the image at the site. Now, the image has been preserved in the Assam State Museum, Gauhati. Here Viṣṇu is shown holding *śaṅkha* and *padma* with upper hands, while the lower hands are made to touch the head of *Gadādevī* and *Chakrapuruṣa*, who are shown standing on either side of the deity. The style of depicting *gadā* and *chakra*, the two *āyudhas* of Viṣṇu in human form was evolved in the Gupta period. After the fall of the Gupta empire also this style continued in various parts for some centuries. Now, it is clear that this pre-Pāla or early Pāla image in style bears Gupta theme.

Gupta art style more or less penetrated as far as Deopanī, east near Golaghat. The inscribed Viṣṇu image, the inscribed image of Harihara (the bigger one), the headless image of Viṣṇu—all of which have been preserved in the Assam State Museum and the images of Kevala Narasiṁha and Vāmana preserved in the Deopanī modern temple should be dated c. 8th-9th centuries A.D., and should be the product of Gupta art formula, of course, with local tribal art style. The script of the Sarupathār inscription.[17] (Nāgajari-Khoni kargāon lipi) discovered in that region have the same type of character that were in use in North India after the Gupta period.

A few years back quite a few gold coins were discovered at Pāglātek to the west of Goalpara town on the bank of the Brahmaputra.[18] After the fall of the Gupta Empire, the rulers of the small kingdom that were so long acknowledging the suzerainty of the Gupta emperor, threw off the yoke of the Guptas and independently started issuing coins in imitation of the Gupta coins. Such type of imitated Gupta gold coins have been found in Bangladesh, Tripura, etc., which are ascribed to c.7th century A.D.[19]

From Tezpur rock-cut inscription of King Harjjarvarman dated 510 G.E.[20] is an eloquent testimony to the fact that Gupta influence or tradition did continue in Kāmarūpa as late as 829-30 A.D. In Nepal and Kāthiawar also late inscriptions bearing Gupta era have been noticed.[21] D.C. Sircar thinks the names of King Samudravarman and Queen Dattadevī of Kāmarūpa were nothing but the imitations of the names of Gupta Emperor Samudragupta and queen Dattadevī.[22]

From the above discussion, it appears true that although the Gupta rulers did not conquer Kāmarūpa, the rulers of Kāmarūpa did acknowledge the suzerainty of the powerful Gupta rulers. That Kāmarūpa was not included in Gupta empire is well documented.[23] As in political field, in the field of art and culture too Gupta tradition influenced Kāmarūpa artists.

Notes and References

1. B.C. Law, "Pragjyohsa" *Journal of Uttar Pradesh Historical Society*: Vol. XVIII Part I-II, pp. 43.
2. Fleet, *Corpus Inscriptionum Indicarum*, Vol. III, 1963, p. 1.
3. *Ibid*, p. 14.

4. *Epigrophia Indica* Vol. XXXI, pp. 67-69, 4a.
5. *Journal of the Assam Research Society*, Vol. VIII, p. 138 and Vol. X, pp. 63-67.
6. *Epigraphia Indica*, Vol. XXVII, p. 19.
7. *Ibid.*
8. *Ibid.* Also P.C. Choudhary, *The History of Civilization of the people of Assam etc.*, 1959, p. 146.
9. *Ibid.*
10. *Journal of Assam Research Society*, Vol. VIII, No. 4, p. 139.
11. Professor S.K. Sarasvati visited the site in the company of Mr. B. Dey of Guwahati University and the present author, He was of the opinion that the three broken pieces of sculptures found at the site bear Gupta features. At his advice one of these pieces was removed to the Assam State Museum. I am deeply grateful to him.
12. *Annual Report of Archaeological survey of India*, 1923-1924, pp. 98-99.
13. *Bulletin of the Assam State Museum*, No. 1, pp. 36-40.
14. *Ibid.*, No. 2, pp. 52-69.
15. Last Year (1976) when he visited the ruined temple in the company of Mr. B. Dey, of Guwahati University, P. Sarma, Dept. of Archaeology, Guwahati, and the present author, he opined this. Also *the Assam Tribune* (a daily) 23 Dec; 1976, p. 1.
16. C.C. Dasgupta, *The Origin and Development of India Clay Sculpture*, 1944, p. 228. Also *Annual Report of Archaeological Survey of India*, 1923-24, pp. 98-99.
17. P.C. Choudhury, Sarupathār Stone inscription, *Journal of the Assam Research Society*, Vol. XX.
18. R.D. Choudhury & M.C. Das, A find of gold coins from Pāglātek, Assam, *Journal of Numismatic Society of India,* Vol. XXXV, 1973, pp. 171-75.
19. "Money in Pre-Āhom Assam and its neighbourhood" D.C. Sircar read this paper in Shillong session of Numismatic Society of India conference 1977. See, *Economy and coinage of N.E. India,* Ed. G.P. Shing, & N. Ahmed.
20. P. Bhattacharji, *'Kāmarūpa Śāsānāvalī, Bengali'* Edn., pp. 180-192.
21. Marshall, *Annual Report of Archaeological Survey of India,* 1902-03, p. 229.
22. *Journal of the Assam Research Society*, Vol. X, Nos. 3 & 4, p. 66.
23. In the Māndāsor Pillar Inscription of Jasodharma of 6th Century A.D. it is mentioned that he extended the limit of his kingdom as far east as the Lauhitya. But it lacks corrborative evidence and hence, it is nothing but an exaggeration. See, *Corpus Inscriptionum Indicarum*, Vol. III, pp. 142-148, also P.C. Choudury, *op.cit.,* p. 157.

3

Assam's Earliest Archaeological Evidence at Śrī Sūrya Pāhār

My explorations and researches have led me to conclude that:

(a) Śrī Sūrya Pāhār was a meeting place of three religions viz. Buddhism, Hinduism and Jainisim. The rock-cut Brahmanical and Jaina sculptures belong to c. 8th century A.D.,

(b) From Śrī Sūrya Pāhār to Marnoi in an extensive area vestiges of ancient culture could be seen. This shows the continuity of settlement in the area, and

(c) The rock-cut votive *stūpas* at the place belong to an early period. At least a few of them belong to the 1st century A.D. - B.C.

My revisit to the place to verify and fix a chronology did not warrant any deviation from my earlier opinion as to the dates of the votive *stūpas,* rock-cut sculptures in a row, the rock-cut Jaina sculptures of Ṛiṣabhanātha and Ādināth at the place.

According to a local legend, one less than one lakh old *Śiva liṅgas* are in Sūrya Pāhār. Local people apparently mistook the votive *stūpas* for big *Śiva liṅgas*. The votive *stūpas do not have* Gaurīpīthas or the lower portions of the *liṅgas.* Moreover, the *Śiva liṅgas* are miniature in size. The votive *stūpas* are quite big in size. Now the local people have accepted the bigger ones as votive *stūpas.*

At Śrī Sūrya Pāhār near the modern sanctuary *(nāmghar)* the rock-cut *Śiva liṅgas,* row of *sculptures* of five divinities, one image of twelve-armed standing deity are found sculptured on huge boulders. At the top of the site two votive *stūpas* (about 8cms) are found sculptured on huge boulder. They are found together. Each of them bears the remnants of the *hārmika* or *chattra* design. The upper portions of these objects are broken or missing, possibly due to weathering effect. At the bottom of each of the stūpas a band is engraved around the object. On a separate boulder at a lower level another such votive *stūpa* can be seen. The beauty and serenity of the site are enhanced by a natural waterfalls and streamlet caused by the water of the falls. Due to sand accumulation at the site one or two small *Śiva liṅgas* are seen half submerged due to the same reason; the two caverns seen at the site are also affected by the water. Similar votive *stūpas* numbering three are seen carved on rock at a distance towards north of the site.

From the natural cave a little to the south, another huge votive *stūpa*, sculptured on a huge boulder has two bands, one on the body *i.e.*, in centre, and the other at the bottom. There has practically no trace of *hārmika*.

This type of votive *stūpas* can also be seen at Dek-dhwā, Bāmun Pāhār, Pañcharatna, etc. These *stūpas* represent the Hiṇāyana phase of Buddhism *i.e.*, the early phase of Buddhism, when image worship in Buddhism was not prevalent. During the period of Kanishka, the famous Kushāna Emperor in A.D. 100 Mahāyāna Buddhism came into being for the convenience of the worship of image by the Buddhist. Thus *stūpa*, worship is an early phenomenon in Buddhism. In Assam except at Śrī Sūrya Pāhār and Pañcharatna no where votive *stūpa*s have come to our notice.

Therefore, at least the two votive *stūpas* at the two of the site bearing hands at the bottom and traced of *hārmika* at the top may on stylistic consideration be dated to 100 A.D. / B.C. The other votive *stūpas* bearing bands on the body or not having any trace of *hārmika* or *chattra* design may be ascribed to a slightly later period *i.e.*, early Christian century.

Some scholars say that Heiun Tsang, the Chinese traveller who visited Prāgiyotishpura in the 7th century, did not mention the existence of Buddhism and the rulers at that time in Kāmarūpa were Hindus. The *Kālikā Purāṇa*, which gives evidence to the socio-culture activities of that period also does not bear any evidence to support our views. But Hieun Tsang was not supposed to visit each and every temple site of Kāmarūpa. He wrote about Assam on the basis of available information collected from the local people. Simlilarly, the author of *Kālikā Purāṇa* was also not supposed to give the description of each and everything of that period or of the period prior to the date of the work. Moreover, the Chinese traveller said that worship of Buddhism was done secretly. The Tibetan historian Tārānāth in his history of Buddhism refers to the prevalence of Buddhism in Kāmarūpa in later years. Tārānāth also compiled his work of the basis of information supplied to him. He did not visit Kāmarūpa.

It is opined that Assam's neighbouring States like Bihar and Bengal have yelled archaeological objects belonging to Maurya and Kushāna periods. Assam also certainly has such objects which need to be revealed through exploration.

The Mahāsthan inscription, found in Bogrā district of Bangladesh belongs to the Maurya period. According to D.C. Sircar, it seems to suggest the inclusion of North Bengal in the Maurya empire. North Bengal was included in Kāmarūpa kingdom or the Prāgjyotisha. He further says "there is little information about the socio-economic life of Assam during the pre-Christian period and about its relations with the Maurtyas."[1]

We have not found any punch-marked coin in Assam, it is true. But we have the votive *stūpas* at Śrī Sūrya Pāhār, which stands testimony to the activities to the time not far from that period. S.K. Saraswati is also of the same opinion. B.N. Mukherjee suggested us to place these *stūpas* in early Christian century. But I prefer to date at least the two votive *stūpas* in Suṅga period, if not in late Maurya period. Further investigation in the hill, would certainly throw more light in this direction. Thus, the relics of Śrī Sūrya Pāhār, are the earliest known relics in Assam, nay, in the entire North-East India or region east of Bogrā in Bangladesh.

Notes and References

1. For details see, my paper "Antiquities of Śrī Sūrya Pāhār: A source of Early History of Kāmarūpa" *Sources of The History of India*. Vol. III Eds. N.R. Ray, Calcutta, 1980, pp. 31-40. Also "Śrī Sūrya Pāhār. *Glimpse of Past*," *Assam Trbune*, a Deily, Guwahati; 27th January 1990, (Sunday Reading) and *Kṛṣṇa Smṛti*, (Prof. K.D. Bajpai Comm. Vol.,) Ed. R.K. Sharma and others New Delhi, 1995, pp. 233-35.

   The Archaeological Survey of India recently has conducted an excavation at Śrī Sūrya Pāhār and found some terracotta sculptures and traces of brick temples or *stūpas* datable to 8/9th century. The excavation is not just completed. It may be a Buddhist site.

4

Recent Archaeological Discoveries in Assam

Operation for the discovery of the archaeological wealth, in the true sense, is yet to be started in Assam. Whatever archaeological finds were discovered hitherto majority are surface collections. The only excavated site is Āmbārī, where from a good number of images, pots and other objects of importance came to light.[1] The surface collections are nothing but the chance discovery. There are many hidden treasures and they should be exposed by means of systematic archaeological excavations and exoloration. In 1960 the Archaeological Survey of India surveyed the Mornoi area in the south bank of the Brahmaputra and decided to excavate the site. But all of a sudden the plan was given up.[2] It is not understood the reason behind. The site, it seems, if excavated, would yield a good result. The State Archaeology Department, have of late shown some interest in small scale excavation.[3] The University of Guwahati though have an excavation branch under the Department of Anthropology, it cannot work independently in the matter of archaeology. However, the wing has shown its proficiency in its own field operations.

On the basis of exploration and, in certain cases, small scale excavation, few scholars have so far conducted researches and completed their works in the field of archaeology both in the pre-history and historical archaeology within a span of about ten years.

In the last decade Garo hill district has yielded many stone tools belonging to the plaeolithic period and neolithic period. A study on them has led scholars to think that the wave of plalaeolithic culture moved towards South-East Asia from South India through Assam. The new discovery has, it appears, played an important role in marking such a new theory.

While digging for the construction of the sanctum of the present Piṅgaleśver temple over the old site of the temple, a few years back many stone blocks were exposed. Some of these slabs bear designs, while many of them are adorned with beautiful sculptures. Of these sculptures many represent erotic scenes. The posture in which the human and animal figures are represented in this group of sculpture can hardly be compared with those of the erotic scenes found in the sculptures at Khājurāho or Konārok. The peculiarity of this group of sculpture is that some of the pieces show scenes of musterbation both by female and male figures. Therefore, this type of depiction in erotic art certainly has become a new element. According to *Matsya purāṅa* a work of 4th century, A.D., a pair of *mithuna* sculpture of amorous figure is to be sculptured on the door of a temple which is known to a art historians. The sacred text like *Kāmasutra* also enjoin the traditional practices of temple decoration with erotic sculpture. At Piṅgaleśver the sculptors went a step further than the textual injunction and tried to depict a real picture of love and passion amongst human being and even animals. Such type of erotic sculptures are also noticed in the ruins at Madan-Kamdev Pāhār. At present all these pieces of work of art, which may, on slylistic ground, be placed in a period ranging from *c.* 8th to *c.* 11th century A.D., have been preserved by the Department of Archaeology, Assam, near the temple along with an inscription of the period. The content of the inscription will be published shortly. In the temple there were some silver objects of late Āhom period along with two copper plate grants of the time of Śiva Siṁha and Gaurināth Siṁha. The first inscription bear some valuable information regarding the price of some commodities prevailing at that time.

Āmbārī archaeological objects discovered by chance in 1969 gave a clue to the archaeologist of the richness of the site. In that year about 38 images in addition to other objects were found. In 1970 a systematic excavation was conducted at the site which revealed as many as 17 images and other valuable materials including potteries. In 1987 excavation at the site was ressumed by T.C. Sharma. It was contained for two years. After this, H.C. Sharma, G.U. excavated the site in 1991-92. Still it is not completed. As the digging at the site is yet to be completed, it is difficult to say about the exact antiquity of the site. However, the site is of great importance of yielding so many images in good condition. It is likely that all these images were collected here for selling or dispatching to other temples exciting in that time. At present N.P. Choudhury is digging at the site.

In 1972 some gold coins were discovered at Pāglātek about 15 km West of Goalpara town on the southern bank of the Brahmaputra. The exact number of discovered coins could not be ascertained, however, 14 coins could be collected for the State Museum. All the coins are same. On the obverse, each of the coins shows a male figure in standing posture holding a bow and an arrow. The reverse of the coins bear a crude female figure in standing posture. They are very much similar to the imitation of the Gupta gold coins which are well known from Bengal and are datable to the post-Gupta period (*c.* 7th-8th cent.). The present coins may also be dated to the same period. Subsequently, several hoards of coins were discovered in Assam and the coins were collected by the State Museum authorities.

At the same time four huge earthen jars were dug out by the Department of Archaeology and State Museum at Mikirati in the Nowgong district. All the jars are full with some articles. On examination, it is revealed that they contain rice starch. It indicates that this was liquid food articles prepared out of ground rice. They may date in *c.* 9th-10 century, on the basis of stratigraphy. However, carbon 14 method of dating will give us the exact information with regard to the antiquity of these articles.

The discovery of a clay boat at Jalukbārī by the department of Anthology, Guwahati University, has indeed become a problem to the archaeologists, as the object is very peculiar and its utility is not known, so also the date. A few years back also two terracotta boats were discovered in the same area one of which has been preserved at the site. At Navagraha within Guwahati a similar object was discovered in 1970. As this type of terracotta object of huge size is not found anywhere, it is very difficult to say at the present state of our knowledge for what purpose these were made.

The discoveries of so many sculptural pieces icons and broken architectural pieces at Madan Kāmdev parvat after jungle clearance and slight digging at the site by the Directorate of Archaeology is an achievement. Recently done excavation in the campus of the Cotton College, Guwahati, has also yielded some valuable materials including some valuable materials including teracotta sculptures. Excavation at Dubarame near Sarupathār has, very recently thrown new lights on the archaeological potentiality of Assam. The excavation is not yet completes.

In addition to these object discovered recently. There are a few stray objects collected from different places or report of discovery of some object of cultural value. It is certain that a systematic plan of the state Government and the Universities in Assam for the excavation and exploration in Assam, will reveal may more important antiquities and will tell the tale of our past history of civilization.

Notes and References

1. The Āmbāri excavation is not yet completed. Still the excavation is going on.
2. However, the Archaeological Survey of India, has been conducting an excavation at Śrī Sūrya Pāhār. Some terracotta sculptures and traces of brick *stūpa* or temples have been discovered. Excavation is still going on.
3. They should publish the reports in the form of research papers.
4. These metallic sculptures of late period were stollen from the temples and police could not trace them out.

5

Archaeological Finds at the Narakāsur Hill*

The Narakāsur hill is situated at a distance of about five miles south of Gauhati. On the southern slope of the hill there is a village, called Kāhilipārā, (also called Odālbākrā), which is adjacent to the Sate Electricity Board's sub-station. The southern slope of the hill is full of huge boulders, scattered throughout. In a hole, caused by the combination of three huge granite boulders, some archaeological objects were found by a local man in 1964. Soon after, P.C. Choudhury visited the site, examined the objects and afterwards, he published a paper on them.[1] It appears from the note of Choudhury that the total number of articles were thirty-seven at the time of discovery. In 1967, it was reported that some of finds were missing. But in our last visit to the site in June, 1971 we could see all the articles. The villagers also denied the report of missing of some objects. Choudhury saw these objects under a temporary shed near the site. But now during our visit we find that they are removed and kept in the house of Śrī Suryakānta Rābhā of the Kāhilipārā village. Choudhury in his paper gave only the sketch of the objects and avoided the detailed iconographical description of the images, as he gave more importance on the historical aspect. Here an attempt is made to deal with the iconographical details of the images, descriptions of the other objects and to give some new interpretations on them.

The finds consist of a *mukhaliṅga,* two *ghanṭās* (bells), a *śaṅkha* Conch-shell), several miniature shells and twenty-two images of various deities.

---

* The co-author of this paper is Dr. D. Chutia, Guwahati.

Except a small image of *Manasā*, which is carved out of a piece of basalt, all the images are of bronze. Amongst the bronze images, four are cast in round plates. The description of the subjects are as follows:

An images of Indra

The biggest image of the group is the icon of *Indra* measures 11" x 7". Here the deity is seen riding on his *vāhana,* Airāvata facing front. He sits astride on the *vāhana*. The deity has two hands, the right hand being held in *varadahasta-mudrā,* resting on the right thigh, while the left in the *abhaya-mudrā,* resting on the left thigh. He is decked with a *karaṇḍa* (?) *mukuṭa, kuṇḍalas, hāras, upavīta, keyūras, valayas* and *nupuras*. His *paridhāna* consist of a *kaṭimekhala* and a *kaṭivastrsa*. He is flanked by two female *chowri* bearers. Both the attendants stand each on a *padma*, so also *Airāvata*. The *aṅkuśa* which was to be placed in one of the hands of the deity, is placed on the head of the *vāhana*. Below the *pīṭha* male a devotee is seen in *añjalihasta* pose. Behind the deity a round splendid *prabhā* is seen which is arranged on an *adhāra* (frame). Above the *parbhā a chhatra* is seen.

According to the *Aṁśumadbhêdagama*[2] the image of *Indra* should be two handed, seated on *Airāvata* and attended by two *chāmara* bearers and his consort. In our image *Indrānī* is not present. Other details of the icon are keeping with the text.

This splendid image is a very rare work of art. Though the *adhāra* and the *prabhā* with the *chhatra* of this image are arranged in the style of sculptures of the Pālas, yet to our knowledge, this type of Indra image is not found in Bengal-nor, in Bihar. None of the authoritative books on Indian bronze images illustrates such figure of Indra. However, the Chidambaram[3] stone image of *Indra* can be compared with ours. The sitting posture of both the images are quite identical. But that is a four handed image. On the basis of the style, this splendid work of art should be placed in the 10th century A.D., if not later.

Four images of Viṣṇu

Next in importance is a beautiful image of *Viṣṇu*. It is 10" in height and 4" in breadth. The deity stands on a *padma in samabhaṅga-sthānaka* attitude. He has four hands. The *āyudhas* are as follows: *padma* in the right front, *cakra* in the right back, *śaṅkha* in the left front and a *gadā* in the left back. The person of the deity is decorated with a *kirīṭakirīṭa-mukuṭa*. His body is beautified with long *kuṇḍalas, hāra, upavīta* and *vaijayantī*. He wears a *kattivastra* and a *kaṭimekhalā* as the *paridhāna* of the lower part of the body. According to the *Agnī-purāṇa*[4] and the *Rūpamaṇḍana*[5] it is *Śrīdhara,* the 9th from of *Viṣṇu*. The *Padma-purāṇa*[6] calls it *Hṛishīkeśa,* the 10th form of the deity.

The next image of *Viṣṇu* is also in *samapādasthānaka* attitude. The deity holds in his four hands clockwise: *padma* (?) *cakra, śaṅkha* and *gadā*. The front hands stretch forward and hold the *āyudhas,* while the back hands hang down and touch the *āyudhas* placed on the *pīṭha*. The *pīṭha* is of a *pūraṇavikasita-padma* (full-bloomed lotus). The deity wears a *kiriṭa-mukuṭa* on the head and other usual *alankāras* on the body and *vastra* to drape the lower part of the body. The *adhāra* behind the deity is quite prominent. Above the *adhāra* a round *prabhā* is arranged. Below the *pīṭha* the *vāhana* of the deity is depicted. According to the *Angi-purāṇa*[7] and the *Rupamaṇḍna*[8] it is a *Śrīdhara* image. But according to the *Padma-purāna*[9], it should be identified with *Hṛshikeśa*, one of the twenty-four forms of *Viṣṇu.*

The *sthānaka* posture and the style of holding the *āyudhas* of this image can be compared with those one from *Nālandā*, illustrated by Banerjea.[10] As in our image, in the case of the *Nālandā* image of *Viṣṇu* also both the front hands stretch forward and the back hands touch the *āyudhas* placed on the *pīṭha.* Both the images from Kāhilipārā or Narakāsur hill can be attributed to the 9th century A.D., from stylistic point of view.

The next image of *Viṣṇu* is also in the same posture. Its style of holding the *āyudhas* is same as that of the previous image of the deity. But in this case we do not see the *adhāra* behind the deity. However, a *prabhā* of palm leaf-tree shape is arranged. No attendant nor the *vāhana* is depicted in this case. Stylistically, the image should date in the 8th century A.D. This image is quite similar to a *Viṣṇu* image from Deopāni, now in the State Museum, Guwahati.At Davaka near Nowgong also an image having the same feature is noticed.

The last image is mutilated. The *pīṭha* of the deity, the *ahdara* and the *āyudhas* of two hands are broken and gone. However, it can be easily made out that the deity is in *samapādasthānaka* attitude. The *prabhā* arranged behind the head of the deity still exists.

Two images of Sūrya

There are two *Sūrya* images in this group of sculptures. The first measures 8" x 5". Here the deity is made to stand in *samapāda-sthānaka* attitude on his conventional *ratha* (chariot) drawn by seven horses. The god holds two *padmas* in both the hands in his usual way. The head of the deity is decorated with a *kirīṭamukuṭa* (?). He wears, as *alaṅkāra* in his body, *keyūras, haras, valayas* and *upavīta*. A *kaṭimekhalā* and a *vastra* are seen around his waist and thighs. Whether he wears a pair of boot is not clear. But the boots worn in North India style are supposed to be hidden by the figure of *Aruṇa*, in case of a eastern Indian *Sūrya* image. Such may be the case in our image. To the right of the deity *Piṅgala* and to the left *Daṇḍa* stand and attend upon the god. *Aruṇa* sits on the middle horse just in front of the deity. The conventional wheel of the *ratha* is not shown here. There is a *prabhā* each behind the heads of the deity, *Daṇḍa* and *Piṅgala*. But in this cases a *chhatra*, seen on the *prabhā* of a Pāla sculpture, is omitted and the *adhāra* is also not clearly visible. The image seems to be little crude in execution. However, it is a rare piece of bronze sculpture.

The next image of the deity does not depict the figures of *Daṇḍa, Piṅgala, Aruṇa* and horses which are represented in the previous case. Here the deity stands in *samapāda-sthānaka* attitude on a simple *pīṭha* and holds two *padmas* in his usual way. The *padma* of right hand, however, is broken. He wears the usual *alaṅkāras*. The *kaṭivastra* worn by the deity is peculiar. Reaching the angles of the deity, it spreads outwards over the knees horizontally.[10a] Around the things a *khaḍgabhanadha* is seen. The boots worn by the deity are quite clear. Behind the god a round *prabhā* is arranged beautifully. Stylistically, both the images can be placed in 8th-9th century A.D.

According to the *Bṛhatsaṁhita,*[11] *Matsya-purāṇa*,[12] *Aṁśumadbhêdagama,*[13] and *Suprabhêdāgama,*[14] an image of *Sūrya* should be two handed and hold *padmas*. The second and fourth texts and also the *Viṣṇudharmottara*[15] suggest that the image should be placed on a chariot drawn by seven horses and driven by *Aruṇa*. The *Viṣṇudharmottara* and the *Matsya-purāṇa* state that the deity should be attended by *Piṅgala* and *Daṇḍa*. All these texts suggest that *Sūrya* should wear northern Indian dress, *i.e.*, a coat of mail and a pair of boots. It shows the sculptor of the first image followed the instructions laid down in the texts. But in the second case, it seems, the sculptor did not prefer to depict the chariot, horses, *Aruṇa* etc.

An image of Gaṇeśa

The group includes only one *Gaṇeśa* image. Here the deity is seated in *mahārājalīlā* posture. *i.e.* putting the right leg vertically and left leg horizontally on the *āsana*. The deity has four hands. He holds in the right front hand an unidentified *āyudha,* in the right back hand a *dhatura puṣpa*, in the left front hand an unidentified *āyudha* and in the left back hand a *triśūla*. The *vāhana* of the deity is exhibited below. Behind the deity a *prabhāvalī* is shown. The image from Pāhārpur, reproduced by Dikshit[15a] is quite similar to ours.

An image of Manasā

The image of *Manasā* is the only stone image in the group. It is chiselled in a piece of basalt measuring 3½ x 3". The deity here is made to sit in *lalitāsana* posture. She has two hands, the right hand being held in the *varada* pose resting on the knee, while the left hold-a *sarpa*. She wears the usual *alaṅkāras* and *vastra*. To the right of the deity a bearded male figure is seen seated in *utkaṭikā* postue. This figure may be identified as *Jaratkaru*. To the left is seen a female figure in the same posture. Behind the head of this figure there is a *three-hooded sarpa*. This figure may represent a *Naginī*. Behind the head of the deity there is a canopy of seven hooded *sarpa*. This image, stylistically, should be placed in 10th/11th century A.D.

Quite a similar image of *Manasā*, from Bengal is displayed in the Dacca Museum.[16] The only difference is that the *śilāpaṭṭa* of the image from Bengal is pointed and decorated, while the *śilāpaṭṭa* of our image is not pointed and is undecorated. The reason of not having a pointed *śilāpaṭṭa* in our image may be that the image is very small. *Bhattasali.*[17] Has quoted a *dhyanā* from the *Tithyaḍḍi Tattvam*, according to which an image of *Manasā* should hold a *sarpa.*[18]

An image of Tārā

This small image of *Tārā* is seated on a *padma* in *lalitāsana* posture. The body of the deity is slightly bent towards the left. She has two hands, the right hand being held in *varada-mudrā* resting on the right knee, while the left hand holds a lotus stalk and plays *abhaya mudrā*. Whether the right hand holds a lotus-stalk while displaying *varadā mudrā* is not clear. But on both the sides of the head of the deity two *padmas* are nicely depicted. The stalk of the *padma* to the left is clearly seen held by the left hand of the deity. The deity is decorated with a *karaṇḍa-mukuṭa, Kuṇḍalas, hārs, valays* etc. She wears a long *kaṭivastra* of thin fabric. The deity possesses youthful beauty.

This image of *Tārā* can be compared with the image of *Tārā* from Khadiravani, Bengal illustrated by R.D. Banerji.[19] Like ours, this figure is also seated on a *padma* in *lalitāsana* and the head of the deity is flanked by two bloomed *padmas*. But this image unlike ours, plays *dhyanā-mudrā* with both the hands and it has a long *śilāpaṭṭa*. It is a stone image. The image of *Lokanātha* (12th century A.D.) from Kurkihar, now in the Patna Museum,[20] also sits in similar posture and on either side of its head a *Padma* is seen as in our case. But the difference is that it is a male figure, while ours is a female figure. Stylistically, our image also can be placed in the same period to which the image of Patna Museum belongs.[20a]

Some unidentified images

There are some images of some deities whose precise identities are not known. The first is an image of a female deity. Here the deity is seated cross-legged in *yogāsana* posture. She has eight hands, two front hands being held in *añjali* pose. The there right back hands, are as follows: (1) raising upwards holding an *akśamālā*, (2) in he *bhūmisparśa-modrā* (?), (3) in the *dyna-mudrā* resting on the lap. The three left back hands, again are (1) raised upwards holding probably a *padama* on which there is another object *damaru* (?), (2) resting on the left knee holding on unknown *āyudha* and (3) in the *yoga* posture resting on the lap. She is decorated with a *jaṭāmukuṭa, kuṇḍalas, hāras* etc. She wears a *kaṭivastra* looking like a *sāri*. Behind the deity a *prabhā* and above it a *chhatra* design are shown. The *vāhana* of deity is not shown.

The second is a seated male figure. The deity sites in *virāsana* posture. The right front hand holding some unidentified *āyudha* rests on the raised knee, while the left front hand simply rests on the left knee which is horizontally placed on the *āsana*. The *āyudha* of the right back hand may be a *cakra*. The left back hand seems to hold a *gadā*. To the left of the deity and to the right there are two female figures attending upon the deity. The *vāhana* of the deity is not shown. On either corner of the *adhisthāna* an unknown animal (?) is seen. Whether the deity can be identified as *Viṣṇu* is not known, because the *vāhana* is not shown and the *āyudhas* of the front hands are not clear. Moreover, one of the female figures, which we could have identified as of *Sarasvatī*, does not carry a *vīnā*. However, this sort of image is rare. This image may, stylistically, be placed in about 10th century A.D., while the former should date in the 9th century A.D.

The next is a female figure. It stands on a *padma* in *dvibhvṅga* posture. The face of the figure is badly corroded. The right hand of the figure hangs down holding some unknown *āyudha,* while the left hand holds a *nīlotpala*. Above the head of the figure, there is a canopy of a hooded *sarpa*. The long *kaṭivastra* looking like a *sārī* worn by the figure is clearly visible[21].

The fourth is a *sthānaka* figure. Whether the figure is of male or a female is not quite clear. Because, the figure seems not to have breasts. It they are worn off is not clear. On the other hand, it wears a long *kaṭivastra* which look like a *sārī*. The *āyudhas* held in both the hands are not at all clear. There must have been a *prabhā* behind the head of the figure. It is evident from its remnants.[21a] There are another two images of little importance. The first is a mutilated female figure behind, whose head there is a *prabhā*, which resembles a palm leaf. The next seems to be a crude female figure. Stylistically, this crude image belongs to a late period.

Four images on plates

Of particular interest are four images cast on four bronze plates. One of these plates contains a high relief of a bust of human figure which is shown to have sprung up from the neck of an upturned buffalo head with horns. The head of this bust wears a *mukuṭa* which looks like a cap. Two *kuṇḍalas* are also seen clearly on the ears of it. From its association with a buffalo head, it may be suggested that the icon is that of the buffalo demon, *i.e. Mahiṣāsura.*[21b] But the presence of the third eye on its head proves that it represents Devi Durgā.

The next plate contains in the same way a figure of a female deity. Here the deity stands in *samapāda-sthānaka* attitude on the back of a buffalo. The deity has four hands. She holds the reins of the *vāhana*, on which she stands with the right front hand, and a *cakra* with the right back hand. With her front left hand she holds a gadā (or a *daṇḍa*?) while with the left back hand she hold a *triśūla*. The *mukuṭa* (*jaṭa* ?) worn by the deity is peculiar. She is decked with all the usual *alaṅkāras* that are worn by a female deity. The *kaṭivastra* or *sārī* worn by the deity has some designs. A line of letters, which are now obliterated to the left of the deity on the plate is seen. D. Chutia however recently has deciphered the letters and expressed his opinion that the icon represents Yakshinī Devi.[21c] According to the Kālikā-Purāṇa (sl. 62 p. 163), buffalo is the *vāhana* of Kātyānī.

The third plate contains a male figure of some deity in high relief. As in the former cases, here also the deity is made to stand on an animal in *samapāda-sthānaka* attitude. The animal may be identified as tiger. The deity in his four hands hold the following *āyudhas* clockwise: an *akṣamālā*, a *khaḍga*, a *cakra* and a *śaṅkha*. The *jaṭa* on the head of the deity is clearly shown. His eyes are big. He has usual *alaṅkāras* including an *upavita* on his body. The erect penis (*urdhava-liṅga*) of the god is nicely depicted. As in the former case, here also some engraved letters are there on the plate.

Most of them are worn out. Stylistically, they belong to 9th-10th century.

The fourth plate shows a male deity in the same style. Here the deity stands on ass (?). He has two hands. With the right hand he hold a long *daṇḍa* and he hold the reins of the *vāhana* with his left hand. The deity wears a *jaṭāmukuṭa* on his head and the usual *alaṅkāras* and *vastra* on the body. Here also two lines of writings are found on either side of the deity. But they are not recognizable.

All these four images are peculiar and such figures are extremely rare. Identities of these images excluding the first, are not known. They are very crude in execution and it seem that the sculptors, who executed these images, were ignorant of the textual injunctions. To our knowledge, such cast figures of deities on plates are not found in Bengal nor in Bihar. Stylistically, they should belong to c. 9th-10 century. The holes on the borders of these plates indicate that they might have been suspended on some temple walls.

A mukha-liṅga

In addition to these images, another attraction of the group is a *mukha-liṅga*. This is the only bronze *mukha-liṅga* found on Assam, so far. The height of it including the pīṭha is 3½'. The *liṅga* stands on the centre of an *astadala-padma,* which is placed on the *yonipīṭha*. Four faces are depicted on the *liṅga*. Four *sarpas*, each in between two faces of the *liṅga* are depicted.

A ghanṭā and a śaṅkha

The *ghanṭā* found in the group is very important, because it bears two lines of inscription. The height and the circumference of the bell are 10" and 1'4" respectively. Choudhury has read the inscription which is engraved on the ghanṭā as follows: *"Sri Kumar Devarājeva Sayatmanā Devāsurarāja (Devayuvarāja) hastyantaka daghyakabhuttacya pujaiyam (iba) tena (yena) devatakāryyādikāntaisa ghanṭāka data..."*[22] The English rendering of the writing is that "Śrī Kumār who was like *Indra* and was the killer of the elephants belonging to the king of *Devas* and *Asuras*, meaning *Indra* again (kings and princes) was or became the protector of this worship of his (*Indra*). This bell was given by him (*Kumāra*) for use of the worship of the deities. The script of the inscription seems to be of eastern variety descending from the *kuṭila* type of Brāhmī. Many letters are similar to those of Hayungthal copper-plate inscription of *Harjjaravarman* (9th century A.D.)

Remnants of two other copper bells (*ghanṭā*) are found along with these objects. The finds include also a big śaṅkha, which is slightly damaged.

Now the question comes as to why and how this collection of portable images and other objects of worship were found together in a hole caused by three huge boulders. Whether they are imported or indigenous. It is not quite easy to answer these questions with conformity.

We have already said that geologically find spot of the objects is quite unfit for the erection of a temple. From the purport of the inscription of the *ghaṇṭā*, it is evident that *Śrī Kumāra*, who is identified with *Kumāra,*[23] successor of *Palaka* mentioned in the Hayaunthal grant of *king Harjjara* of *Kāmarūpa*, donated the *ghaṇṭā* for the worship of *Indra*. On this basis, Choudhury wants to prove that the image of various deities found along with the image of *Indra* centred round the latter; in other words, the image of *Indra* was installed in some temple as the chief deity and other images were kept in the same temple and were worshiped as the subordinate deities. But is seems Choudhury's view is not fully convincing. Because, these image belong to different periods from stylistic point of view. Secondly, the image of *Tārā, a* Buddhist deity, was definitely not worshipped in a Hindu temple. Moreover, these images have varied physiognomy, indicating that they were executed in different periods in different places. However, it may be said that some temple was definitely dedicated to *Indra* where the present image of *Indra* was kept. The *ghaṇṭā* was also kept in the same temples. We can suppose that the big *śaṅkha* also belonged to the same temple. It may be mentioned that in the Vidic period *Indra* was a very important deity. But in the later periods his position was lowered and was treated as a Dikapāla only. Therefore, though the present image of *Indra* was worshipped as the chief deity in some temple, yet it seems not likely that the other deities centred round him. Because, the importance of *Indra* had already been reduced. Though *Hiuen Ts'iang* mentioned about the existence of *Deva* temples in Assam, yet we cannot say that all the temples housed *Indra* as the presiding deity. The Buddhist pilgrim might have meant Brahmanical gods by the term *'Deva'*.

Our conjecture is that the finds might have been collected by some person, who was interested in the metallic art or image and due to some political or religious upheavals of external invasions they were kept hidden under the boulders. Assam in the Ahom period fell victim to many external invasions, particularly from the Muhammedans from the west, by whom most of the Hindu of the temples were largely destroyed. The legend of the renegade Kālāpāhār and his atrocities are still prevalent in Assam. Therefore, it is highly likely that during the Muslim inroads and the subsequent atrocities to the populace and their faith, the collector kept these images and other associated objects in the hidden place to save them from the iconoclasts, with the hope of recovering them after the panic was over.

The person who collected these objects was interested specially in the metallic art and the objects of worship. The miniature stone image of *Manasā* which looks like a metallic image, was probably collected by the person out of interest. The *śaṅkhas* and the big *ghantā* (*bell*) might have belonged to the *Indra* temple where the present *Indra* image was installed.

All the images, excluding the figures of four plates and the crude female figure, bear the characteristic features of the Eastern school of sculpture. They are similar to the metallic sculptures of Bengal and Bihar. But we cannot boldly say that they are imported into Assam from those States. Because, our images have some regional variations in style and so, the minute details of the images do not resemble those of Bengal and Bihar sculptures. However, we can say that the image of *Tārā* was imported, as is evident from the comparison of the image of *Tārā* of ours with the Bihar and Bengal sculptures, as shown above. This view is substantiated by the fact that Buddhism was not accepted by the Hindu people of Assam, though its smell was in the air of the State.

It is true, whatever may be the accuse of hiding, that such an instance of a hoard of metallic sculptures along with other objects of worship is rarely found. The entire hoard some years back, was removed to the State Museum, where they are on display.

Notes and References

1. "Archaeological Finds in Narakāsur Hill, *Journal or Assam Research Society,* Vol. XVI, pp. 57-50.
2. Rao, *Elements of Hindu Icnography,* Vol. II, Pt. II, pp. 510.
3. *Ibid*, Pl. CL.
4. B.B. Bidyabinod, *"Twenty four form of Viṣṇu,"* M.A.S.I. 2, p. 25.
5. Rao, *op.cit.,* Vol. I, pt. 1, p. 229.
6. Rao, p. 232.
7. Bidyabinod, *op.cit.*
8. Rao *op.cit.* p. 229.
9. *Ibid.,* p. 232.
10. *Benerjea, Development of Hindu iconography* Pl. XXII No. I

10. *Benerjea, Development of Hindu iconography* Pl. XXII No. I
11. Banerjea, *op.cit.,* p. 437.
12. Bhattasali, *Iconography of the Buddhist and Brahmanical Sculptures in the Decca Museum, 1929* Pl. LXXIII, Fig. (a).
13. *Rao, op.cit.*, Vol. I, Pt, II, p. 308.
14. *Ibid.*
15. *Banerjea, op.cit.*, p. 437.
15a. *Excavation at Pāhārpur*, 1938, Pl. LVIII, f.
16. Bhattasali, *op.cit.*, Pl. IXXIII, Fig.(a).
17. Ibid., p. 227. It may belong to a late period.
18. It is to be noted that the cult of Manasā became popular in Bengal and Assam the 11th century A.D. and it was introduced by the Senas who came to Bengal in the middle of the 11th century from South India where Mansha was prevalent Ibid., pp. 221-4.
19. *Eastern Indian School of Medieval Sculptures,* Pl. XVII, Fig (d).
20. P.L. Gupta, Patna Museum cataloge of Antiquities Pl. XXXI.
20a. Interestingly, the iconographic description of the present image tallies to some extent with that of Mangalcandi or Lalitakanta as found in kalita Pūrāṇa. See, *Kalika Purāṇa*, Venkatesvar Edn. Sl. 83 pp. 52-54.
21. If is doubtful, if it is a representation of Manasā
21a. The border of the *prabhāvalī* of our first Sūrya image and the fourth identified image is quite similar. This type of design on the border of present is seen in some bronze images from Bihar. Sec J.C. French, *The Art of the Empire of Bengal*, Pl. IV; Benerji, *Eastern Indian School* of the Sculptures, *Pl. LXIX* and Gupta, Patna Museum Cataloge *Pl. XXX;* Arch. 9739. The Buddha image found at Kutch, has the same type of design in the broader of the *prabhā*. Gujarat Research Society, *Vol. XXIX*. Probably it was imported from.?
21b. This bust of *Mahiṣāsura can* be compared with this of the image North Cachar hills, once dominated by the Kachāriā. See R.M. Nath. Back ground of Assamese Culture, Pls. XXVI.
21c. D. Chutia, "A study on some early medieval inscriptions" *Studies on Indology (Professor M.H. Sharma Feleciation Volume),* Guwahati, 1996, pp. 219-220.
22. *Op.cit.,* pp. 58.59.
23. *Ibid.*, p. 59.
24. With regard to the proper identification of some of the icons of the hoards, see R.D. Chaudury, *op.cit.*, pp. We also propose to give a clear picture in the proposed monograph on the hoard to be published soon. After giving readings of the few letter inscriptions three scholars have given different, inter-pretations with regard to the identifies of the deifies depicted on the

four bronze round shaped casts with boarder holes for suspending on the temple walls. See D.C. Sircar, *Journal of the Ancient Indian History*, Calcutta University, Vol. X, p. 115. B.N. Mukheriji, *Eastern Indian art Style*, 1980, pp. 23, 36 & 55. D. Chutia 'A study on some early medieval inscriptions studies on Indology (Prof. M.M. Sharma Felecitation Volume), 1996, pp. 218-227. For the present we have reserved our comments on their identifications. We shall discuss about this in our proposed monograph on the hoard of metallic sculptures at Kalilāpārā

6

Archaeological Objects from Bargāng T.E.*

On 15.3.76. the Government of Assam have formally received the archaeological objects from Mr. J.P.P. Leitch, the General Manager of the Bargāng Tea Estate about 96 km east of Tezpur on way to Lakhimpur. On behalf of the Government of Assam, Śrī Bijioy Chandra Sarma,the then Minister of State for Finance, Assam received the objects. All these objects have been brought to Tezpur.

In all there are eight pieces of stone bearing sculptures. Another piece of stone rectangular in size bear an inscription in Tibetan language and script. All the pieces are preserved on the lawn of the bungalow of the General Manager. The stone pieces are of almost same height measuring 135 cm and are four-sided. These stone pieces were originally brought from Nakṣā-Parvat, to the north of Ketelā Tea Estate of the bank of a tributary of Bargāng river, by Mr. E.J. Nicholls, the then Managing Director of Bargāng Tea Estate and kept in Ketelā Tea Estate. Subsequently, these were brought to the Bargāng Tea Estate. It is said that still there are remains of old relics in Nakṣā-Parvat. Probably the four side stone pieces bearing geometrical design preserved in Phulbari Tea Estate were also brought from the same place. Nakṣā-Parvat is in Arunachal Pradesh now. The description of the objects are given below.

Pillar No. 1: It bears on one side the representation of a tree. The small branches and the leaves are well depicted. Above the tree a design is shown. It comprises seven carvings, each of which is like a *chitya*. The

* The co-author of the papar is Sri C.R. Samaddar I.A.S.

top portion of this design is almost conical and above it is shown a vase (*kalasa*). The entire design resembles the upper portion of a temple *i.e.*, *śikhara* and the *kalasa*. This type of seven arched design we have seen in Bāmunī hill ruins at Tezpur.[1] But unfortunately this rare piece of stone carving is not to be seen in the ruins now.

Another side of it also bears the sculpture of a tree with the *śikhara* and *kalasa* motives as mentioned above. Here the tree is shown in the shape of a betel leaf, probably it represents a pipal tree. The third-side bears two snakes coiling with each other. The other side is blank. It shows that tree and snake worships were popular amongst the people of the area.

Pillar No. 2: This pillar bears on one side a scene showing two male human figure fighting hand to hand. The right hand of the figure to the left holds the hair lock of the other, while the left hand of the other figure holds the hair lock of the figure to its left. The other two hands of the figures are also shown engaged in fighting.

The right leg of the figure to the left and the left leg of the other figure are also in action. Above the scene the same motif, arched *śikhara* and *kalasa*, are shown. The sculpture represents a scene of wrestling. Just below the arches and above the heads of the fighting figure there is a lotus design. Probably, it is done to fill up the vacant portion. The figure to the left is mutilated. One of the other three sides of the pillar bore some human figure, but they are badly mutilated and nothing can be made out except the lotus design in the upper level. The other two sides of the pillar are blank.

Pillar No. 3: This pillar bears three human figures on three sides. The first figure represent a male human figure-standing erect and holding something on the chest with both the hands. It wears a turban like a conical shaped crown on head. The body of the figure is draped in tight fithing shirt and a *dhoti*. The second side of the pillar is adorned with a standing sculpture of a female human figure. With its left hand holds probably the *hāra* worn on its neck. The other hand holds something, which is not clear. The third side shows a female figure (?). The objects held on the chest are not clear. The hair lock is shown to the left side of the figure's head. The pillar is slightly broken on all sides.

Pillar No. 4: This pillar shows three figures on three sides. On one side a male standing human figure is shown. Here the figure is made to stand on its left leg, while the right leg is kept bending over the right. The objects held in the hands of the figure are not clear. But the sacred thread worn on the body of the figure is quite prominent.

On its head is shown a short *mukuṭa*. Another side of the pillar shows a male human figure wearing a sacred thread. The hands of the figure are made to hold probably a shield on the belley. The legs are also kept on outward bent. The third side of the pillar depicts a woman with a child. Here the standing figure holds a *kalasa* with its left hand. To the right of the figure a small figure of a child is shown in the standing posture.

Pillar No. 5: One side of it shows a male human figure holding a stick (?) on chest and pushing it forward. The legs are shown moving. The figure has a prominent hair lock. The face of the figure has a monkey look. The other side bears a female standing figure. Below it is seen a goose. The third side of it also depicts a female human figure.

Pillar No. 6: It bears three figures on three of its sides. The figure in the middle shows a male human figure probably, in the same attitude. But the middle figure is shown facing front and the other two figures are in profile. Evidently they are made to face to the side of middle figure in devotion to some god (?). The half of the pillar is sunken in the earth. So the figures are half exposed only.

Pillar No. 7: It shows a male human figure in profile moving forward. The right hand of the figure holds something, which is on the right shoulder. The left hand is shown holding a *daṇḍa*. The head of the figure is armed with a helmet and the body is covered with armour. So, it is clear that the figure represents a warrior. The face of the figure looks like of a monkey.

Pillar No. 8: It hows a emaciated male figure in profile. The figure is shown moving towards left. The ribs and the veins of the figure are well exposed. The face resembles a monkey. The objects held in hands are not clear. The second side the emaciated standing female figure. The figure is made to face front. The exposed ribs and veins of the figure shows an uncanny feature of it. The objects held in hand are not clear. The face is slightly mutilated. However, the hair the sunken belly and reduced breasts are clear. Both the figures have terrible look like that of Camuṇḍā. Probably, they represent some tribal divinities in terrible look. The other side bear a male human figure in profile wearing a helmet on head and armour on its body. Both the hands of the figure are holding a sword (?). The figure is shown moving to the right. The figure represent a warrior like the other described above. The face of the figure has a same look like the other.

At the place an inscription on a stone block is preserved. It is inscribed in Tibetan script and language. The General Manager of the Tea-Eastate had sent an impression of it to some Tibetan Scholar, who gave the English translation as below:

> "Oh! Thou who was born in the Bull-wood year in the era of the king of the sky. The employer of the man who engraved this six-letter-stone is the lady Wangyal Jhamu, the incarnation of the Goddess of wealth. The life of Jo-Jo-Rie has passed away. The beneficence of this writing will cause the gate of hell to be closed against him and bring prayers that he may be born in the heaven where Chengregzi resides. The suppliers of funeral liquor are Sanghu Shari Bhuti and Ama Tinpang Jam Dhou with her sons Rinchen and Lasemo and her daughter Gagso."[2] The inscription on the mane stone are motive offerings made on the memory of departed relatives. Mostly these are inscribed with a prayer. Śrī G.G. Gatsov[3] gave the above reading of the inscription. As the last line of the inscription is not very clear, so he could not read it. From the palaeograpic style, it can be said that the inscription in question is not very old.

R.M. Nāth[4] has given a description about the Varāhas and their kingdom. He has said that the kings of the Varāhapāla dynasty many enterprising princes had an admixture of blood with the Boḍos and thus, a race of children of Varāhapāla fathers and Boḍo mothers grew up and was known as the Varāhas. Their males took Boḍo girls as wives but were reluctant to give their daughters to Boḍo youths.

After the Pāla dynasty was ousted, Babhru-Vāhana organized the Varāhis and Boḍos and established an independent Kingdom with his head-quarters at Ghughuragrah, somewhere to the North West of Dibrugarh. Afterwards, they made their stronghold at Mājulī and ultimately the main capital was shifted to near about present Śimaluguri. On a hillock near the capital was installed the stone image of Viṣṇu mounted on the ride Garuda in a brick built temple. The image was popularly known as "Charāideo" or the bird-god. When the Āhoms came to this area their chief Sukāphā made friendship with them and later usurped the throne. The sanctity of this hillock was, however, retained for ever.[5]

After this sad incident the poor king of the *Varāhī* have fled to the north bank of the Brahmaputra and established a capital somewhere in the present district of Darrang. Here during the reign of Virhas (1375-1385), a prince of the Kamatā royal family established a city Pratapgar, now occupied by Pratapgarh Tea Estate. When Boḍo son-in law and minister Vīrochan fled with his Boḍo people to the South bank, while the king with his followers faced Pratāp Sing and was killed.[6]

The above historical back-ground lead us definitely to say that the remains belonged to some tribal dynasty. But Nāth has not given a single reference of the source of the history of these Boḍo people. This has put us in some confusion.

It appears that Nāth personally visited some sites in the north. G.C. Talukdar also visited the area and located the actual site of the ruins on the boarder of Assam and Arunachal Pradesh.[7] Talukdar says that in that region there is another archaeological site on the bank of Namurā river. He has not given the description of the ruins.

The ruins of our discussion do not have any relation with the pre-Āhom remains scattered throughout the Darrang district and elsewhere as far as the stylistic consideration is concerned. The style of these pieces of sculptures lead us to purt them in a later period ranging from 14th century to 16th century. These sculptures so not have any stylistic resemblance with the Āhom and Koch sculptures. However it can be postulated that they were product of the Boḍo or the Varāhīs who had been ruling in the region in the late madiaeval period.

From these pieces of sculptures we can assume that like other rulers the Varāhīs were also fond of songs and music, gymnasium, social & religious functions etc. Their priests with the sacred-thread on the chest and the pig-tail like hair tuft on head ministered to their religious needs. Worship of snakes and trees was popular amongst the people. Though this group of sculptures, brought from Nakṣā-parvat, where still ruins of old architecture lie scattered does not represent high class art, yet it represent a style with degenerated workmanship in tribal affiliation. Further field study in the region will tell the tale of the past tradition and culture of the area. Now all these sculptures have been brought to the Assam State Museum and are on display.

Notes and Refrences

1. See K.L. Barua, *Early History of Kāmarūpa*, 1966, Guwahati, pp. 112-113, also, R.M. Nāth, *The Background of Assamese Culture*, 1948, Shillong P1. XI.
2. This translation is by some scholars of Tibetan script as is learnt from Mr. Leitch, General Manager, Bargāng Tea Estate. But he has not given the name of the scholar. Probably G.G. Gatsov gave this reading. He is expected to write a paper on this subject.
3. According to Bhiksu Kaundinya, this reading was given by G.G. Gatsov. See *Dainik Asom,* an Assamese daily 1st April 1976.
4. *Op.cit*, p. 61.

5. *Ibid.*, pp. 61-62.
6. *Ibid.*, p. 63.
7. 'Nakṣā Parvator dhaṅsāvaśesh.' *Dainik Asom, an Assamese daily* 7th December, 1975.

7

Archaeological Remains at Bhuvan Pāhār*

Bhuvan Pāhār is situated on south-eastern border of Cachar district under Sonāi Police station, Assam. From Sonāi one can go to this place via Motinagar bāzār which is in the valley. From this place only jeep can ply along the P.W.D. gravel road which terminates just on the foot hill. Thereafter, visitors to Bhauan or the temple of Bhuvanbābā have to climb about 3000 feet high hill on foot through forest path. Up to Khāsipuñjī (puñjī means village), inhabitated by Khasi people, which is about one km off from the foothill, the path is quite wide. Possibly, it will be made jeepable very soon. From the Khāsipuñjī one has to climb up about 4 to 5 kms to reach Trivenī or Trikonī. From Khāsipuñjī the path is stiff. From Trivenī point one path goes to Bhuvan temple towards west, which the other goes to the Nāgā temple eastward. Since this point is the junction of three paths, it is called Trivenī or Trikonī. The path from this point of Bhauan shrine is almost plain. It runs along the top of the hill.

We (C.D. Tripathi & R.D. Choudhury) along with Mr. G.M. Srivastava, the then D.I.G., Southern Range, Silchar, paid a visit to Bhuvan shrine on 1st November, 1985 after climbing the stiff hill. We were accompanied by Dr. S. Choudhury, Deptt. of History, Karimganj College and the Assistant Conservator of Forest and Mr. Gautam Sarma, Photographer and a Ranger. Our journey were made comfortable by the staff of the Forest Deptt. and the police personnel, without whose assistance it would not have been possible to reach the site. We had to make a night halt in the forest Guest

* The co-author of this paper is Sri C.D. Tripathi, I.A.S.

House, just near the shrine of Bhuvanbābā.

The shrine is of recent times having tin roof. Inside it a *sādhu* (monk) stays, who looks after the shrine and the images of the divinities installed inside it. The construction of the shrine is very ordinary. It is an Assam type house without any Śikhara design. It does not have *ardhamaṇdapaḍ* too.

But the so called *Garbhagṛha* where the images are installed, is quite spacious so that the devotees can sit there comfortably and the *sādhu* can also sleep. The shrine is facing to the west. Near the eastern wall inside the shrine (or the sanctum) there is a row of stone sculptures numbering four.

To the extreme left of the row a bust of Hanumān (53" x 50 cms) in a very bad shape is seen. Due to the presence of thick layer of vermilion on it, image is not easily recognizable unless one closely observes the figure. The second image (80" x 32 cms) represents a crude male human figure. The figure does not have arms and legs. Some engraved lines, possibly meaning male organ are noticed clearly on it. The image is worshipped by the people as Rāma. This crude female figure, which is slightly shorter than the figure of Rāma, is worshipped by the devotees as Sītā. On the body of the figure similar engraved lines are shown meaning probably female organ. The fourth figure of the row i.e., the figure to the extreme right is of Garuḍa (146 x 40 cms) which is the tallest of all the images of the group. The image is broken into two (or three) pieces, which were later joined together with cement plaster. The wings and the body portion of the image is lost. Only the head was straight way joined with waist. The body portion of the figure is missing. The legs are kept apart. The figure is shown as standing. The short lower garment worn by it is very clearly shown. The physiognomy of the image papers to represent Garuḍa, the vehicle of Viṣṇu and it has resemblance, in so far as the facial expression is concerned, with the image of Garuḍa found commonly elsewhere.

The main deity, of the shrine is Bhuvan (or Bhuvanbābā or Bhuvaneśwar) whose image is installed towards the central place of the shrine, which faces to the west i.e., front entrance of it. Here the two armed deity is shown as seated in *lalitāsana* posture, placing the left leg horizontally with a bend at the knee on a lotus seat, while the right leg is kept pendant. The body was possibly detouched from the head of image and later it was joined with cement plaster. Unfortunately, both the hands of the figure are broken so that we have no idea about the objects held in the hands. The right hand of the deity is broken at elbow, while the left is broken at wrist. The deity wears garlands, ear rings and lower garment, which is not very clear. The crown on the head of the deity can neither be called *Kirīṭamukuṭa,* nor *jaṭāmukuṭa*. It is short and only three cones can be seen The waist of the figure is round and slim, while the chest is broad. Since the quality of the stone is bad, the details of the face and other parts of the figure of the deity are gone. In the absence of the vehicle of the deity and the objects held in the hands, it is very difficult to know about the real identity of the deity. We can only surmise. The local people worship it as Bhuvanbābā, i.e. Śiva. The image is installed in a slightly lower level than that of the floor. Just near the image of the deity there is a small carved block of stone. It is sadly damaged However, one can make out that the sculpture represents a seated elephant.

The next image represents a female figure in standing posture having three bends of body (*tribhaṅga*). This is placed almost in front of the image of Bhāvanbābā, described above, facing to the row of four images to the North. Like the image of Bhuvan it is also placed in a slightly lower level than that of the floor. Like the previous case, in this case also both the hands of the two armed deity are sadly mutilated so that we can not have any idea about the objects held. The ornaments and the dress worn by the figure are not at all clear. There is a trace of a necklace around the neck of the deity. Earrings worn by the deity can be recognized. The crown on the head of the deity has good deal of similarity with that of the image of Bhuvanbābā. The bosoms of this female deity are almost natural and not like the stylized ones as noticed commonly in sculptural art of India. The navel of the figure is, clearly seen. Local people worship it as the image of Pārvatī. But the difficulty in identification is that there is no trace of the vehicle.

On stylistic consideration both the images of Bhuvanbābā and Pārvatī may roughly be assigned to the 12th-13th century tentetively. Both the sculptures appears to have borne Pāla characteristic features. The cylindrical body shaped image of Bhuvanbābā can be compared with the Pāla sculpture of Bengal or Bangladesh or Kāmarūpa, although it appears to have some local tribal trait on the face. The physiognomy of both the sculptures have some tribal affiliation, as it appears. The style of the crown and the earrings in both the cases seems to be local and has no relation with the Pāla school. The shape of the bosom of the Pārvatī, which have almost a realistic look, do not have any relation with the Pāla style or with any school of Indian art. One should attach more importance to this phenomenon. This female figure is portrayed in an elegant posture.

But the figures of so called Hanumān, Rāma, Sītā and Garuḍa, in so far as the style is concerned, had no relation with the figures of so called

Bhuvanbābā and Pārvatī. All these figures except the figures of Bhuvan and Pārvatī are very crude in execution. The face of Hanumān is corroded so much so that the details of the face are lost. The images of Rāma and Sītā are very peculiar as they are carved in two blocks of stone in the shape of bottle without hands and legs. If I have not mistaken, they were executed in the style of the images of Kṛṣṇa, Balarām, and Subhadrā of the temple of Jagannātha of Puri, although they were not exactly similar to the images of Jagannāth temple and there are lot of differences in other details. We have not come across the symbolic images of Rāma and Sītā in Assam sculptured in tribal style. Because of the sadly mutilated condition of the image of Garuḍa, it is difficult to say anything with definiteness regarding its age. However, we can say that it has no stylistic relation either with the images of Hanumān or Rāma-Sītā. The head-gear of the image and the style of the lower garment indicate about its date in an earlier period than that of the images of Rāma-Sītā, which are of very late period. The style of the image of Hanumān is also of a late period. To get a clear picture of all these images, they must be chemically cleaned and the layers of dirt and vermilion etc. should be removed.

Just behind the shrine there is a small cave temple. The cave is natural, but a stone door-frame is fitted in the front of it (the lintel is not there) and above the natural ceiling of rock there is a trace of *śikhara* like supper structure made of chiselled stone blocks. These were hidden under thick vegetation. After the clearance of the vegetation only the shape of this small cave temple could be clearly seen. Inside the cave to support the loose earth carved stone refters are fixed just near the entrance. In the central and rear portions of the cave we do not notice such ceiling support. Such stone rafters are joined each other with some substance of liquid object, white in colour, which can be chemically examined. In the rear portion of the cave loose earth from the ceiling had fallen. Two three persons can easily enter the cave at a time and they can easily stand inside it. The height of the cave temple (from the ground to the top of the super structure) is 126 cms, while the breadth of the supper structure is 86 cms. The measurements of the entrance is 140 x 94 cms. The two door jambs measure 151 x 48 cms each. The lintel of the door frame is found lying at a little distance. It was possibly removed by some one, with a view to worshipping separately for monetary benefit. The door jambs are plain and each of it has three bands. Inside the cave no icon is installed. If it is under the fallen earth is not known.

Just in front of the door frame of the cave temple there is a trace of an almost square courtyard, trace of a stone wall is also noticed. It was covered with vegetation. After the clearance of the vegitation, the outline could be traced. But there is no trace of any pillar. There are also traces of two small and shallow drains on the rock for the outlet of rain water falling from the upper part of the temple. We are of the opinion that this is a significant discovery.

The lintel (91 x 48 cms) of the doorframe which is found to the west of the tank, which is in the front of the shrine bears the figure of Gaṇesha in the centre. From stylistic consideration, it cannot be placed with the images of Bhuvan and Pārvatī, as there is marked deterioration in its execution. Nor it can be placed with the images of Rāma-Sītā Hanumān etc. It can be placed in the period in between, as I think. In the front of the shrine (slightly to the right) there is an old tank. On the left bank of it, stone slabs used earlier in temple structure, are placed in rows for making some steps for the benefit of the visitors for using tank water.

The shrine of Bhuvan is worshipped by the Manipuris and Nāgās. The Khasis also visit the temple as we were told by the *Sādhu* who stays at the place. The *sadhu* is a Bengali gentleman from Cachar district. He is a graduate. We were informed by him that Manipuri king, Buddha Chandra worshipped in the shrine of Bhuvan Pāhār. He stayed form sometime in the place and repaired the shrine. The present tinshed structure of the tank at the place was erected and the dressed stones at the steps arranged by him. Nāgā Rājā and Khasia Rājā also offered worship here. Every year at the time of Magha Pūṇimā a *melā* is held here. The *melā* is known as *Bhuvan melā*. During the *melā* period the place become overcrowded. Even people from various places of Barak Valley visit the shrine during that period in good number. During rainy season only a few tribal worshippers-Manipuri and Nāgās occasionally visit the place. The *sādhu* stays in shrine. He stays in the shrine alone even during the rainy season fighting against many adds in the deep forest.Even sometimes he has to eat roots of wild plants for his survival. Thanks to this real devotee of Bhuvanbābā for his penance.

From this place Manipur is only 2 km as the crow flies while Mizoram is about 10 km off. On the way to Triveṇī from this place to the left side of the way, there is a big rockshelter. We visited it. But there is no trace of human habitation. As the rock is sedimentary in formation and very loose it is not possible to draw painting inside the shelter on the wall. The shape of this shelter (*ardhacandrākriti*). At least one hundred people can take shelter in it. We were told that there was another such shelter on the other side of the path which was known to the forest guards.

Towards the east of Trivenī, if one walks about 1 km he finds a streamlet on the bank of which a modern Nāgā shrine is constructed. It is well looked after and the Zemi Nāgās regularly visit it. Inside the shrine two modern images are installed. They are worshipped as Bhuvanbābā and Pārvatī. Here goat, chicken, pegion etc. are sacrificed. It is being looked after by a Zemi Nāgā priest. Further to the east if one moves, he will find a big natural falls and a natural tunnel through which the water passes. This is locally called *hrad* (in Bengali?). There is another smaller falls of similar type near it. It is called Nāgā cave. Both of them are interesting for geologists.

Late Dr. V.S. Wakankar, an eminent archaeologist, specially known for his contribution for discovery of pre-historic shelters, it is learnt, which was later confirmed, visited these two sites (but not the Bhuvan shrine nor the half circular rock-shelters). He was also shown some photo copies of manuscript by one Mr. Sapre, who obtained from Bhuvan Pāhār. We had no information of this writings. However, later on Mr. Tarun Goswami, Director of Cultural Affairs, N.C. Hills District Council, Haflong, Assam gave us this piece of information and the copies of the photograph of the writings. Since the letters of the manuscripts are very peculiar it is difficult to say anything about this at this stage. I have not come across such writings. I was told by Mr. Goswami that they are known as Nāgā script. But this will have to be confirmed. This was also shown to Dr. P.C. Choudhury, Guwahti and Dr. J.P. Singh (N. E. H. U.) who are also of the opinion that this script mist have been used by some local people, and it had no relation either with Brāhmī or *Shaṅkha* script of central West India, as is opined by Dr. Wakankar. I am also of the view that this script has nothing to do with *Brāhmī or Śaṅkha lipi.* It may be some script affiliated to possibly Burmese culture. If it is so, it will be really very important. Dr. Wakankar was, however, making a study of the script. But his effort to find its roots in the Brāhmī or Śaṅkha lipi will go in vain.

Thus, the ruins of Bhuvan Pāhār shows that:

1. There must have been a Hindu temple around 12/13th century in which the so called image of Bhuvan (Śiva) and Pārvatī were installed. They were worshipped by the local tribal populations-mainly by the Manipuris and Nāgās. It must have been visited by the Khasis also, as we were told. At the foot hill there is a Khasi village. The sculptures have

no stylistic relation with the sculptures of Khāspur of the capital of Kachārī kings.

2. The original temple must have been fallen down due to natural calamity and subsequently Manipuri king, Buddha Chandra erected the tin-shed shrine wherein the present images were installed. He also renovated the bank of the old tank by making steps with the stone blocks used in the old temple at the site. The images of the so called Rāma and Sītā were installed by him. The images of Hanumān and Garuḍa should also be placed in a later period. They cannot be grouped with the images of Bhuvanbābā and Pārvatī.

3. It appears that both Śaivisim and Vaisnavism were popular here as in the other places of Assam, Bengal and other parts of the country. Saivism must have attracted the tribal people much earlier. Still Śiva is popular here as Bhuvanbābā and that is why the Zemi Nāgās have constructed a modern temple on this hill wherein the images of Bhuvanbābā and Pārvatī are regularly worshipped. From here at a distance Manipur border can be seen.

4. This is perhaps the highest hill in the entire N. E. region to have the ruins of a old Hindu temple.

5. The cave temple at the site is the only example in N.E. region. Although it is small in size, it has proved that the architect or the mason of those days tried to learn the technique of this architecture also. But it has been constructed in a peculiar method. Above the ceiling of the cave there is a super structure which must have been the *Śikhara,* which is damaged. This should be immediately conserved either by the Archaeological Survey of India or by the State Archaeology Department.[1]

It appears that before our visit no archaeologist visited the site. Even late Upedra Nath Guha, the author of the *Kāchārer Intibṛtta,* wherein he gave a description of the ruins, it seems did not visit the site.[2] He must have relied upon others. This ruins require detailed study.[3]

Notes and References

1. Mr. Mitra, the then Dy. Superintending Archaeologist, Archaeological Survey of India, Guwahati Circle visited the site later and took good photographs.
2. U.C. Guha, *Kāchārer Itibṛtta* (Bengali), 1971, pp. 11-15.
3. We are grateful to Mrs. Mandira Bhattacharya, Reader, Deptt. of History, North Bengal University for giving the valuable information of the ruins

and the caves at Bhuvan Pāhār. We are indebted to Mr. G.M. Srivastava, D.I.G. for his valuable help without which our trip would not have been possible. We are also grateful to the Superintending Archaeologist, A.S.I., Guwahati Circle for supplying the photographs used in this paper. Thanks are due to the officers and staff of the Forest Deptt., Silchar.

8

Assam Sculpture: An Outline

Looked from the point of view of styles the sculptures of Assam can be divided broadly into two groups, (a) Pre-Āhom sculptures and (b) Āhom sculptures. In the pre-Āhom period the kings of Kāmarūpa patronized art and culture and maintained its Indian tradition. In the Āhom period, the old tradition of Indian art suffered a set back due to various reasons. However, some Āhom and Koch and Kachārī rulers patronized art and culture in tune with their own tradition based on mainly Hindu religion.

The art history of Assam dates back to *c.* 6th century A.D. It is evident from the standing temple door frame at Daparvatīā near Tezpur. This ornate door frame carved out of three separate pieces of stone, depicts the standing figures of Gaṅgā and Yamunā, the two river goddesses, commonly found in the temple gate in the Gupta period at the bottom of the jambs in elegant posture each holding a garland with their hands. The figures along with the dwarf figures of attendants of the goddess are in high relief. Above these figures on either jamb of the door frame are seen three bands,—the middle one showing some human figures toped by the figures of Ganesh and Kārtikeya—the two sons of Śiva. On the topmost band on the lintel are seen some miniature figures of which a seated image of the Sūrya and that of a Lakuliśa, an aspect of Śiva., are clearly visible. In the centre of the lowest band of the lintel is seen a winged figure holding the tails of two snakes running as bands, on either jamb. The workmanship of details of the door frame is of high standard and such type of beautiful well proportionate lively figure of Gaṅgā and Yamunā as depicted on this piece are really rare treasures. This can be placed in the later half of 6th century on stylistic consideration.

The figure of a dvarapāla standing on the side of the Badgaṅga rock-cut inscription dated as belonging to the 6th century is also an example of the early sculpture of Assam. The style of the mated hair of the figure and the beaviness of the sculpture seem to bear the characteristic of early Gupta art style. A few terracotta plaques were discovered in the ruins of the temple at Daparvatiā. One of them shows a seated cross legged figure. Stylistically, it belongs to the 6th century A.D.

Sculptures of pre-Pāla style, are also found in Assam. Recently a stone image of Viṣṇu with two *āyudha purushas, i.e.*, in human form, was discovered at Khārāmedhipārā near Dudhnoi. Now, it is being preserved in the Assam State Museum Guwahati. In this image the figure of standing Viṣṇu is shown touching the miniature figures of Gadā Devī and Chakrapuruṣa with its lower hands, while the upper hands are made to hold *padma* and *śankha*. The image, on the basis of style, can be placed in *c.* 7th century A.D. This type of Viṣṇu images sculptured in Gupta styles during pre-Pāla period have been found in some places of Bengal and Bihar. However, the image in question is the only example of Viṣṇu of this type found in Assam. In the temple ruins of Deopānī a few stone images are found sculptured in the fashion of the late Gupta styles during the pre-Pāla period, *i.e. c.* 8th century. Of these images four have been preserved in the Assam State Museum.

Two images represent Viṣṇu, while the other two represent Harihara. Both the images bear inscriptions on their back. The image of Viṣṇu which does not bear any inscription is headless. The broken head is missing. All the images are chiselled after late Gupta style mixed with the local Mongoloid trait. Considering the character of the script of the inscriptions and the style of execution of these two images plus the headless Viṣṇu image, they may be paced in c. 8th century. The other Harihara images, appear to have borne inscriptions of a slightly later date. The execution of this image were found in the same place, where still two images, one of Kavala Narasimha and the other of Vāmana executed in c. 8th century sculptural style can be noticed. Similar sculptural style influenced by Gupta characteristic feature can be seen in a row of rock-cut sculptures representing Viṣṇu, Harihara and Śiva at Śrī Sūrya hill. Above this row of sculptures is seen a multi-armed standing deity canopied by a seven hooded snake. The identity of this deity is not very clear. By the side of these images a few votive *stūpas* datable to about 1st or 2nd century A.D. are noticed. Towards a little south of this site are seen another group of rock-cut sculptures representing Nemināth, Ṛisabhanāth and Gaṇeśa datable to about 8th century. It is to be noted that sculptural representations of Jaina divinities in Assam is found only at this site. Thus, the archaeological evidences show that Śrī Sūrya Hill was a centre of three religions, Hinduism, Buddhism, and Jainism. The existence of a pocket of Buddhism in that area is further substantiated by a recently discovered terracotta piece bearing Buddha and Boddhisattva images, the type of which are commonly found in Bengal in the early Pāla period.

As in other temple sites elsewhere in India, in Assam also erotic sculptures are found in some ruins of temples belonging to pre-Āhom period. The ruined stone temple at Piṅgaleśware presents some interesting erotic scenes. Here, there are scenes showing coition between man and women, women and other animals. Also, there are some scenes depicting masturbation. The presence of an image of Kārtikeya and another image of Gaṇeśa tends to prove that it was a Saiva temple. A few sculptures showing erotic scenes are also being preserved in the Assam State Museum, Guwahati. These are very similar to the erotic sculptures from Piṅgaleśwar. On the basis of the style, these pieces of art can be placed in c. 8th and 9th century.

Pre-Āhom sculptural style can be seen in the stone images from the ruins of a Śiva temple at Madan-Kāmadeva Parvat near Baihātā Chāriāli, Numalīgarh, Cole-Park, Tezpur and Bāmuni Hill near Tezpur. Rock-cut sculptures of the same period are also noticed at Śukreśver ghāt, Urvaśī island, Guwahati, and at Kāmākhyā. The Umā-maheśhvar image of the temple ruins at Madan-Kāmadeva Parvat and the seated rock-cut image at Sukreśver ghāt are very big sculptures. In the first case Umā is made to sit on the lap of Śiva in the usual posture, while the second sculpture represent Viṣṇu seated in *padmāsana* posture holding his usual *āyudhas*. On either side of Viṣṇu are seen the figure of Gaṇeśa, Sūrya, Mahiṣamardini, etc. in a a row. The hoard of bronze sculptures from Narakasur hill proves that metallic sculpture as art form was popular in the Pāla era.

The art style in eastern India reached its zenith in 12th century A.D. during the rule of the Senas in Bengal. The artists patronized by the Sena rulers who came from the South continued the style of art formulated by the artists of the Pāla period in Bengal and Bihar. These artists of the Sena period added more ornamentation and details to it. Such type of beautiful stone sculptures are not wanting in Assam. Three images sculptured in this style have been presented in the Assam State Museum, Guwahati. The first image representing Viṣṇu hails from Barpetā. Here the God is made to stand erect and to hold the usual *āyudhas, i.e. Śaṅkha,*

Cakra, Gada and *Padma*. The figure of the deity is well decked. The second image, which was collected from Budhābudhī, near Nowgang, is also of th same style with detailed ornamentation. The last image, which hails from Davakā, in the Nowgong district and which is identifiable with Davakā mentioned in the famous Allahabad pillar inscription of Samudra Gupta, represents Sūrya in standing posture holding two lotuses in the hands in the usual way. All these sculptures are carved on black basalt blocks with great care. Such types of sculptures are also reported from some other places of Assam.

The Chutiās ruled in the north-east corner of Assam, *i.e.*, the region around Śadiyā with their capital at Bhismak Nagar where ruins of that period have come to light. Tāmresvarī temple at Śadiyā is said to have been built during their rule. From the broken door jamb of that temple, it appears that during that period also the style of the eastern school of medieval sculpture was continued, but in a degenerated form. The best period of the said school of sculpture was the 12th century in Bengal as well as in Assam.

Later, it appears that Assam did not witness much art activities at least for a few centuries. Although the Tāi speaking people of Shān tribe from upper Burma entered into the Brahmāputra valley of Assam in 1926 A.D. they could spare very little time to augment art activities, as in the beginning they were busy with consolidation of their power and with administration. However, since the reign of Rājeśvar Singha from the 17th century onwards, we find regular work of art. The copper gate of Kamalabari Satra shows ten incarnations of Viṣṇu. The style of the figures of these incarnations have no resemblance with that of pre-Āhom sculpture. They are quite inferior in workmanship. In fact, the Āhoms used Tāi language for many years in the beginning. Hence, the Āhom artists were not acquainted with the Sanskrit text wherein the description of the various icons of Gods and Goddesses were given. They created a new style of art by imitating the pre-Āhom tradition and adding certain new elements to it.

The brass images of Mahiṣamardini from Tinsukia and the Viṣṇu image from Laruā Mauza, Dibrugarh should find a special mention. The representation of the fighting scene between the goddess Durgā and the buffalo demon is well depisted. But the treatment of 'topi' (cap) of the demon and its foot wear seems to bear Moghul style. The style of the lower garment of the goddess also shows similar trait. The short cones of the crown, a characteristic feature of late Āhom sculpture is evident in the image. The image representing the assimilation of two styles, Moghul and Āhom, may be dated in *c.* 18th century.

The icon of Viṣṇu, collected from Laruā Mauza, Nowgonh *Dilrugarh* district,now being preserved in the Assam State Museum, expresses typical Āhom style and so also the brass image of Arjuna from Puthimāri.[1]

There are three more sculptures of this period preserved in Assam State Museum. All of them are stone sculptures and they are from Tezpur. The first one represents a standing image of Parsurāma. Here, Parsurāma is shown holding his Paraśu, an axe. The axe is disproportionately bigger than the size of the body of the figure. The other two images, *i.e.*, the images of Brahmā and Agni are also sculptured in the same style and possibly by the same sculptor. It appears, that the sculptor while making these images did not pay heed to the anatomical measurements of the figures. This is a common style in case of any late medieval sculpture.

From Bāghapārā a few terracotta plaques have been collected and now being preserved in the Assam State Museum, Guwahati. Most of the pieces bear late medieval terracotta style created by the Moghal artist in Bengal region.

The temple at Hazo popularly known as Hayagrīva Mādhava, was built in 16th century under the patronage of Koch King and so also the famous Kāmākhyā temple on the top of the Nīlāchal hill. There are many sculptures struck into the temple walls of both the temples. These sculptures are chiselled in the same late medieval art style that prevailed in Assam. The stone sculptures collected from Bargang which was originally brought from Naxaparvat bear tribal trait. The peculiar type of art in the monoliths sculptured and erected at Dimapur and Khāspur during the rule of the Kachārīs are also worth mentioning. The monolithic columns bear geometric floral and animal designs which are quite different from Āhom, Koch or other sculptural style. Such art style is seen in any contemporary art.

In the late medieval period another type of sculpture mostly of wood and metal work came up with the setting up of the Vaiṣṇava *sattras*. This was the creation of the great art master, Śri Śankardeva. Sattriyā is art mainly of religious nature. It was created for the spread of Vaisnavism.

Thus, from the above discussion, we find that the sculptures of Assam bore the same style of art of the medieval period that was popular in Bengal and Bihar in the pre-Ahom period with some regional variations. In the

Āhom period it took a different style. It shows the influence of pre-Āhome, tribal and also Moghul style that prevailed in Bengal in the late medieval period.

Notes and References

1. This miniature image was stolen by miscreants by entering into the State Museum at night, when Mr. G.N. Bhryan was the Director. Police came to investigate, but no trace could be found them.

9

Some Folk Sculptures Preserved in the Assam State Museum

The practice of folk art in the ancient period in Assam is not known. Not only Assam but the entire North-East India is yet to be properly explored and the hidden treasures of this region dug out. From the exciting materials that are available in the Assam State Museum, which are described below, we get a clear picture of folk art tradition existing from *c.* 9th century.

First, let us examine a sculpture from Deopānī preserved in the Assam State Museum. The Deopānī ruins, about 26 km from Golāghāt on the Golāghāt-Dimāpur road have yielded quite a few stone images bearing such trait. The presiding deity of the temple is Durgā in *śānta-rūpa* (pacific form). Two images of Viṣṇu are also seen in the *garbha-gṛha* (sanctum) of the temple. On the right and left half walls of the *maṇḍapa* (hall) stone images of Kevalanarasimha and Vāmanāvatāra, respectively, are seen in *sthānaka* attitude.[1] Four images have already been removed from this site to Assam State Museum. Brick-bats are also noticed scattered about the place.

The image in question carved on a block of stone (14½ x 8cm) from Deopānī also represents Hari-Hāra. The right half of the image represents Viṣṇu, while the left represents Śiva. Garuḍa and Nandi are also seen flanking the deity. The *urddha-liṅga* of *Śiva* is clearly visible. Here also we find that the standing posture (*samapādasthānka*) and that of holding the *āyudhas*, are based on the classical formula. But the physiognomy of the figure of the God and His attendants are quite peculiar. They bear the similar local features. Of all the four images from Deopānī that are preserved in the Assam State Museum, the present one is the crudest in execution. The face of the deity is almost square. The forehead is a little projected, the eyes are a little bulging, the cheeks are a little sunken, and the closed lips are slightly projected. The miniature figure of Garuḍa is very crude. There is an inscription on the back of the image, the script of which bears the character of *c.* 9th century according to P.C. Choudhury.[2]

It may be noted that Deopānī lies closer to Dimāpur (now in Nagaland) and Kāchamāri, where still exist the ruins of the distinct culture associated with the Kachārīs. But the sculptures of Kāchamāri-pathār have nothing to do with the present group of sculpture from Deopānī. The Dimāpur and the Kāchamāri-pathār ruins belong to a much later period. However, the physiognomy of the sculpture bears an eloquent testimony to the fact that about 8th-9th century A.D. the Deopānī region must have been inhabited by tribal population (Kachārī) and possibly it was a pocket of some Tibeto-Burman people, who embraced the *Āryadharma* already popular in the rest of the country. Even if one does not think that the extra-Aryan physiognomy depicted in the sculpture from Deopānī has nothing to do with the folk element, it is sure that the image of our discussion, although chiseled in the classical formula, was sculptured by the local artist who added some amount of tribal feature to it, mixed with folk elements. R.M. Nath has given a description of the images that are found at Deopānī,[3] but he has not taken the folk element, noticed at least in a few of them,into consideration.

Next, we come to the group of Narakāsur bronze sculptures. This group of bronzes consists of a good number of metal sculptures, which on stylistic ground, belong to a period ranging from c. 9th-10th century to *c.* 11th A.D. Most of the images of this group represent various Brahmanical and a few Buddhist deities. Some of them are pleasing works of metal-art and have similarity with the Pāla school of Bengal and Bihar. However, a few pieces of sculptures do not bear classical Pāla trait. They are crude in representation. Specially, four medallions represent such type of sculptures, as we show below.

The first medallion (17 x 16 cms) shows a human head. Below it, the head of a buffalo with its two horns are seen. The neck of the human bust and the neck of the head portion of the buffalo are joined together. The human head is seen wearing a cap or (short *mukuṭa*) with flame-like decoration on either side. On the forehead, it has the third eye, if not a *tilaka*. The *kuṇḍalas* that are hanging down from its ears are quite clearly visible on either side. The eye-balls are slightly bigger in size. These features, definitely represent some folk motifs. The eyelids are not very clear. The lips are closed and a little projected.

Now, there lies the difficulty with regard to the identification of this icon. It is sure that it has not been sculptured in the classical form. The buffalo head may represent Mahiṣāsura, the demon, who was killed by Goddess Durgā. In that case, the human head with the third eye should represent Durgā with a terrible look. This type of iconographical representation is very rare. It is entirely based on folk style, as it appears.

The second medallion (21 x 18.2 cms) shows a four armed female goddess standing in *samapādasthānaka* attitude on the back of a buffalo. The objects held in the hands of the deity are clock- wise (upper left) *triśul*a, *gāda,* rein of the buffalo vehicle and *cakra*. The face of the goddess is cylindrical. The eyes are bulging and the nose is disproportionately pointed. The *mukuṭa* worn by the deity is of a peculiar type, the back of which is joined with the border of the medallion. The body of the deity is bedecked with the usual ornaments. She wears an *ūpavita* (?) on her body. The lower drapery of the goddess is well designed, the like of which is not usually found in the Pāla sculpture. Below, the buffalo which is in moving posture from the left to the right is also crudely depicted. Below it the medallion is slightly damaged.

Two lines of indistinct inscribed letter are noticed to the right of the figure of the deity on the vacant portion of the medallion. D.C. Sirear has given a reading of third inscription.[4] The script is not at all similar to the old Assamese script. Rather, it appears that the letters, though crude, may be similar to the letters of the 9th/10th century inscription found elsewhere in Assam.

The third medallion (22 x 17 cms) represents a four handed male deity standing on an animal in *samapādasthānaka* attitude. The deity holds clockwise (from upper left): *cakra*, *śaṅkha, akṣamālā* and *khaḍga*. On the head of the deity a mark is clearly noticed. He wears a hāra around the neck, a *kaṭimekhala* on the waist, and possibly a thin *kaṭivastra* is shown as his lower drapery. An *ūpavita* is also noticed on the body of the deity. The *ūrdhva-liṅga* is very clearly shown. The eyes of the god are large and so are the eyebrows. The nose is disproportionately raised but blunt. The face of the animal, which is moving to the left raising its tail and on the back of which the deity stands, is peculiar. The face of the animal, (if it represents a face of a tiger) is not very clear. The body portion of the animal looks like that of dog or tiger. Had the animal represented a bull, the deity could have somehow been identified as Hari-Hāra. Now the identification of the deity has become a problem, although some iconographic details of Śiva are found in this image. On either side of the god a line of indistinct inscription in the Brāhmī script of about 9th century A.D. is seen which has been read by D.C. Sircar.[5] Whatever may be the real identity of the god and the purport of the two-line inscription, it is true that the sculpture, bears a good deal of folk element in it.

The last medallion (20.5 x 19.5 cms) represents a two armed male figure standing in *samapādasthānaka* attitude on an ass or a donkey. With the right hand the god holds a stuff, while with the left he holds the rein of the ass. A pair of *kuṇḍala*, a *hara* and a pair of *valance* are seen worn on the various parts of the body of the god. On the waist a belt like *kaṭimekhala* is noticed. On the body an *ūpavita* is shown. The head of the god carries a simple conical *mukuṭa*. The eyes of the god are large and bulging. The nose is almost flat. The *vāhana*, an ass, is also crudely represented. From the style of the execution, it can be safely concluded that whatever may be the identity of the image, the sculpture differs significantly from the classical plastic art and it was done by some artists, producing folk art. All the four medallions depicting the figures in relief, show a clear line of folk-art tradition in Kāmarūpa in *c.* 9th/10th century A.D.

Among the same group of images there is a miniature bronze image. It represents a female (?) figure. It has two arms, abnormally long, which are hanging down below the knees. The hands of the figures are crudely depicted. The face of the figure is round. On its head there is no trace of hair. The mouth is open and the chin is very short. Traces of breasts in low relief are noticed. The legs are short. The style of the sculpture is plain. The present miniature figure, stylistically contains folk elements in it. It is likely that the image belongs almost to the same period to which the major images of Pāla style belong.

A miniature stone image of Sūrya from an unknown place Bhavānīpur of Assam datable to *c.* 8th century, preserved in the Assam State Museum with its depiction of the seven horses, the figures of Daṇḍa and Piṅgala, etc., show some affiliation to folk art treatment although the icon is sculptured in classical formula. So also is the depiction of the style of horses of the Sūrya icon in bronze from Narakāsur hill, preserved in the same museum, as that of the Sūrya image from Haharā, as we shall show. However, the other details of the Narakāsur Sūrya image belong to the mediaeval period.

Folk style can be traced in the terracotta sculptures from Bhishmaknagar, too. A plaque showing a rowing enjoyed by a couple, the second depicting a dancing female and another mutilated plaque carrying a couple, depict folk treatment in them. All these pieces were collected from Bhishmaknagar near Śadiyā from an extensive brick work that is now in complete ruins. These and the ruined Tāmreśvari temple at Śadiyā (now not to be seen) have been attributed to the Chutiās who ruled over this region in *c.* 13th century A.D.

Terracotta plaques from Jogījān in Nowgong district showing a warrior with a quiver and a bow, a seated image of Gajalakṣmī and a female seated figure, whose hair is being held by a male figure with its right hand, surely bear popular folk art traits. Unlike the figures from the Bhishmaknagar terracotta plaques, here each of the figures has a pair of bulging eyes. These plaques were discovered underground while clearing the debris of the sanctums that are in rows at Jogījān. The ruins of Jogījān, from the nature of the antiquities, may belong to early mediaeval period, *i.e.*, *c.* 9th century A.D., if not earlier. The terracotta sculptures from Bālujorā mauza, Goālpārā district, showing Śiva in crude form, bear the same popular style.

A brass image (8.7 x 5.8 cms) of a female deity from Māghnowā in *samapādasthānaka* posture is preserved in the same Museum. Here the deity is shown holding an arrow (?) in her right hand and a ring in the left hand. The deity wears a peculiar *mukuṭa* on her head which has three cones—the middle one being the shortest. The forehead is short. The *puṣpakuṇḍalas* that deck the ears of the deity are of a peculiar style. The flower of each *kuṇḍala* is shown with branches, either end of which have outward band. The cheeks are broad. The eyes are bulging. The nose is slightly damaged. The lips are closed. The arms are outwardly bent at elbow level in angular form. The feet of the deity are missing along with the lower portions of the *ādhāra* (frame) and the pedestal. The almost pointed *ādhāra* joins the main sculpture, it is difficult to say whom actually it represents. However, it is sure that the sculpture is devoid of classical treatment. It must have been worshipped as some folk goddess of late period.

A four-armed stone image (25.5 x 15 cms) hailing from Deopānī shows Viṣṇu in *sthānaka* attitude in a crude form. The deity is made to hold clockwise (from upper left): *cakra, gāda, padma, śaṅkha.* The upper hands are shown with outward angular bend, while the lower hands are shown below these two hands in the same fashion as seen commonly in the sculptures of the Āhom period. The cones of the short *mukuṭa* worn by the deity on his head are very short. The forehead of the deity is short, while the cheeks are broad. The eyes are amall but bulging. The nose is disproportionately long. The lips are closed. The lower portion of the deity wears a *dhoti*, a fold of which is prominently shown in between the legs which are shown apart. The chest portion of the god is a little projected. The style behind the god, of which the breadth of the lower portion is lesser than the upper portion, has for holes—two on either side of the neck and two on either side of the waist of the god. The physiognomy and other details show that the style of depiction of the image has nothing to do with the classical style. It is a typical folk art piece. The style of holding the *āyudhas,* it appears, has similarity with the Āhom sculpture. However, the facial expression shows its tribal or folk-art affiliation. Stylistically, it should belong to late mediaeval period, *i.e.*, 18th century or so.

The execution of the *jaṭā* with a crescent moon, the trunk and other details of each of the two metallic miniature images of Gaṇeśa from Haharā shows some folk elements. The Sūrya images (9 x 8.5 cms) from the same hoard portrays some folk elements mixed with classical one like the two Gaṇeśa images. Here above the row of seven horses who draw the symbolical chariot of the Sun-god, is shown a disc-like object on the edges around which are seen lotus petal-like design. The round disc rests on a stalk which is fitted on the back of the middle horse. On the back of this horse is seated Aruṇa, the chariot driver, who is not clearly visible from the front. In the centre of the disc, on a full-blown lotus is seen Sūrya seated crosslegged holding a lotus in each of his two hands, who is flanked by seated figures of Daṇḍa (?) and Piṅgala (?). The seated figure of the Sun-god on a lotus which again rests on one inch long stalk is of extremely rare type. This treatment is not to be seen in any image of Sūrya sculptured in classical style. The entire sculpture has undergone folk influence, as it appears from its representation. The same type of combined folk and classical treatment is found in the representation of Gajalakṣmī, a metallic image of the same group. Here, folk element is clearly seen in the crude depiction of four elephants (one being missing), each standing on a corner and pouring water on the head of Lakṣmī, who is shown seated in the centre. Usually in the image of Gajalakṣmī sculptured in the common classical form, two elephants are shown.

One of the most interesting sculptures of the Assam State Museum is a ten handed deity (20 x 18 cm). It is from Mangaldoi. The figure of the deity is shown as standing erect. All the hands are shown stretched outward horizontally with a grip in each hand. The arms of each of the hands are shown issued from both the sides of the body portion, *i.e.*, from the actual arm to the belly portion, which is an extremely rare instance. The chest and the belly portion is almost "U" shaped. On the chest portion in all 13 nails are shown fixed on the body. Four blank small holes are also seen here. Evidently, in these holes some nails were put, which are now missing. On the belly also is seen such a nail. Whether these iron nails were put for ornamentation or some other purpose is not clear. The deity has two eyes. The eyes are represented by two golden nails fitted into the actual eye-sockets. On the forehead of the figure a very small hole is seen. Undoubtedly, there was also a golden nail which represented the third eye. There is no trace of a *mukuṭa* on the head of the deity. However. it appears that at the top of the head the hair knot is shown. The peculiar ears are of big size. The mouth is slightly opened. The nose is almost flat. The entire face is almost round. The neck is abnormally long. Another peculiar feature of the sculpture is that around the neck and the waist of the figure the style is cut deeper and perforated possibly to show the figure in relief. The perforation is continued in two rows on either side of the chest and the belly portion of the figure in between the horizontally stretched arms. In all, there are 24 perforations (small holes). Below the lowest left hand are seen two crude two-armed human figures in shallow relief. Below these figures is seen a dog (?). On the other side, under the lower right arm of the deity is seen a miniature standing human figure in dancing posture (?). Two round flower motifs are seen in shallow relief in front of and above these figures. Below, at the level of the feet as on the other side, a crude representation of an animal (tiger) is seen. The style is pointed and surmounted by a *liṅga*-like thing. From the technique of the sculpture, adopted in this work, it is clear that the artist did not touch the classical style at all and this art product is the result of the translation of his idea in his mind into an art form of his own. The identity of the divinity, depicted in this work, is not very clear. Whether it represents a male or a female deity is also not known. However, it appears that the artist tried to work out an image of Durgā. The ten arms, the third eye on the forehead of the deity and the presence of a crude figure of tiger (?) below the right side of the leg of the deity show that it bears the fundamental iconographical features of Durgā. However, the common fighting scene between the goddess Durgā and Mahiṣa (buffalo demon) is not shown, and as such, it should be taken as the pacific form of Durgā. Two images of Durgā in pacific form from the medieval period are noticed in Assam, one at Deopānī as stated above, and the other at Dimāpur.[6] which have, of course, stylistic differences from the present one.

The back of the style of the sculpture bears a nicely designed tree motif. On either side of this motif are seen two rows of lotus (?) petals in conical shape. In all, there are 16 perforation marks. The tree design or motif is executed on a tiered base. In the locality amongst the tribal people this piece of icon was known as Buḍhī Gosānī, *i.e.* Durgā. The style of depiction of the arms of the goddess shows that the folk artist believed in simple expression and to some extent in abstract art, too. Stylistic consideration leads us to place it in a very late period.

In the same Museum two miniature metal images—one representing Kṛṣṇa and the other Veṇugopāla (from Billveśvar *devālaya*)—show the same trend of the popular art style. The same trend is depected in the art style of the metal sculptures belonging to *c.* 18th century, preserved in the *Piṅgaleśvar-devālay*a, Assam, which were donated by the royal authorities of the late Āhom period (now These are stolen from the temple).

The above study of the art pieces of the sculptures collected from various places of Assam, now preserved in the Assam State Museum, Gauhati, shows that side by side with the classical art practised by the professional artists under the patronage of the royal authorities in the medieval period, *i.e.*, pre-Āhom period, in Assam, a tendency of folk art, or at least the folk art with tribal affiliation, did exist, as is evidenced by the Deopānī and Narakāsur hill sculptures. In fact, the Deopānī art is the work done by the Kachārī (Tibeto-Burman) artists, on the principle of the Brahmanical iconography keeping their own identity in the representation of at least the faces of the sculptures. From this it is also proved that the Kachārī people in that area accepted Hinduism as early as the 9th century.

The existence of this art form is also proved by the sculptures from Jogījān. As in other parts of India, it is sure that here, too, archaeological excavation will throw more light on this aspect of the local or popular art tradition. The art depicted in the terracotta plaques from Bhishmaknagar reflects the same tendency that existed in the 13th/14th century. During the Āhom period, although in some places by some artists the pre-Āhom art formula (eastern Indian medieval art) was continued in a degenerated form, as evidenced by some Āmbāri sculptures, the general style of the art got much deteriorated and it has no stylistic relation with the pre-Āhom art style. Rather, the art style that developed in this period, it appears, had a leaning towards the tendency of the folk art. By the end of the Āhom rule, *i.e.*, 19th century, the style adopted by the artists, who were patronised by the royal authorities, deteriorated so much so that it was almost fully absorbed in the folk-art form.

Notes and References

1. R.M., Nath, has described five stone images preserved in the place. They are: two Viṣṇu images, one Durgā image, one Śiva image and an image if Umā-Maheśvara. See, *Journal of the Assam Research Society,* Vol. VIII, No. 4 pp. 130 f.
2. *Sāptaāhik Nīlācal,* An Assamese Weekly, Sreeguru Press, Guwahati, Chaitra, 1819 *saka.*
3. *Op.cit.*, Vol. XIX, 1970, pp. 23-24.
4. *Journal of the Ancient India History,* Vol. X, 1976-77. pp. 114-22. Also see, B.N. Mukharjee, *East Indian Art Style*, 1980, Calcutta, pp. 28-30, Fig. 77-80 for identification of some icons of deities from Kāhilipārā.
5. *Ibid.*
6. Nath, R.M. *The Back-ground of Assamse Culture, Shillong,* 148.

10

Some Wooden Sculptures Newly Collected for Assam State Museum

The Assam State Museum authorities have recently collected some old wooden sculptures from Sundarīdiā *satra* and Janiā *satra* near Barpetā, which is the district headquarter of Barpetā district. The village Janiā is located at a distance of 8 km west of Barpetā, while Sundarīdiā village is situated about 3 km east of Barpetā across the Chāulkhowā river. Both the places, well known for the sacred *satras* or Vaiṣṇava monasteries, can be reached by vehicular traffic. This type of *satras* or the Vaiṣṇava institutions were introduced by Śrī Śaṅkardeva, the great Vaiṣṇava saint in Assam for propagating Vaisnavism in the 16th century and these *satras* are seen throughout the Brahmāputra valley in great numbers. The Berpetā satra is said to be the biggest and well maintained *satra* in Assam.

In all, in the past few months 14 pieces of old art, *i.e. Satriā* art were collected for the Assam State Museum. Of these 5 pieces were collected from the Janiā *satra,* while 9 pieces were collected from the Sundarīdiā *satra.*

Sculptures from Janiā Satra

The first piece of work of art (43 x 15 cms) represents Garuḍa, the vehicle of Lord Viṣṇu. Here Garuḍa is depicted in the usual style *i.e.,* kneeling with *añjalī-hasta mudrā* out of reverence to his lord, the figure of which is, however, is not depicted along with him. This mythical figure is always depicted in hybrid form. Here also he has been depicted in the same style. However, his wings are not seen. At the back of the figure there are two nail marks. Possibly, the wings were fitted with the nails, and they are now detached due to rough handling. This piece of wooden sculpture must have been painted, for, the trace of yellow colour can be noticed on the eyes, the short *mukuṭa* and the folds of his lower garment seen falling down in between his kneeling legs. The right ear of the figure is broken.

The second piece of sculpture (30 x 43 cms) shows a scene of killing of a man by an elephant. The man is falling on the ground and the elephant is standing on the legs of the man and with its trunk it is trying to catch hold of the neck of the man. On the other hand, the man is also seen trying to fight with the elephant. He is holding the trunk of the elephant with its left hand and exercising a sword with the right hand. The head and the face of the man are damaged. The figures are not proportionately carved. The figure of the man has become big compared to the figure of the elephant. Both the figures are in low relief. The style is slightly pointed. On the other side of this object, the trace of a painting showing the figure of Garuḍa is noticed. The painting in pink and ash colour is almost fade up. Possibly, this wooden piece was placed on the wall of the *satra* so that from either side the painting and the carving became visible to the visitors.

The third work of art (42 x 26 cms) shows the Gaja-vyāla motif *i.e.*, the popular motif in the sculptural art of Assam or other part of the country. Here the lion is shown riding over the vanquished elephant. In *Satriā* art this motif was very popular. The lower portion of the sculpture is slightly damaged. A burning mark is also seen on it.

The next piece of sculpture (20 x 10 cms) shows a scene of lion riding over or jumping over (or treading over) a retreating deer. During pre-Āhom period this deer and elephant motif was not used in sculpture. This motif was created, it appears by the *Satriā* artist.The last piece of wooden sculpture (25 x 18 cms) from Janiā also shows the same lion and deer motif. Here the face of the lion is mutilated.

Sculptures from Sundarīdā Satra

The first sculpture shows the figure of Viṣṇu (75 x 34 cms). Here Viṣṇu is depicted in *samapādasthānaka* attitude on a lotus. He holds *padma, gadā, cakra and śankha* in his four hands clock-wise. The *Kīriṭa-mukuṭa* and the *vanamālā* worn by the deity are clearly visible. The remnants of the stele on either side of the figure of the deity show two miniature figures of combined figures of *Makara* and *Siṁha* at the top. The style must have been tapering, but unfortunately this portion is broken. The *Makara-Siṁha* motif is not found in the pre-Aom or Āhom sculpture, as far as our knowledge goes. It is the creation as *satriā* artist. The entire figure of the deity is under deep blue colour, which is now slightly fade up.

The second sculpture (67 x 28 cms) from Sundarīdiā Satra represents *Balarāma*. He is depicted in *samapādasthānaka* attitude. He is holding a gadā with his right hand and a plough with his left hand. Above the *mukuṭa* worn by the God, three hoods of a snake are canopying. Two hoods of the snake are broken. The figure of the God must have been in white colour which is completely fade up.

The third sculpture representing the figure of four armed Viṣṇu (48 x 26 cms) seems to be carved only a few years back. The deity is made to stand putting his legs apart on a lotus. The *āyudhas* of the hands are not sculptured by the artist along with the hands. The hands are shown gripping the *āyudhas*. The *āyudhas*, made of iron are put in the grip of each hand. Now, except for the *cakra* held in the upper right hand, other *āyudhas* held in the other hands are missing. This type of style of holding *āyudhas* became popular in the later phase of the *satriā* art tradition. The *Kīriṭa-mukuṭa* worn by Viṣṇu is replaced by a very short *mukuṭa* with a symbolical peacock feather in the middle of the present case. This is also a very late characteristic feature. Behind the head a round halo (*Śira-Cakra*) made of tin is seen. Behind the body of the figure of the deity a long *chivara* type back cloth can be noticed. It is a very late phenomenon. The body of the figure of the God is in blue colour while his lower garment, a *dhoti*, is depicted as yellow.

The next figure in *sthānaka* attitude represents Ananta Nāgā in human form. Here the male human figure is shown as holding a *gadā* with its left hand, while the right hand is made to hold a *daṇḍa*. Above the *mukuṭa* of a late style worn by the figure a canopy of a five-hooded snake is seen. The body position of the snake is made such a way that it looks as if it has emerged from the human body of Ananta. The eyes of Ananta look a little bulging. The body of the figure is in white colour, while the lower garment, a *dhoti* is in deep blue colour.

There is a solitary stone sculpture (57 x 19 cms) depicting a human figure in *sthānaka* attitude in group. If it represents a male figure is not very clear. For, the breasts are slightly raised and a *hāra* is also traced around the neck of the figure. The lower drapery must be a *dhoti*. The elongated eyes, nose, chin etc. lead us to think that image must have been brought from Utter Pradesh, or Bihar some years back. As the projected hands of the figure do not hold anything or if any objects were fitted into the grip of the hands are not known, it is not possible to know its identity.

The group of sculptures includes three wooden panels too. All of them were used on the walls for decoration purpose. The first piece (52 x 62 cms) shows the most bulky figure of Rāvana with ten heads and twenty arms. Rāvana is made to sit cross-legged. His belly and the chest portion of the body is shown as very wide and flat. Compared to the size of the body the figure, the heads and arms are quite small. The tenth head is put above the middle head of the row of nine heads. The combination of yellow, red and blank colours are seen on the sculpture in bad state. Below, on either side of the figure of Rāvana a stylized lion, the symbol of *Vaiṣṇava* seat is shown. Two corners of this panel are slightly mutilated. The entire figure is carved in low relief in a chamber or *Khaṭṭaka* measuring (38 x 36 cms).

The second piece of wall panel (68 x 50 cms) shows Viṣṇu in a peculiar seated posture flanked by his consorts, Lakshmi and Sarasvatī (Plate 165). The deity is made to hold the usual āyudhas in his four hands *i.e., Śankha, chakra, Gadā,*and *Padma* clock-wise. Lakshmī is seen holding right leg of Viṣṇu with both of her hands. On the other side Sarasvatī is shown as holding the *Cāmara.* It appears, Viṣṇu is made to sit on an *āsana* (seat) higher than the *āsana* over which the consorts are sitting. On either side of the *āsana i.e., simhāsana* over which the entire scene is depicted are seen two stylized lions. The scene is carved in a niche or *Khaṭṭaka* in low relief. The colours put to decorate the figures are fade up. A similar scene depicting Viṣṇu seated in a peculiar style along with his consorts are seen. But here his consorts are made to stand. The god is very crudely depicted and the scene is also not carved well. Possibly, it is not properly finished. On each of the four corners of the wooden plaque there is a hole for fixing on the wall with nails. The last wooden panel (58 x 53 cms) shows peculiar scene. Here two stylized lions are seen in a moving posture on side *i.e.,* in opposite direction. The hind portions of both the figures are touching each other and over the backs of those lions a human figure is seen sitting in a peculiar *lalitāsana.* The left leg of the figure is streetched downwards in 45 degree. The figure with its two hands holds arrows and a bow. On the head of the figure a turban is noticed. The *uttareya-bastra* on the body of the figure is also clearly visible. It has a moustache. The front fold of the *dhoti* worn as lower drapery of the figure is shown as flying due to the movement of the lions while running. To the right of this figure is seen a seated male figure on a chair putting a turban on its head. The figure is putting a long sleeved coat of mail (?) as his upper garment. The right hand of the figure is holding something which is not clear. The figure has a moustache. Whom these two figure represent is not clear. If the artist tried to depict Sūrya or Arjuna or some royal figure is also not clear to us.

The last one represents a figure of Hanumān in seated posture. He is eating a *ladduka* or some other object which is seen placed between his two lips. The figure is half burnt.

The study of these sculptural pieces described above reveal that in these two *satras*, as in other *satras* in Assam, mainly two styles of making of sculptures were practised by the artist *i.e.*, the sculptures representing gods, Viṣṇu and other Vaiṣṇava gods meant for worship (?) inside the *satra* or its *Manikut* (sanctum) and the decorative panels for stucking on the walls of the main building of the *satra*. The images of gods held in worship were carved out from solid block of wood, while the panels were prepared from the wooden planks. The figures on the panels are always carved in low relief. The panels are heavier. The presence of folk elements in the sculpture made of wood is a common affair. But, it appears, these elements can be seen more in the panels. For, the artists found more liberty while carving panels. But, the artist carving icons held in worship had to follow certain iconographical texts or tradition. The panel showing the figure of Rāvana is full of folk elements and so also the other panels. While the first icon of Viṣṇu and Balarāma are carved almost in classical style although it has undergone some changes with additions of folk elements. However, in later phase of the satriā art the icons held in worship also were greatly influenced by the folk art tradition, as is evident from some sculptures of our discussion. From stylistic point of view, all the sculptures discussed above should belong to the latest phase of the Āhom or Koch rule. Some of them even should date in the first half of this century.

The *satras* were the great centres of music, dance and wood carvings. A good number of old wood carvings used as decorative wall panels are still to be seen in *situe* in *satras at* Soālkuchi, Barpetā and other places of Assam. Some of the valuable wood carrings used as the decorative panels on the walls of the original *satra* building at Bardowā, the great centre of *satriā* art tradition, are seen in bad state. However, the Directorate of Museums, Assam has taken up a new plan to preserve them by setting up a local museum at Bardowā. As the use of wood carving in Āhom temples was not common and the wood carving belonging to the pre-Āhom period did not exist due to peculiar climatic condition in Assam, it has become the urgent necessity to preserve wood carvings, which are easily perishable. The Directorate of Museums, Assam, has taken up a project to collect these objects in phased manner.[1]

Notes and References

1. Dr. Naren Kalita has made a study on these wood art works and recently written a monograph on them. But his monograph has been published in Assamese. See N. Kalita, *Bardowār Śilpa-vastu*, Nagaon, 1985. Kalita has made a detailed study on the objects in depth. For the first time Kalita has made a study on wood art in Assam. But the book is in Assamese.

11

Some Buddhist Sculptures Preserved in the Assam State Museum

The Assam State Museum, located in Guwahati, the most important city of North-Eastern India, is the treasure house of the past culture of the Brahmaputra valley of Assam and its neighbourhood. This museum has a good collection of sculpture, amongst other things. Majority of the sculptures preserved in this museum represents Brahmanical deities. In quantity next to Brahmanical gods and goddesses, comes the Buddhist deities. Not a single Jaina sculpture is preserved here. Only three Jaina icons have been noticed in entire Assam so far. All of them represent Riṣabhanātha which are cut on rocks at Śrī Śūrya Pāhār.[1]

Although the rulers of Kāmarūpa kingdom were Hindus and patronized art and culture, yet they did not hate other faiths. They had a sense of tolerance. A section of people did believe in Buddhism and they worshipped Buddha, as is known from both written records and archaeological evidence, as we shall show. This is also supported by the records of Hieun Tsang,[2] who visited Kāmarūpa and stayed in Prāgjyotiṣpura, now identified as Guwahati, during the rule of Kumār Bhāskara Varmana, an illustrious king of Kāmarūpa in 7th century. The Āhom rulers who belonged to the great Tāi race entered the Brahmaputra valley in the beginning of the 13th century (1228 A.D.) and ruled till 19th century, when the administration went to the hands of the British government. Although they practised their own faith (Pagan religion-not Buddhism) in the first part of their rule, later they accepted Hinduism and patronized art and culture through Hindu religion. During the late phase of their rule, Buddhist people, such as Khāmtis, Norās, Phākiāls etc. from Burma entered into the Brahmaputra valley and still they are seen settling in some pockets in upper Assam and Arunachal Pradesh.

It will not be out of place, though the scope of our present paper is very limited, to mention that the earliest evidence of Buddhism in Assam is noticed at Śrī Śūrya Pāhār. Here quite a few votive Buddhist monolithic rock-cut *stūpas* and a few rock-cut caverns can be seen. Stylistically, they should date in early Christian centuries.[3] Next early evidence is found at Da-parvatiā.[4] It is a terracotta sculpture representing a torso of a male seated figure, which can be taken as a Buddhist deity.

The first icon of our discussion is a beautiful brass image of Buddha (55 cms x 48 cms) found at Chābuā near Tinsukiā in upper Assam. The face of the god is mutilated. The lord Buddha is here shown as seated cross-legged in *vajraparyāṅkaāsana.* The right hand is in *bhūmiṣparaśa mudrā.* The left hand is resting on the lap. The top right corner of the head is broken away. The deity wears the usual elongated ear-lobs. The left eye is seen half-closed. The chins and the folds of the neck are clearly visible. The figure is clad in a garment that leaves the right shoulder and breast bare. The folds of the drapery are depicted in a conventional fashion on the left shoulder and arm. The garment is highly sophisticated from the stylistic point of view. The border of the garment was decorated with artificial gems or glass, as it appears. The elegance and grace of this image reflecting sublimity proves that this piece of metallic art is an work of high order. Stylistically, the image may be placed around 11th century or so.

The second image of the lord is carved on a white marble (46 cms x 31 cms) over which some coatings of paints are put. It is from Arunachal Pradesh. It is a bust and the lower portion is not shown. The image is from some place of Arunachal Pradesh which is not known. The *uṣṇīṣa, ūrna* and the elongated ear-lobs are most artistically carved. The nose is flat and the eyes are half closed. The *uṣṇīṣa* here has some striking similarity with that of the seated Buddha in stone from Chābuā.

The next icon of Buddha hails from Golāghāt.[5] The image measures 43.5 x 26 cms. This image is very much similar to the image of the lord found at Chābuā, described above. Here also the deity is made to sit in *vajraparyāṅka sana* and forming *bhūmiṣparśa mudrā*. The half closed eyes are beautifully depicted. The *uṣṇīṣa* and the elongated earlobs are clearly shown. Above the *uṣṇīṣa* the symbol of flame is noticed. The folds of the drapery are not so prominent as we see in the case of the image from Chābuā. This metāllic image is smaller than the image from Chābuā. However, the physiognomy of the sculpture, though little different from the other, yet we can say that South-East Asiatic style is very much clear. Stylistically, it should date in c. 13th century or so. The present image compares well with Buddha image sculptured in Simese style.[6]

There is a miniature sculpture (12.5 cms x 6.4 cms) of Buddha made of lead. This is from Arunachal Pradesh. Here the deity is shown in the usual posture *i.e.*, seated in *bhūmiṣparśa mudrā*. The ornaments and *uṣṇīṣa* are not clear. The deity is made to sit on *bhadrāsana*. Behind the deity a snake hood (?) a pointed stela is clearly seen. The back of the sculpture shows a votive *stūpa* design. It may be Muchalinda Buddha

About two years back, the Assam State Museum collected as many as 64 images of Buddha from Barphākiāl (Tāi-Phāke) Buddha Vihār, situated on the western bank of the river Dihing near Mārgheritā. Dibong Buddha Vihār is about 3 k.m. from Mārgheritā and one can reach this place along Mārgheritā-Tengākhāt P.W.D. road, a motorable road. From this Buddha Vihār, the Barphākiāl Buddha Vihār is about 2 km. The road to Barphākiāl Buddha Vihār is not good.[6]

When we first visited Dibong Buddha Vihāṛ in connection with my study, I met Mr. Varanachar Bhikshu, who on my request readily presented three old images of Buddha lying in the Vihār. These images were discarded and not held in worship at the time of their collection. The first one is a standing image of Buddha made of wood. Here the deity is shown in *sampādaṣthānaka* attitude. Both the hands of Buddha are shown hanging down without forming any *mudrā*. The *uṣṇīṣa* of the head of the deity is very clearly shown. The elongated earlobs is nicely depicted. The *chivara i.e.*, the entire dress worn by the deity, is also nicely depicted. The border of the *chivara* is dotted with glass chips for decoration. The physiognomy of the sculpture has clearly depicted Burmese affinity.

The second image of the Buddha is depicted as seated in *bhūmiṣparśa mudrā*. The *uṣṇīṣa* in not shown. In its place on the head a pointed crown is shown. The dress wron by the figure is different from that of the previous one. The dress worn by the deity here is akin to the dress used in mythological *khon* dance drama of Thailand. On shoulders, elbows, wrist and knees of the attire flame like objects are used. The attire is bedecked with dotted glass chips. The deity wears *hara* on his neck. Like the former image this is also coloured with yellow pigment. The image is made in paperpulp, saw-dust and clay technique.

The third one is again a seated image in the same style. It is made of wood. The deity has *uṣṇīṣa* on his head and wears *chivara* of which the border is dotted with glass chips. The folds of the *saṅghāṭi* is very clearly shown. The elongated ear-lobs are also shown in the usual manner. The image is under the usual colour *i.e.*, golden, which has been raced in some places. All these three images bear physiognomy of Burmese affiliation.

After getting an information from Śrī Varanachar Bhikshu of the Dibong Buddha Vihār regarding more such images in the nearby Barphakial Buddha Vihār, I could not resist my temptation. After some days I paid a visit to the Buddha Vihār in the company of Śrī G.C. Sarma, Assistant Political Officer, Mārgheritā and after seeing a good number of discarded images of Buddha kept in a neglected condition, we requested the Barphākiāl Buddha Vihār Committee to handover these to the Assam State Museum in a formal function. They agreed to do so. Subsequently, they were handed over to the Assam State Museum in a formal function.

In all 64 images of Buddha of various sizes were collected from the Barphakial Buddha Vihār. The material used for making these images are wood, paper-pulp, saw-dust, glass and marble. The images are in *samapadsthānaka* and *vajraparyāṅkasana* attitude forming *bhūmiṣpar-śamudrā*. We have not come across any image of Buddha in *Śayana* or reclining attitude in this group. The number of seated images is high. There are only two images in *sathanaka* attitude. Only one image of marble is seen. The number of glass image also is one. It is a torso.

The majority of the seated images are draped in the dress akin to mythological *khon* dance drama of Thailand, which symbolises the deity as having super-hunman quality. The style of this type of image has already been mentioned while describing the seated image in royal dress used in dance from Dibong Buddha Vihār. There are also quite a few seated image showing *uṣṇīṣa* on head and wearing *chivara*. These are quite similar to the first images from Dibong Buddha Vihār described above. Both the *sthānaka* images are wooden. They wear *chivara*. In both the cases the deity has *uṣṇīṣa* on head. The elongated ear-lobs is also shown in each case. In fact, both the images are sculpture in the style of the *sthānaka* image of Buddha from Barphākiāl Buddha Vihār.

The biggest image of the group as depicted in the *bhūmiṣparśa mudrā* in usual way. It measures 1.75 cms x 74 cms. It is made of paper pulp and saw-dust. Here the deity is made to wear the royal mythological dress used in *khon* dance drama. There is another image of Buddha made of Sandal wood. It represents the bust portion of the deity measuring 29 x 37 cms. The *saṅghāṭi* worn by the deity and the *uṣṇīṣa* on his head are clearly shown.

The lone glass image, a torso, although seated, is not shown in *vajraparyāṅkasana* forming *bhūmiṣparśa mudrā* with his right hand, as we noticed in majority of the images of the group. Here the deity is shown seated simply cross-legged. The image carved on marble is also depicted in the *asana* attitude wearing a *chivara.*

From the above discussion, we find that the images collected from Dibong Buddha Vihār and Barphākiāl Buddha Vihār go together in the matter of style, material used and periodicity. The images made of pulp are holo and they are cast images. All these images are executed in Burmese style. On stylistic consideration and the consideration of the material used to carve them, these images are not very old. They may be placed between 50 to 100 years in age. However, they are important because, they are mostly executed in wood and paper-pulp which are easily perishable in the damp climate of Assam. Their preservation will definitely carry some benefit to the scholars of the future generation. The local people of the Barphākiāl village told these image were brought from Burma and some of them were carved in the Buddha Vihār by Burmese artisans or carpenters. The materials used in these Buddha images, *i.e.*, paper-pulp, is not common in Assam.

There are many Buddha Vihārs in upper Assam. Buddha Vihārs are also called *Bapu-Chāng* in Assamese language. *Bapu* means Buddhist monk and '*Chāng*' means a wooden or a bamboo platform. Thus, *Bapu-Chāngs* or the Buddha Vihār are double storied building made of wood and bamboo. They may be C.I. Sheet roofed or thatched roofed.

Apart from the images of Buddha with South-East Asiatic affiliation there are also a few also a few images of Buddha or Buddhist deities with Indian or Tibetain affiliation. They include the image of stamped Buddha on terracotta tablet, Khadiravani Tārā, Jānguli Tārā, Bodhisattva, Chuṇḍā, et. All these icons of the Buddhist deities had mahāyana affiliation. During the Pāla regime mahāyana and *vajrāyana* form of Buddhism be came very popular in Bengal and Bihar. Though the ruler of Kāmarūpa, the old name of Assam, were Hindus, due to their tolerance for or respect to other religion, Buddhism could gain some ground in the Brahmaputra valley of Assam. This mahāyana form of Buddhism came to Assam from the western side of the home land. But the therāvādin from of Buddhism came to the Brahmaputra valley from the east, *i.e.*, South-East Asia-mainly bordering Burma. The Siāmese cultural contact with this region of India is also proved cultural by the sculpture of Buddha which bears the *Sakhodaya* style of Thailand. Not only in the field of art history but also in the matter good deal of similarity with South-East Asia. This shows that Assam and South-East Asiatic countries had cultural contact in past which is still being continued in various ways.[7]

"Sarve sattva sukhita Hantu"

Notes and References

1. R.D. Choudhury, "Antiquities of Śrī Śūrya Pāhār: A Source of Early History of Kāmarūpa", *Sources of the History of India,* Vol. III (Ed. N.R. Ray), Calcutta, 1980, pp. 37-38. Facets of Indian History, culture and Archaeology Ed. by S.P. Gupta & K.S. Ramachandran, New Delhi, 1991, p. 62; *Kṛṣṇa Smṛti,* Prof. K.D. Bajpai Felicitation Volume, Ed. R.K. Sharma & R.C. Agarwal, New Delhi, 1995, pp. 233-235. Assam Tribune, a daily, Guwahati, 27th January, 1990 (Sunday Reating).
2. Watters *On Yūan Chwang's Travels in India,* Vol. II, London, 1904, p. 186f. Also see, R.D. Choudhury, *'Archaeology of the Brahmaputra Valley of Assam'*, Delhi, 1985, p. 19.
3. R.D. Choudhury, *op.cit.,* pp. 112-13.
4. *Annual Report of Archaeological Survey of India,* 1925-26, p. 110.
5. This image is strikingly similar to that of the image of the deity printed in the folder of "Thailand" published in connetion with the International Conference on Thai Studies held in Bangkok from 22-24 August,' 1984.
6. R.D. Choudhury, *"Barphākiāl Buddha Vihārar Murti,"* *Batori* (An Assamese Bi-weekly), Guwahati, 24th January, 1982.
7. I am very much greatful to Shri G.N. Bhuyan, Director of Archaeology, Assam, Guwahati, Mr. Pradip Chaliha, Director of Ajanta Kala Mandal, Golāghāt, Assam and Mr. B.K. Malakar, the then Librarian-cum-Publication Officer of the Directorate of Museums Assam, Guwahati for their valuable abvice and co-operation.

12

Terracotta Sculptures from Assam (pre-Āhom-Chutiā-Koch Period)

Terracotta sculptures as in other parts of the country, in Assam too have been discovered. Since, except archaeological excavation at Āmbari, Bhaitbari Cotton College Campus, and Śrī Sūrya Pāhār no systematic excavation in Assam has been conducted to unearth the hidden past treasures, number of terracotta here is very less compared to the other parts of the country. That this great art was practised to a great extent by the artists of old Assam or Kāmarūpa is a fact. Only the archaeological excavation will be able to reveal its potentiality.

The earliest terracotta sculpture of this region comes from Da-parvatīā, famous for the temple door frame depicting lovely figures of Gaṅgā and Yamunā, while clearing the debris at the site of this ruined temple R.D. Benerji, the then Superintending Archaeologist, Archaeological Survey of India, discovered it in 1926 and published it in his report.[1] Alongwith it possibly few more terracotta figures were discovered of which a photograph of a broken piece was published. About the rest he has not given details. The first figure is shown as seated cross-legged. The head of the figure is lost. It is a male human figure. "The modelling of this figure which consists in the broad chest, the proportionately thin waist, the well framed hands and the style in which the hands and legs are kept necessarily connect this figure with some of the medieval stone-sculptures."[2] Benerji has further remarked that "The style of the representation of these figurine shows a very close connection between medieval art of Bengal and Assam (reported in the same volume) and at Pāhārpur."[3] A comparative study of the figurine in question with a figure of Buddha from Pāhārpur[4] proves that Banerji's remark holds good. But slight difference is also noticed. The Pāhārpur figure seated in *bhumiāparṣamudrś*. But our figure is in a peculiar pose. Both the hands of the figure are made to hold something and rest on the respective knees. However, seated cross-legged figure holding *āyudhas* forming peculiar *mdurā* are found in many places in Assam.[5]

Of late in the Daparvatīā village, near the ruined temple site two more pieces of terracottas are noticed. S.C. Bhattacharya published a preliminary report on them.[6] Subsequently, both the pieces of sculptures were brought to the Assam State Museum with his help. The first plaque (31 x 25 cms) shows two female figures riding on elephants. Both the elephants on which the female figures are sitting, are shown facing to the opposite direction so that the back portions of the bodies touch each other. Their rear portions touches each other with heavy pressure and so the tails are not seen. Each of the female rider places one hand on the waist and the other hand rises above head in an attractive posture possibly holding some indistinct object. The upper portion of the breast of the image of left side is mutilated, while the face of the other figure has been disfigured. Bhattacharya has identified this as figures Gajalakṣmī which is not at all tenable. This may be some decorative piece, but certainly very peculiar. The plaque shows a human figure of which the upper portion is mutilated. Only the lower part of the abdomen of the figure is visible. The number of hands are also not clear. Stylistically, both the plaques may be placed in 6th/7th century. In the same village, separately, I saw some more terracotta plaques which are mutilated depicting animals and (tiger and monkey) human figure etc. These plaques are now worshipped by the people of the village placing them under temporary sheds. All these plaques show the same style. They are sculptured in high relief.

There are three terracotta plaques in the Assam State Museum collected long back from Yogījān in Nagaon district. The first plaque shows a male human figure. It is in half-kneeling posture with folded hands, as if praying to somebody in *añjalihasta,* pose and in ālīdhā attitude. The figure bears a quiver with arrows on its back. The bow is shown behind the figure. The second plaque shows two human figures. Both the figures seem to be male. One figure is seated cross-legged keeping both the hands over the knees. The other figure stands to the left of the former and touches its headgear. The last terracotta plaque (29 x 24 cms) shows an image of Gajalakṣmī. The goddess is seated and her head two elephants pour water.[7]

At Kenduguri just near Yogījān three terracotta plaques have been noticed. These plaques are weathered. One plaque bears a human figure, while other two show the figures of a bird and a tree respectively.[8]

P.C. Sarma has recently exposed a ruined temple site at Na-nāth Yogījān. Yogījān area includes the ruined temple site of the Na-nāth (nine Yogīs) and a ruined temple at Kenduguri. The entire area is archaeologically very rich. The ruined nine shrines show rows of terracotta sculptures stuck into the walls. Sarma has published a preliminary report[9] on these terracotta plaques.[10]

The clay sculptural pieces depicts variety of subjects, sometimes we see human figures, birds, animals trees, flowers etc. Sometimes depiction of mythical and grotesque figures of these human figures appear to have dominated the series. Figures of *dvārapāla* are also found in different posture. Two conch blowers and other human figures are also seen in dancing, leaning and bending postures. Hunting scene is also not wanting. A scene depicting the scene of imparting training to an elephant is of special interest. A human figure sitting on a stool is very interesting.[11]

Figures of divinities are also depicted in the clay sculptures of Na-nāth. Figures of Ganesha, Narasimha, six armed Natarāja and Nāgarājā with a servant hood over his head. "A less distinct figure," Sarma says "may be identified as Hanuman in flying posture holding Rāma and Lakshmaṇa on his either hand". Sarma further says " female standing figure with a javelin in her hand could not be identified."[12] Another figure in the form of subjugating two trees standing flanking him and still another, a baby suckling the breast of a stout female are also in the group. This possibly draws the picture of *Putanabadh* by Lord Kṛṣṇa and the subjugation of two trees represent Kṛṣṇa's Arjūnabhanjana episode.

Among the mythical figures, *Kirttimukha* and a few elephant-faced lions are noticed in the group of sculptures. Animals like goat, deer, horse, buffalo, lion, bull, monkey, tortoise etc. are also vividly portrayed in the plaques of Na-nāth. A plaque depicts a monkey, teasing a sleeping goat. Vegetables and floral motives do not seem to have found a good place in the terracotta art at the place. However, a banana tree has been executed with commendable grace and proportions. The terracotta figurines are executed in high relief and it bears stylistic affinity to some extent with Daparvatīā clay sculptures. However, this group of sculptures may date back to C. 8th-9th century. We have used the article by Mr. Sarma liberally.[13] I had visited the site long back when these plaques were not exposed. A terracotta plaque of the similar style was discovered at Sarupathār gaon which is being preserved in the District Museum, Jorhat. This plaque depicts possibly

Parvati.[14] In 1988 again I visited the site and studied the sculptural wealth of Na-nāth. Details are available in my paper.[14a]

Two terracotta sculptures were collected from the residence from Śrī Debes Das, Mornoi, for the Assam State Museum. The first terracotta plaque which is half broken shows a seated female figure, which is depicted in profile. The hands of the figure seems to be empty. The face of the figure is mutilated. The second plaque depicts two male figures seated very close, one behind the other. It is also mutilated. Both the sculptures with the figure in high relief. On stylistic consideration, these terracotta plaques may be dated to a period slightly later than that of the Pāhārpur terracotta sculptures. The other three broken pieces of sculptures[15] of the same group bear some geometrical designs.

The same museum houses three very good pieces of terracotta art. All these three sculptures were collected from Kukurmūtā, now Chenikuthi, Guwahati. The first plaque shows three female figures standing in *tribhanga* posture. The middle one is taller than the other two figures who are attending upon the central figure. All these figures have each two arms and wear usual ornaments and dress. The lower drapery is a long *sārī*.

The hands of the central figure seem to be busy in fixing the hair-knot. All the figures have high breasts and all the figures are cylindrical in body shape. The lower and upper borders as the plaque bears each a row of lotus petal design. The entire scene, it appears depicts an aristocratic lady in toilet. The middle figure commands a fair feminine beauty.

The second plaque shows a dancing scene. Here a lady is shown as dancing, in front of a male seated figure displaying *vākhyāyana* pose with his hands, while a male figure is shown as playing *pākhowāj* or *mridaṅga*. The facial portion of the figure of the male seated figure, evidently *Guru* (teacher), is mutilated. This is an unique piece. The third sculptured bears an emaciated male figure with exposed veins and ribs in dancing posture. The two armed figure holds a *triaṇḍa* and a *kamaṇḍalu*. The figure may represent an ascetic or Brings. The lotus petal design on two borders of the plaque, as seen in the first and second plaque are not see here, as the borders are broken. Stylistically, all these three pieces of art belongs to 11th/12th century.

From Bhāitbārī quite a few terracotta plaques were collected by G.N. Bhuyan[16] for the Assam State Museum. Bhāitbārī region in the plains of Garo Hill district contiguous to the plains of Assam in Dhubri district in the Southern bank of the Brahmaputra, is a very potential archaeological site. We shall describe the pieces of the sculptures collected from Bhāitbārī, which are being preserved in the Assam State Museum. Recently, The Archaeological Survey of India (A.S.I) has conducted an excavation and discovered a good number of antiquities including terracotta sculptures of the same style. The A.S.I. also has recently found a number of clay sculptures from an excavation at Śrī Sūrya Pāhār datable to 8th/9th century Rearing Buddhist affiliation.

The plaque shows a beautiful image of Manasā. Unfortunately, the lower half of the image is broken off. Above, the head of the deity, the snake hood is beautifully done. At the top we see the design of a *Śikhara* of a temple. The upper border of the plaque bears a row of lotus petal design. The second image is of Kārtikeya. It is a very beautiful work of art like the previous one. In this plaque the God is made to site in the usual posture on his *vāhana*, a *mayura*. The objects held in the two hands of the deity are not clear. On either side of the figure of the God there is a standing female figure. Unfortunately, the upper portion of the plaque is broken and gone. On the lower periphery of the plaque, in the same way as in the previous case, we get a floral design depicting lotuus petal in a row. The third plaque shows the figure of Ganesh in his usual seated posture on his *vāhana*. The figure is weathered. But the plaques is in better state of preservation. The upper and lower borders of the plaque are adorned with the lotus petal design. Another plaque (26 x 27 cms) shows a human figure, if divinity, identity not known, of which the legs are broken. The figure is seen bending its lieft leg, while standing and leaning the head backward. The objects held in its right hand is not clear. But it looks like a thread which is near his right thigh. The left hand is seen holding something on the right thigh. The figure wears a *karaṇḍa mukuṭa* (?) on its head. The body of the figure is slim. Above the head of the figure *chāitya* design and further *āmalaka* are noticed, as in the other cases. Most probably this terracotta figurine represents some deity, the identity of which is not very clear. The next plaque (25 x 24 cms) from the place is also broken. It depicts a mutilated female figure. The head of the deity is missing. Possibly, it was an attendant of some divinity. Another plaque (13 cms long) show a similar female figure in mutilated condition. Its left breast, legs and upper part of the head are mutilated. The bottom of the right hand is also missing. The raised left hand on its palm, possibly, holds a pot. The face of the figure is slightly unshaped due to baking effect. The figure is slightly bulky. The next (11 cms long) plaque shows the lower portion of some figure. The upper part of the plaque is broken off. Looking at the attractive thighs and hips, one can guess that it represents a female attendant. In addition to these mutilated figurines, there are a few fragments of terracotta sculptures from Bhāitbārī area, which are not worth mentioning here. From stylistic point of view, this groups of sculptures may be dated in 11th/12th century A.D.[17]

We have another image of crude variety from Bālujorā mauja, Bhāitbārī. This terracotta piece was collected by Mr. Sibananda Sarma and was handed over to the Assam State Museum authority. The plaque depicts the seated figure of Śiva along with the figure of Nandī, the bull vehicle of the God. The God is seated in *mahārājalīlāsana*. The *kuṇḍalas* worn by the deity are very clearly seen. The figure is bulky. The plaque appears to represent crude representation of art and it cannot be compared with the other terracotta pieces from Bhāitbārī described above. Few pieces of terracotta figurines from Bhāitbārī are in the Dhubri District Museum.

The Assam State Museum houses two terracotta votive tables. These were found in Guwahati. The first tablet (17 x 11 cms) is punched on a terracotta plaque. The deity is shown in *bhumiśparsamudrā*. The raised rim of the tablet is mutilated. Three symbols of *stūpas* are noticed on both the side of the figure of Buddha. Below the figure is inscribed the wellknown *Mahāyāna* creed in the character of 11th century. Such terracotta plaques with the stamped images of Buddha, exactly similar to this are found outside Assam also. Impressed almost with the same stamp, tablets have also been discovered in large numbers in Bengal and Bengladesh. The second figure of Buddha (23 x 10 cms) stamped on terracotta plaque is like the former one. It does not bear any inscription. But the other features are quite common. It appears that the present tablet is a part of a big terracotta plaque which is broken. In fact, it is the remanant of a big terracotta plaque containing more stamped figures of Buddha.[18]

Śrī Bijan Dey of Calcutta University a few years back donated a very interesting terracotta plaque the State Museum. He collected it from Śrī Suyra Pāhār. The plaque has a band, which may suggest its basement on some circular *stupa*. The plaque (33 x 19 cms) shows eight miniature figures of Buddha in two tiers. The first tire shows four figure, while the second tier depicts other four figure at a lower level. All the figures are in *bhumisparasa*-mudrā and stamped in the same way. The lower portion of the plaque is broken off. Such terracotta plaques carrying Buddha figures were very popular during the Pālā rule in Bengal and Bihar region.[19] The terracotta plaque from Sābhār illustrated by Bhattasali[20] is strikingly similar to the plaque in question. Possibly, the broken plaque bearing only one figure of Buddha described above were sculptured in the same way as the present one.

In addition to the terracotta sculptures described above some terracotta *Śiva liṅgas* have come to light from the Āmbari excavations, which is still being conducted. The excavation site of Āmbari is in the heart of Guwahati and very close to the Assam State Museum. In 1970 in the first phase of excavation some terracotta sculptures were found, which were briefly noticed by Sipra Sen and T.C. Sarma.[21] They have also given three illustrations of the terracotta fragmentary pieces. These includes the upper portion of a miniature image of Ganesh. The *siracakra* around the head of the deity is very clearly shown. Unfortunately, the sculpture is sadly mutilated. The illustrations have also shown some decorative objects. But the two important terracotta discoveries are neither included in the paper nor their photographs are published.

One terracotta plaque depict a dancing female figure. The figure is very beautifully sculptured and it is in perfect state of preservation. Another terracotta pieces shows a tapering head of a holo object with hair like thing. The precise identity of the object is not known. These are not mentioned by Sarma and Sen. Recent excavation at the site has revealed more miniature clay sculpture, particulary icons.

The above brief discussion and description of the terracotta sculptures from Assam belonging to the pre-Āhom-Koch and Chutiā period lead us to say that:

(a) The Da-parvatīā terracotta figure is the earliest known terracotta sculpture in Assam. We may agree with R.D. Banerji[22] and C.C. Dasgupta[23] in respect of its dating (6th century).

(b) The newly discovered Da-parvatīā terracotta sculptures in the nearby village bear stylistic relation with the terracota art from Yogījān. Both the group of sculptures are sculptured in high relief. Both the group bears post Gupta characteristic feature. So they can be placed in *c.* 8th century.

(c) The terracotta sculptures from Pāhārpur appears to be very bold and in higher relief than the Yogījān and Daparvatīā sculptures.

(d) There is a marked similarly of style between the terracotta art from Chenikuthi (Kukurmūtā), Guwahati and Bhāitbārī, now politically in Meghalaya, but culturally very much with the plains Dhubri District of Assam. Both the groups of sculptures show refined treatment in workmanship. It shows that as stone and metal art reached its zenith by

12th century in Assam and Bengal region, in case of clay art also in Assam we get the same picture. But to our knowledge, such refined style in terracotta art is not found in Bengal in 12th century S.S. Biswas,[24] who has made a thourough study of terracotta art of Bengal has not illustrated any sculpture in his work which is similar to Bhāitbārī or Chenikuthi clay art. Recently, discovered terracotta sculptures in the excavation in the cotton college campus by the Directorate of Archaeology, Assam have proved that they are strikingly similar with the Kurkurmuta (Cherikuthi) sculptures preserved in the State Museum. These pious are now in the college.

(e) The votive tablets bearing the figures of Buddha found in Assam are commonly is noticed in Bihar and Bengal region.[25]

(f) Terracotta art, therefore, in Assam, stylistically, reached its zenith, unlike Bihar and Bengal region, by 12th century and it become sophisticate art based on almost classical style. However, in Āhom-Koch period the standard fell down and folk elements become heavy in certain cases. We shall discuss it separately in future. The number of the terracotta plaques belonging to the pre-Āhom period in Assam are quite limited. More excavation will surely throw new light in this direction.

Notes and Refrences

1. *Annual Reports of Archaeological Survey of India (ARASI),* 1925-1926, p. 110, Pl. LIV.
2. C.C. Dasgupta *Origin and Evolution of Indian Clay Sculpture* Calcutta University, 1961, pp. 227-28. Also see, R.D. Choudhury, *Archaeology of the Brahmaputra Valley of Assam*, 1985, pp. 167-68.
3. *Ibid.*, Also see Dasgupta, *op.cit*
4. R.D. Choudhury, *op.cit.*
5. *Ibid.*, It is not known, now the figurines are preserved where.
6. "Two New Terracottas of Da-parvatiā", *Assam Tribune*, Guwahati, January, 29th' 83.
7. R.D. Choudhury, *op.cit.*, p. 169.
8. *Ibid.*
9. "The Terracotta treasure of Na-nāth", P. Sarma, *Sintinel*, a daily Guwahati, 13th April '86 also a news item published in *Dainik Asom.*
10. Also see, R.D. Choudhury *"Park-Āhom Yogar Silpa Kalā" Ājir Asom* (Assamese Daily) Guwahati, 21st April'88.
11. Sarma, *op.cit.*
12. *Ibid.*

13. *Ibid.*
14. *Assam Tribune,* a Daily from Guwahati,. dt. 8th May, 1985.
14a. *Jornal of the Indian Society of Oriental Art,* Calcutta, XX & XXI, New series., pp. 19-25.
15. Also see R.D. Choudhury, *op.cit.*, p. 170. These two pieces neither could be traced in the museum, nor they are catalogued. I think, they are misplaced.
16. G.N. Bhuyan, *Jurnal of Assam Research Society*, (JRAS) Vol. XX, 1972, pp. 8-14.
17. R.D. Choudhury, *op.cit.* pp. 169-70.
18. *Ibid.*
19. *Ibid.*
20. N.K. Bhattasali, Iconology of the *Boddhist and Brahmanical Sculptures in the Decca Museum*, 1929, Pl. X (b).
21. *JRAS*, Vol. XIX, 1970, pp. 46-48, Pl. I-III.
22. R.D. Banerji, *op.cit.*
23. C.C. Dasgupta, *Origin and Evolution of Indian Clay Sculptures, Calcutta University*, 1961, p. 228.
24. See, S.S. Biswas, *Terracotta Art of Bengal,* 1981.
25. Dr. N.P. Choudhury, has said that he wrote an article in the Cotton College Magazine recently, who conducted the excavation which was not even seen by him. But I personally saw the sculptures, which are similar to Bhāitbāri and Kukur muta (now in A.S.H.) sculpture as mentioned above. From Birupur, in Garo Hill district of Meghalaya, a number of fragmentary pieces of terracottas were collected by Dr. H.C. Sarma, who showed me in the Anthropological museum, Guwahati University. These were noticed by me See, Rabin Deve Choudhury, *Asamat, Purātāttik Adhayanar Agragati*, Guwahati, 1992, p. 37.

13

Elephants in the Art of Assam

The position of elephant in Indian art is very high. It has also occupied an important position in the art of Assam. In archaeological objects, paintings, literature, folk-literature, fiction etc. elephant is popular in all the parts of Assam, including the hilly regions. It is regarded as a symbol of peace, might, auspiciousness and wisdom.

In the pre-historic period elephant must have been plentifully available in the forests of north-east India. However, we have no corroborative evidence to prove it. But we can infer it, as in many pre-historic sites of India remains of elephant bones have been discovered, which conclusively prove the existence of elephants in those days in India. From the *Mahābhārata* period or the early historical period downwards, we have literary evidence pertaining to the availability and importance of elephant. For instance, king Bhagadatta, of Prāgjyotiṣa fought for the Kauravas in the great *Mahābhārata* battle riding an elephant at his old age.[1] This shows that at the time of the *Asura* rulers in *Prāgjyotiṣa*, elephant was available and it was regarded as a very important animal for warfare in this region.

In the *Kālikāpuraṇa,* a 9th-10th cent. work composed in Assam, we have a reference to the four-toothed white elephant of the *Kirāta* king, Ghaṭakāsura, the legendary Dānava king of *Prāgjyotiṣa*. Naraka is said to have killed Ghaṭaka in a battle and acquired the mount of the Dānava king for his own. The elephant is described to be as large as the Airāvata, the mount of Indra and as fast as Garuḍa, the mount of Viṣṇu.[2]

In the pre-Āhom as well as the Āhom periods, the importance of elephant increased to a great extent, as in other parts of the country. Even the great Vaiṣṇava Saint of Assam, Śrī Śaṅkaradeva, was asked by the

Āhom kings to catch elephants for the use of the kings (evidently for warfare). His son-in law was put to death by the royal authority for his failure to do so and Śaṅkaradeva had to flee to the Koch kingdom to save his life.[3]

Elephant occupied an important position in the sculpture and architecture which were patronised by the royal authorities. Both the sculptures and temple architecture belonging to the pre-Āhom period, *i.e.* the period of the Varman, the Sālastambha and the Pāla dynasties and the Āhom-Koch-Kachārī period, reflect this animal in various ways. The Assam State Museum (A.S.M) houses quite a few figures of elephant in different forms. The big stone image of Gaja-Lakṣmī preserved in this museum shown an elephant pouring water on the head of the deity. The elephant to the right of the figure of the deity is, however, badly broken off. However, we can easily infer that the broken figure was that of the other elephant, as two elephants, iconographically, pour water on the head of the goddess. The next image of Gaja-Lakṣmī is a miniature metal sculpture from Haharā, collected a few years back. Here two elephants are clearly showns pouring water on the head of the goddess Lakṣmī. Stylistically, the previous image may be dated in *c.* 8th century, while the image from Haharā, crude in execution should be dated to a very late period. Two terracotta plaques from Jogījān showing the image of Gaja-Lakṣmī are preserved in the A.S.M. In both the cases, the elephants are in a good state of preservation.

The A.S.M. houses a beautiful bronze image of Indra. This image of exquisite beauty was found along with other bronze images to Kahilīpārā (Odalbākrā or Narakāsur-hill). Here the god is made to sit on his *vāhana*, Airāvata, in a graceful posture. This is one of the most beautifully sculptured metal images of Indra in India. There is another image of Indra (Pl. XIV) in the same Museum. It is a stone image, which was found in Guwahati, while digging near the Guwahati Railway Station. Here the deity is in *sthānaka* attitude. Below the deity, the figure of the elephant *i.e.*, Airāvata is shown. Stylistically, the image of Indra from Kāhilīpārā may be placed in *c.* 11th century, while the stone image of Indra may be placed in *c.* 10th century A.D.

An interesting stone image of Manasā from Śilghāt has been preserved in the A.S.M. Here the goddess Manasā is shown in *sama-pāda-sthānaka* attitude. The *vāhana* of Manasā is a snake. But here an elephant is shown as the *vāhana* of the deity. The *Brahmavaivarta-Purāṇa,* however, mentions that the *vāhana* of Manasā should be a *nāga*, which means ordinarily a huge snake and also an elephant.[4] Here, perhaps the sculptor preferred to put an elephant, as the vehicle, interpreting the meaning of *nāga* as elephant. However, to our knowledge, this is the only image of Manasā in eastern India, nay, India, bearing the figure of an elephant as *vāhana*. Stylistically, it belongs to *c.* 12th century.

A few years back, a terracotta plaque (broken into two halves) was discovered at Da-parvatīā village, not far from the famous ruined temple at the place. It was deposited in the A.S.M., by S. Bhattacharya, who also published a note on it.[5] In this plaque two elephant female riders are shown. Both the elephant are facing each other and so also the riders. Bhattacharya has identified the female riders with Gaja-Lakṣmī. The figures cannot represent goddess Gaja-Lakṣmī. In any case, Gaja-Lakṣmī never rides an elephant, as far as we know. Two elephants pour water on the figure of Gaja-Lakṣmī which is flanked by both the elephants. Stylistically, this piece of clay sculpture may belong to *c.* 7th-8th century, if not earlier. The same museum holds two panels of *gajathara* motif mounted on either side of the main entrance of it. This *gajathara* motif supposed to carry the weight of the superstructure of a temple, symbolically, with their backs, perhaps means the strength of this auspicious animal. These two pieces of sculptured panel, must have been used as architectural members of some temple belonging to *c.* 9th/10th century. The style of this panels showing *gajathara* motif can be easily compared with those of Ellora temple. The only difference is that the *gajathara* motif of the Kailāśa temple is rock-cut as the entire temple is cut out of a solid huge rock, while ours are sculptured on stone. The Kāmākhyā temple and the Hayagrīva Māndava temple, Hājo, also have each a panel of *gajathara* motif in the same style sculptured in stone and placed at the *adhisthāna* of the *vimanas*. However, the *gajathara* sculptures of the Kāmākhyā and Hājo temples belong to 16th century,[6] while the Kailāśa temple belongs to *c.* 8th century or so.[7]

The Assam State Museum holds a beautiful terracotta plaque showing a hunting scene (Pl. XVI). The plaque is displayed in the miscellaneous gallery. Here an elephant is shown as moving forward and before it an animal is shown running. The elephant is mounted by a male human figure dressed in Mughal style, possibly representing some royal family member going for hunting. The sculpture may, stylistically, be placed in *c.* 18th century. The A.S.M. also houses one stone image from Numaligarh. It may be identified as *Gajāntaka-cum-Tripurāntaka*[8] aspect of Śiva. Here Śiva is seen dancing on the Gajāsura, who has been killed. Only the head of the elephant demon can be traced below the feet of Śiva. In the image, it appears that the sculptor could not give the finishing touch. The sculpture, on stylistic consideration, should be placed in *c.* 9th-10th century. At Madan Kamdev ruined temple a standing icon of Indra with his elephant vehicle, Airāvat is noticed.

Depiction of elephant is noticed in various archaeological sites in Assam. For instance, just in front of the Kāmākhyā temple, there is a rock-cut image of Viśvakarmā, who is riding his *vāhana,* an elephant. This may, stylistically, belong to a late period. The *gaja-vyāla* ,motif is very popular in the sculpture of Assam as in the sculptures of other parts of India. In temple *dvāra-dehalī* (door-sill) also elephants are depicted. Such a *dehalī* is preserved in the Ma'rar Park. Nagaon.[9] Here two elephants are shown facing each other. In between them there is the *Kalpavṛkṣa* motif. *Dehalīs* depicting *ghaṭa* in between the figures of elephants are also noticed elsewhere in Assam. Stylistically these *dehalīs* should be placed in a period ranging from *c.* 9th-10th to *c.* 12th century A.D. Corner stone of the *adiṣṭhānas*, of pre-Āhom temple bearing *gaja-vyāla* motif are frequently met with. Almost all the ruins of pre-Āhom temples have at least one or two pieces of sculptures, if not more, depicting the elephant. It figures either as the *vāhana* of some deity or as a decorative motif. In the temples constructed during the regime of the Āhom and the Koch kings, the elephant is depicted mainly as a vihicle or a decorative motif. Representation of elephant was so popular that even the ruins of Bhuvan Pāhār[10] located in the border of Mizoram, Manipur and Assam in Cachar district, at a height of 3000 feet inside dense forest yields a chiselled stone block showing a seated elephant. It is, however, very badly weathered. Behind the Tourist lodge at Kajiranga on the hillside a rock-cut figure of an elephant is noticed.[11] It is a huge sculpture.

Elephant was not only depicted in stone art and architecture. In wood art, which is mostly used for the decoration of the *satras*, Vaiṣṇava monasteries in Assam, depiction of elephants are found mostly in the scene of Gajendramokṣa wherein the elephant, which is attacked by a crocodile, is shown worshipping Viṣṇu by offering a lotus with its trunk. Viṣṇu who rescued the elephant, is shown as seated on Garuḍa. This scene is sculptured in most of the *satras,* possibly to attract the attention of the visitors to the *satras* and to teach the lesson of *bhakti* (devotion) to Viṣṇu. Interestingly, not a single stone, terracotta or metal sculpture depicting the scene of Gajendramokṣa is noticed in Assam belonging to the pre-Āhom and pre-Koch period. Representation of Gaja-Lakṣmī in the wood art of the *satras*, it appears, was not very popular. But it did find a good place in wood-art in the *satras*. For the purpose of decoration also the figure of elephant was sculptured in the *satras*. For instance, the Bardowā site Museum houses two wooden panels of which the first one shows two elephants fighting each other, while the second panel depicts a single elephant with *patralatā* design.[12] Such elephant figures are found in almost all the famous *satras* of Assam, particularly the *satras* of Barpeta and Suālkuci, and Mājulī. Figures of elephant occur in wood-work of the British period, too. For instance, two panels showing the figures of elephants are seen on the verandah of the Silcar Normal school silear. These are suspended on the wall. Stylistically, they do not go with the *satriyā* art.

As in other parts of India, in Assam also icons of Gaṇeśa is found abudantly. Right from 6th century to the modern times, this elephant-headed deity has been occupying a special place in the art of Assam. The earliest figure of Gaṇeśa in Assam occurs in the ornate Da-parvatiā *dvāra,* which is dated in 6th century A.D. In stone, rock, wood and metal, the image of this deity was sculptured in the past. Perhaps, the images of Gaṇeśa will outnumber the images of all other deities in Assam.

The most prestigious position was given to the elephant by the kings of Kāmarūpa through its depiction as the royal insignia in the copper-plate inscriptions.[13] All the kings of Kāmarūpa from Bhāskar Varma (7th century) to Dharmapāla (12th century) had one and the same type of royal seal in their copper-plate grants. Each seal depicts the head of an elephant and below it, the legend is inscribed giving the name of the king and the genealogy. Perhaps, only the Kāmarūpa kings used elephant as their royal insignia in India. We have no knowledge of elephant being used as royal insignia by the kings of other dynasties in India in the past. This is a very important phenomenon. The Āhom kings had the dragon as their royal symbol.

In painting also elephant occupied a very important position. In many illustrated manuscripts of Assam elephants are depicted in various ways, as in other parts of India. The *Hastividyārṇava,*[14] a famous illustrated manuscript of Assam done under the patronage of the Āhom king, Śiva Singha, is well known. This manuscript was composed by Sukumār Barkāth in A.D. 1734. Its paintings were done by Dilbor and Dosāi, two artists from Rajasthān. This is a treatise on elephantology. It may be possible that the original compilation of the manuscript in Tai-Āhom language was without paintings of elephant. The treatise was recomposed by Sukumār Barkāth (Kāyasṭha) with materials drawn from Gajendra-Cintāmaṇi.[15] This book gives detailed description of various types of elephants, their different types of disease and descriptions of cure of the diseases.[16] Here descriptions are also given as to how elephants are to be caught and how they are to be trained.[17]

As in other parts of India, in Assam also elephant tusks are treated as valuable materials for decorative art. In the past also elephant tusk was treated as a valuable object. In other parts of India still many valuable ornaments and other decorative objects are made out of ivory. In Assam this art is almost dead. Barpeta was a seat of ivory art and industry. But after the death of the last reputed artisan, the industry also almost has come to an end. The Assam State Museum houses an ivory fan, made out of ivory strips, a pair of sandal *(pādukā)* and a hollow cylinder used in weaving. We have also noticed four miniatures in ivory sculptures of lion, which are in a very bad state of preservation, in the Hayagrīva Mādhava temple, Hājo. Ivory decorative art-works are still in the possession of many residents in Assam.

Elephant cart was possibly an important vehicle in Assam in the past. Because of the bad condition of road and the peculiar condition of climate, elephant cart was used to a great extent. However, we have neither come across any inscriptional reference, nor have we found any depiction of such cart in sculpture or painting in Assam, as far as we know. The Assam State Museum possesses an excel of Elephant Cart with out wheels.

Use of elephant was very important in warfare in India, as we have mentioned above. In Assam also this animal was treated as an important vehicle in war. The strength of the armed force depended on the strength of elephant. Elephant was also used by the royal authorities and the rich class of the society as vehicle. It was used as a mode of transport to reach inaccessible areas.

Considering all these factors, possibly, as in other parts of the country, in Assam also in the past, elephant was treated as a very important and auspicious animal. The elephant headed god Gaṇeśa noticed in the Daparvatīā *dvāra* should be the earliest icon of the deity. Prior to that also, we can assume that elephant was given an important position in Assam. The most important factor is that all the Kāmarūpa kings right from Bāskarvarman to Dharmapāla used elephant motif in their royal seals which were attached to their copper-plate grants. This is very significant. For, to our knowledge, no rulers of any dynasty in India used elephant as royal insignia like the Kings of Kāmarūpa. If shows that the royal authorities in Kāmarūpa understood very well the importance of the animal and that is why they gave this prestigious position to elephant. It is sure that in addition to the already discovered stone, metal, wood, illustrated manuscripts depicting elephants, many such objects will come to light in future. The climate and environment of Assam region favoured elephant to live in this region in the past, as in the present.[18]

Notes and References

1. Sharma, M.M., *Inscription of Ancient Assam,* 1978, pp. 6-7, Barua B.K. *A cultural History of Assam,* 1969, pp. 18-19. Also see, *Mahābhārata,* Santiparva, xc. 27-30.
2. cf.
   तमः स नरकोवीरः आमारू दय सितं गजम्
   चतुर्दन्तं मकाकायं किराताधिपवादनम्
   पेरावत समं वीर्ये वेजेन गरुडीपमम्
   pp. 38, 110-11.
3. Barua, B.K. and Murthy, H.V.S., *Temples and Legends of Assam,* 1965, p. 96.
4. Bhattasali, N.K., *Sculpture of the Iconography of the Dacca Museum*, 1929, p. 219.
5. *The Assam Tribune,* Guwahati, dt. 29th Jan; 1963.
6. Barua, B.K. and Murthy, H.V.S., *op.cit.,* pp. 32, 61.
7. Siddiqi, S., *A pictorial Guide to......Ajanta*, 1962, p. 18.
8. Choudhuty, R.D., *Archaeology of the Brahmaputra Valley of Assam*, 1985, *p. 70.*
9. Choudhury, N.D., *Archaeology of Central Assam,* 1985, Pl. XIX, Fig. 9.76.
10. Choudhury, R.D., *'Archaeological Remains at Bhuvan Pāhār'*, Sentinel, Guwahati. Also see *Studies in Indian History and culture* (K.L. Barua Comm. Vol.). Ed. R.D. Choudhury & S.B. Sing, New Delhi, 1990, pp. 1-10.
11. This information was given by Professor J.P. Singh, Deptt. of History, N.E.H.U., Shillong. I am grateful to him for giving the information. Later I examined the sculpture personally.
12. Kalita, N., *Bordowār Śilpa Vastu* (Assamese), 1985, Pls. 39 and 40.
13. See, Barua P., "*Elephant-the royal insignia of the Kāmarūpa kings*" *Sentinel*, 17th Nov; 1985. The article was published by the present author under a pseudonym. Another article Asamar Sanskritit hātīr sthān' by the present author was published in *Dainik Asom* Guwahati (D.A.), 29th Dec; 1986. Also see, D.A., Dec; 12th 1985. This was reprinted in the *Souvenir, Asamar Sahamajdar Samaj aru Sahkriti,* Ed. B. Mahanta, 1986, pp. 53-60. D.C. Sircar Comm. Vol., Studies in Ancient Indian history, Ed. Dasgupta and others, p. 236.

14. Choudhury, P.C. (ed.), *Hastirvidyarnava,* 1976, see the plates.
15. P.C. Sarma, 'Paintings in Assam' *Journal of Assam Research Society*, (Proc) of the seminar 2, IV '22 Feb; 13, 181, p. 18.
16. *Ibid.*
17. Pālakāpya, the author of the *Hastyāyurveda*, a treatise on the treatment of diseases of elephants, is said to have hailed from ancient Prāgjyotiṣa. The sage declares: "In the country which borders on the Himalaya and through which the Lauhitya flows towards the sea, there lived a *Muni.* He was my father, my mother being a *Karenu* or she-elephant. I leave and move with elephants. They are my friends, relatives and companions. My name is Pālakāpya. I take care of elephants and nourish and cherish them, hence, my name is Pāla and the suffix *Kāpya* denotes the *gotra* or family in which I was born, I am an expert in the treatment of elephants". Tr. H.P. Shastri, vide *JBORS,* V. 311-2 (*JBORS-Journal of the Bihar & Orissa Research Society*). See for a picture of Pālakāpya Ṛṣi, See, A Panchanathan Guide Book to Sarasvati Mahal, Thanjavur, 1993, Pl. No. 14. In the Borgāon copper plate charter of Ratnapāla we have a reference to a particular disease of elephants, *Kūṭa-Pākala.*

    दुंर्दान्त गौड़ेन्द्र-कूटपाकलेन-करेलेयच्चल्

    (cf. 11-34f.).

    Pālakāpya, the author of the *Hastyāyurveda*, discusses this disease in his treatise (I. viii, 3-4). According to this, *Pākala* is a particular fever *(Jvara)* of the elephants Kūtapākala is one of the ten varieties of the *Pakala-jvara* and is considered fatal.
18. In the month of December 1985, when I met Dr. N.R. Banerji, Rtd. Director, National Museum, New Delhi, he told me that one of his students has submitted a Ph.D. thesis on the *"Elephant in Art of India"* a few months back. But he did not consult any material from Assam region. Edgerton, F has made a study on elephants. See his *The Elephant lore of the Hindus*, Motilal Banarasidass, 1986. The jacket of the book shows a sene from *Hastividyārṇava.* Elephant in terracotta sculptures are reported from Da-parvatiā and Na-nath. See, *History and Archaeology* (Prof. H.D. Sankalia felicitation volume) Ed. B. Chatterjee and others, Delhi, 1989, p. 410 and *Journal of The Indian Society of Oriental Art*, Calcutta, New series, Vol. XX & XXI, 1991-93, pp. 19-24.

I am grateful to Dr. D. Chutia for his valuable information regarding some references—Author.

14

Decorative Elements in the Art of Assam: A Survey

As in other parts of India, in Assam too, decorative elements are found in the works of in various ways. It occurs in stone art objects, metal work, paintings and wood work. Textile works are also decorated profusely.

The decoration on art of Assam can be traced as early as 100 B.C. or 100 A.D. in the rock-cut votive *stūpas* at Śrī Sūrya Pāhār.[1] These decorations include only a few bands going around the bodies of the *Stūpas* and the *Hārmikas* on the top of the *stūpas*. These bands are no doubt simple, but it is certain that these were chiselled out only for decoration of the votive *stūpas*. A votive *stupa* cut out of a solid rock found standing in between the site of the row of rock-cut icons and the natural cave show two such bands, one in the middle and the other at the bottom. From stylistic consideration, we can assume that it was cut out a few centuries later than those mentioned above. It shows that sculptors of later age gradually started using more decorative elements in the interest of the beautification of the object. However, at this stage, as shown above, the decoration was in a very simple form. As in other parts of India in Assam too, in the work of art belonging to the Gupta period, we find different picture.

This is evidenced from the Da-parvatīā ruined temple door frame. Da-parvatīā is a village near the Tezpur town. "Here is noticed a most ornate free standing *dvāra* of a ruined temple belonging to the late Gupta period. The two *dvāra-śākhās* (161 cm x 41 cms) have five *paṭṭas* or *śākhās* each. Above the *śākhās* a *śirapaṭṭi* (125 x 41 cms) which shows a *lalāta-bimba* is horizontally placed. The outermost *paṭṭa* (vertical band) on the *dvāra-*

śākhā extends beyond the *śirapaṭṭi* and runs above the same. The first two inner most *paṭṭas* are adorned with *patralatā* (scroll) design. The second *paṭṭa* at the bottom a figure of *nāga* in the hybrid from *i.e.*, the face and the upper part of the body resembles a man and the hoods being the head resembles a *sarpa*. This figure is in *añjalihasta* (folded hand out of reverence) pose. The tail of this *nāga* shoots up on the *śirapaṭṭi* horizontally like the first two. The fourth *paṭṭa* is embellished with the tiny human figure and *padmakośas* springing out alternatively. This sculptured *sākhā* is surmounted by an ornamental *ghatta-pallava* design. The last *paṭṭa* shows richly carved *puṣpa* which springs up and spreads across the *śirapatta*. At the bottom of the (either) *dvāraśākhā* are carved graceful images of Gaṅgā and Yamunā with attandents.

The topmost horizontal *paṭṭa* on the *śirapaṭṭi* contains *candra-śālā* motifs housing the figures Lākuliśa, Sūrya and other mythical figures. The whole *dvāra* is minutely sculptured and both the *śākhās* display most varied decorative details. The extended *śirapaṭṭi* though not prominent, is a typical Gupta feature. The figure of a flying *gandharva*, holding the tails of the *nāgas* on the *śirapaṭṭi* is also a Gupta feature. This figure with two visible wings in a flying posture may be of Garuda".[2]

From the above description and looking at the photograph of this ornate *dvāra* and the figure of Gaṅgā and Yamunā standing in elegant posture, one must be inclined to say that this is a unique work of art in India which is executed with detailed decorative elements *i.e.*, mainly floral animals, birds etc. The same type of modelling of ornaments we find in a torso, a stone sculpture from Mikirāti now being preserved in the Assam State Museum. Da-parvatiā *dvāra*, thus stands as one of the best examples of the decorative art belonging to late Gupta period, *i.e.*, 6th century.

More decoration we find in the Pālā art of Assam. Right from 10th to 12th century the stone art of Assam was influenced by the art of the Pālas of Bengal. In so far as the decoration is concerned, the Pālā art of Bengal got lavish ornamentation in the Sena period (11th-12th century). We get the same picture in Assam also. The sculpture belonging to 11/12th century are more ornamented and decorated. The ornamentation and decoration in art reached its zenith by the 12th century A.D., in Assam as in Bengal. In the sculptures, belonging to this period the figures of the gods and goddesses found properly ornamented and the *śilāpaṭṭa* and the *pīṭha* are found beautifully decorated with floral, animal and geometrical designs. Floral designs dominate the *pīṭhas,* while the *sirapattis* depict floral and animal and geometrical designs. The top of the *śilāpaṭṭa* of a sculpture is invariably dominated by the figure of *Kīrtimukha*. The artists of this period mostly used basalt and granite rock, as it was easier to execute the work with even minor details. In case of medium and miniature sculptures, basalt was preferred, while for execution of bigger sculptures, granite blocks were used. Evidently, basalt was more precious than granite. The quarry of basal rock was located in Rajmahal hill.[3] It was not found in the Brahmaputra valley. So, it must have been imported to Assam valley.

The pre-Āhom art style that developed in the Pālā period in Assam was continued in a degenerated form in some pockets in Assam to even 13th/14th century. This is well evidenced from the Āmbari sculptures. The Āmbari sculptures that are being preserved in the Assam State Museum, can be ascribed to 13th/14th century. All the sculptures are, however, sculptured in pre-Āhom Pālā style in a degenerated form. Although they are sculptured in Pālā formula, yet they do not depict the perfect picture of Pālā sculpture of Assam, as they are devoid of decoration. The *silapattas* and *pithas* of the icons are devoid of decoration. Unlike the icons of the Pālā period, they are not in some cases, proportionately sculptured. Thus, the Āmbari sculpture should be the last phase of the sculpture carved in Pālā style.

After the Āmbari sculpture in the Āhom period, in so far as the execution is concerned, we get altogether a different type of sculpture. These sculptures belonging to 17th/18th and 19th century are less ornamented and less decorated. The sculpture belonging to the Āhom-Koch period are not sculptured in classical formula like the Pālā sculptures. These sculptures have absorbed folk elements to a great extent. The stone sculpture belonging to this period mainly represent divinities. These sculptures are not decorated like the Pālā sculptures. In most of the cases, *silapattas* are not seen. Even if there is a small śilāpaṭṭa, it is not decorated at all.

As compared to the number of stone sculptures the number of metallic sculptures is quite small. We have no evidence of any early medieval metal sculpture. We have some metallic sculptures belonging to the Pālā period. All these sculptures were found a few years back all Kāhilīpārā (Narakāsura hill or Odālbākrā). On the *adhāra* (frame) of the sculptures in certain cases we notice decoration with floral and animal motif. For instance, the *adhāra* of the icon of Indra, which is one of the finest examples of metal work in eastern India is decked with floral and animal motifs. Because of the space problem, decoration in metal sculpture was not possible. Decoration in the metal sculptures belonging to the late medieval period was practically done away with.

Wood was another material commonly used by the artists. Due to the peculiar climatic condition, wood work belonging to medieval period does not exist in Assam, However, extensive wood work are found in the late 17th, 18th and 19th centuries. The wood art became very popular in Assam with the preaching of neovaisnavism by the great saint Śrī Sañkardeva. This art is not at all connected with the temples. A vaiṣṇava *satra* (monastery in Assam) is commonly decked with wooden panels of sculptures. The sculptures, bearing a trait of the late period are mixed with the folk elements. The style of the wood art is quite similar to the stone art belonging to the late medieval (17th/19th century) period. The wooden images of Viṣṇu are sometimes decorated with floral, animal and geometrical motifs. The walls of the *satras* are beautified with the floral designs and creeper-motifs.

In the case of terracotta, we find the same picture. There is a solitary case of terracotta plaque belonging to the Gupta period found in Assam. The provenance of this plaque is Darparvatiā. However, there is no trace of decoration in the figure representing possibly a Bodhisattva. In the terracotta sculpture belonging to the Pālā period, we get decoration like the stone sculpture belonging to the same period. There is a peculiar characteristic feature in so far as the decorative elements is concerned in some terracotta plaques belonging to 11th/12th century. Below the scene depicted on the lower periphery of the plaque there is a row of lotus petal. This feature is not found in the terracotta sculpture belonging to a late period. The terracotta sculptures belonging to 17th/18th century, however, shows Mughal influence in some cases. There are cases of terracotta plaques belonging to the period where in even fauna and flora are depicted in its natural form. There is a beautiful terracotta plaque in the Assam State Museum where in a royal hunting scene is depicted in the midst of fauna and flora. However, geometrical designs are also noticed in the same plaque. Mughal style is depicted in some terracotta plaques from Sibsagar Joysāgar area also. This influence came from the contemporaneous terracotta Mughal style from Bengal, which is also know as Bengal terracotta.

Textile was another important medium through which artist or artisans depicted decorative elements in various ways according to their taste. We do not have any piece of textiles belonging to the medieval period in Assam. It is not at all possible to find even the remnants of old textile belonging to that period in Assam due to its damped climatic condition. Old costume belonging to the Āhom royal families are still found here and there in Assam. A few pieces of such clothes are being preserved in Assam State Museum. Some of them bear Mughal characteristic features *i.e.*, having embroidery of gold thread.

The embroidery shows floral motifs mostly. In the Mekelā-chāddar, Rihā, typical Assamese ladies dress, various beautiful designs are depicted. Flower and creeper designs dominate here over the geometrical designs. Designs depicting animals are very scarce. In case of tribal garments some times we get the designs of bird and animals in addition to geometrical and floral motifs.

Illustrated manuscript painting in Assam has already occupied a good place in the history of art in Assam. Mainly we notice in the painting of Assam three distinctive styles—Tāi, indigenous style mixed with folk and Mughal style. Artists according to their taste depicted fauna and flora in their paintings in various ways. Unlike the sculpture, paintings are drawn depicting various scenes such as hill, sea, royal court, portrait of kings and queens, animals and so on. While doing so artists depicted scenes in stylized forms.

From the above discussion,we find that as in other parts of India, in Assam too, fauna and flora was used as decorative elements in sculpture, architecture, painting and textiles. Floral, animal, bird and geometrical motifs were commonly used as decorative elements, architectural motif, like *candrasālā, bṛittakkhands, gavāksha, āmalaka, viśvapadma* and miniature *śikhara* are commonly noticed in the sculptural art of Assam,[3] particularly belonging to the pre-Āhom period. The ornate Da-parvatiā *dvāra* is one of the best examples of the Gupta period, which is profusely decorated. Two beautiful and very bold designs of creeper (scroll) are noticed to the right side, while going to Kāmakhyā temple outside the front *torana* and inside the *torana*. They are fine examples of decorative elements of the art of Assam belonging to the pre-Pālā period.

Thus, from stylistic point of view, art in Assam has found an all India position through the ornate *dvāra* at Da-parvatiā belonging to 6th century, while as in Bengal in the Brahmaputra valley of Assam too, sculptural art reached its zenith by 12th century A.D. in so far as decoration and ornamentation are concerned. In Assam the earliest decorative designs or elements are noticed on the body of the votive *stūpas* at Śrī Sūrya Pāhār datable to c. 100 A.D. or so. These are geometrical simple lines only as described above. The decorative elements used in the art of Assam are not quite different from the other parts of Northern India. However, local variations are also noticed. An extensive study on the subject is sure to throw new light on the subject.

Notes and References

1. R.D. Choudhury, *Antiquities of Śrī Sūrya Pāhār: A Source of Early History Kāmarūpa,* Sources of the History of India Vol. III, *Institute of Historical studies, Calcutta, 1980, Ed. N.R. Ray.*
2. R.D. Choudhury, *Archaeology of the Brahmaputra valley of Assam*, Delhi, 1985. p. 135.
3. *Ibid.,* p. 184.

15

Art in the Royal Seals of the Inscriptions from Assam

The copper-plate stone and rock inscriptions issued by the Kāmarūpa rulers and the Āhom kings are important source materials for the reconstruction of the social, political, cultural and economic history of Assam. These inscriptions also furnish important information relating to the development of art style of the region. Particularly, the copper-plate inscriptions throw important light on the subject. All the copper-plate grants issued by the Kāmarūpa kings belonging to the Varman, Śālastaṁbha and Pāla dynasties have each a seal depicting an elephant, while the copper-plates issued by the Āhom rulers bear such a seal each showing a dragon. The rock inscriptions of Assam do not have such seals, nor the stone inscriptions bear such royal emblems. However, a stone inscription, which is known as Nāgajarikhanikargāon fragmentary stone inscription and dated in the 5th century A.D., considered the earliest inscription in Assam, has a *cakra* like relief, possibly representing a lotus.[1]

The earliest copper-plate seal is found with the Doobi copper-plate grant of Kumār Bhāskara Varman,[2] which is placed in the first quarter of the 7th century. The shape of the seal is roughly oval and measures 3.4" by 3.1". The seal has a raised circular border and is separated into two parts. The lower part contains the legend of the seal and the upper part an elephant head with a frontal view. Above the elephant head and outside the circle, there is an object which tapers onto the apex and resembles the upper portion of a Śiva liṅga. This is actually an end of the ring that binds the plates. The elephant head is in low relief.

The clay seal of Kumār Bhāskar Varman found at Nālandā[3] depicts an elephant in the same way and the legend on the lower half. The seal is almost circular and half thereof is sadly broken. The figure of the elephant is depicted in the same way as in the Doobi plates. The original seal is being preserved in the Nālandā museum. The Assam State Museum displays only a plaster cast of the original seal. The style of the seal of the Nidhānpur copper-plate grant of Bhāskar Varman[4] is exactly similar to that of the Doobi plates. However, the seal is broken into two parts. The shape and other details of the seal of the Nidhānpur plates are strikingly similar to the Doobi lates.

Now it is clear that all the three seals, viz., the seal of the Doobi plates, the seal of the Nidhānpur plates and the Nālandā clay seal were executed in the same way. They were all issued by the same king, Kumār Bhāskar Varman in the 7th century. All of them are of oval-shaped and there is no point at the tops. In the case of the Doobi and Nidhānpur seals, however, the tapering ends of the rings to which the plates are fixed can be seen at the tops above the elephant figures. In all the three cases they are in low relief. The Nālandā seal does not have a raised rim around the legend and the figure of the elephant within the border circle.

Copper plates of the 8th century have not come to light so far in Assam. A few inscriptions issued by Vanamāla Varman in the 9th century have come to light. The seal of the Parvatiyā plates of Vanamāla[5] is slightly oval and has some similarity with the seals of Bhāskar Varman described earlier. This seal has been divided into two equal halves by a distinct line unlike the other seals described above. Thus, the seal has two chambers. The upper one is occupied by a figure of the elephant while the lower one contains the legend of the seal. The rim on the periphery of the seal is raised and in high relief. The figure of the elephant, the dividing line of the two chambers and the bordering rim are also in high relief unlike the other seals of Bhāskar Varman. There is no tapering end of a ring to which the plates are fixed on this seal as are seen on the Bhāskar Varman's seals. Instead, the artisan has made the top of the rim, just above the figure of the elephant, slightly pointed. The Parvatiyā plate inscription was issued in the middle of the 9th century.

There is another inscription of Vanamāla Varmādeva, which was recently found at Koliābar in Nagaon district of Assam.[6] The seal of this set of copper-plates also depict the figure of an elephant and the legend in two separate chambers. The shape of the seal is more oval with a slightly raised point just above the elephant figure as in the preceding case. This seal is better finished than the others. The last seal of the same king, attached to the Tezpur grant is also executed in the same type.[7] But the raised border which is in relief, has become pointed just above the figure of the elephant giving the seal a look of a betel leaf.

The seal of the Uttarbarbil grant of Balavarman III, which is placed in the last quarter of the 9th century,[8] is also more oval with the rim slightly pointed above the elephant figure and giving the entire seal the look of a betel leaf.

No copper-plate inscription belonging to the 10th century has so far been discovered in Assam. A few inscriptions of the 11th and the 12th centuries, however, have come to light. The seals of Saratbārī copper-plates[9] and Bargāon copper plates issued by Ratna Pāla[10] in the middle of the 11th century depict the same theme of a figure of an elephant and the legend and in two parts. The seals pointed like those of Vanamāla Varmādeva and Bala Varmādeva III, are described above. The seal of the Guākuchi grant of Indrapāla also shows the same picture. This may be placed in *c.* 1071 A.D.

The seals of the Khanāmukh grant[11] and the Pushpabhadrā grant[12] of Dharmapāla, the last ruler of the Pāla dynasty in Assam, belonging to the 12th century, were more developed. Dharmapāla issued another inscription, of which the seal is partially broken and the upper part with the figure of the elephant is missing.[13] The other two seals, viz., seals of the Khanāmukh grant and the Pushpabhadrā grant are more pointed giving a look of a pointed betel leaf. In both cases the elephant is shown in high relief and the border is much raised giving a security to the legend and the elephant motif to a great extent.

The Śubhāṅkarapātaka grant and the Puspabhadṝa grant belong to the first half of the 12th century. We can very well assume that the seal of the Śubhāṅkarapātaka grant, which is sadly broken, must have been executed in the same way and it must have been pointed, as the other two seals issued by the same king.

Apart from the artistically executed copper plate seals from which we can get an idea about the craftsmanship and art style of the period in question, we can also get some information and idea about the art style of some Vaiṣṇava symbol from an inscription. The Guākuchi grant,[14] at the end of the last plate, depicts the figure of *Garuḍa a*nd the *Vaiṣṇava* symbols of *Śaṅkha, Padma* and *Cakra*. All the symbols and the figure of *Garuḍa* were engraved possibly to show respect to *Vaiṣṇaivsm*. To the right of the figure and at the same level, three names are written. They are *Sani*, *Dani* and *Ani.*[15] It is difficult to say as to what these names are relevant. Below the figure an inscription is engraved which reads "Pustā Śrī aṣṭahenta". P. Bhattacharya has suggested that it is a prakritisd version of a sanskrit expression 'pustaṁ śrī aṣṭakeṇa,' meaning that the pictures have been drawn by one named Aṣṭaka. The word Ṗustā' means plastering or painting or any work of clay.[16] The presentation of the Vaiṣṇava symbols smply prove that although the king Ratnapāla was a devotee of Śiva and Śakti, yet he had regards for Viṣṇu.

The earliest inscription of Assam, *i.e.*, the Khanikargāon-Nāgājari stone inscription, referred to above, bears the design of a full blown lotus (?) in a fragmentary piece. The inscription is broken into several pieces. The engraved lotus symbol, with 15 petals is found in a broken piece. The petal of the lotus symbol are within a slightly raised border, which again is pointed at the top resembling a copper-plate seal.

The royal seal of the Āhom period is differently depicted. Unlike the seals of the Kāmarūpa kings, the seals of the Āhom rulers are shown engraved on one side of the plate itself. The royal insignia of the Āhom rulers—a dragon or a winged lion is shown inside engraved encircling lines in a separate chamber, while the other chamber shows the name of the king issuing the charter. A good number of copper-plate grants belonging to the Āhom period have been published so far.[17] Still many more are in the possession of old families of Assam, which are not published. All these plates depict the royal insignia—a dragon and the legend bearing the name of the king in the same way.

Like the stone and rock inscriptions of the pre-Āhom period, Āhom-period stone and rock inscriptions are also found, but without the royal emblem of the figure of a dragon. Some of the stone inscriptions issued by Āhom king invariably bear the sculptual depiction of a full blown lotus. The Kūrma-Janārdana Phalgutsava stone inscription of Pramatta Siṁha (1750 A.D.) is of this type.[18] There are some stone inscriptions around the borders of which beautiful creeper designs are engraved. For instance, the stone inscription of Barphukan's Durbar's Vijayadvāra (1735 A.D.) display beautiful floral and creeper design all along the borders on all sides.[19] This type of design are common to Moghul art, and must have been borrowed from the Moghul school. Instances of depicting the figure of lord Gaṇeśa in some copper-plate inscriptions of the Āhom period are also found. The Nīlāchala copper-plate of king Mādhava Deva (15th century), for instance, shows the engraved figure of Gaṇeśa on the right upper corner of the plate just at the beginning of the legend.[20]

The above discussion shows that the inscriptions from Assam give us valuable information on the art history. The royal emblem of the Kāmarūpa kings found along with the copper-plate grants are, indeed, unique. The depiction of the elephant motif can be seen on the royal seal of the Salem plates of Gaṅgā Śrī Purusha plates of Śaka 693 from South India.[21] On the surface of the seal is carved in relief the figure of a standing elephant facing the proper right. The seal is ovalshaped. The figure of the elephant, depicted in profile, has covered the entire seal area leaving no space for engraving any legend. It is also evident that the artist while making the seal did not pay much attention to its esthetic aspect. The designers of the seals of the Kāmarūpa kings, however, took sufficient care to give them a pleasing artistic look. D.C. Sircar mentioned that the Nesari plates of Rāstrakuta Govinda III[22] show that the Pallavas, Gaṅgās, Cālukyas, Colas and Pāndyas had the bull, elephant boar, tiger and fish respectively displayed on their banners. But he has not given illustrations.

The Sasankota plates of Gaṅgā Mādhavavarman,[23] Anantapur district, Andhra Pradesh, had the seal depicting an elephant. The seal is oval-shaped and measures 1-7/16" x 1-1/4". On its counter-sunk surface is carved in relief the figure of a standing elephant facing the proper left. On the top and bottom side of the seal small projections are noticed, of which the one at the bottom looks like a small knob and bears carved on it a spiral. The significance of the presence of the spiral is not known. The elephant is shown standing and facing left. The seal carriers no legend.

None of the two seals, namely, the seal of the Salem plates and the seal of the Sasankota plates, bearing the elephant figure as the royal insignia, offers any resemblance to the seals of the Kāmarūpa kings so far as the style is concerned.

The rings binding the copper-plates generally are round in shape. D.C. Sircar[24] has rightly pointed out that the copper-plate grants of the kings of Kāmarūpa and Kāthiawar (Gujarat) exhibit longish rings. The side of one end of the ring touches the side of the other end and not the face of one end. The rings of Māliya copper-plate of Mahārājā Dharsena II[25] has a good deal of similarity with the ring of the copper-plate rings of the Kāmarūpa kings.

Regarding the style and shape of the seal of the kings of Kāmarūpa, one must say that it has no affinity with the seals of the Pāla kings of Bengal and Bihar which bore the representation of the Buddhist wheel of law.[26] It also has no similarity with the seal of the kings of Sylhet and

Tripura. Our conjecture is that the seal of the Imperial Guptas had some influence over the seal of the Kāmarūpa king Bhāskar Varman, in so far as the style and shape are concerned. For example, the seals of Kumargupta[27] offers a good deal of similarity to the seal of Bhāskar Varman, in so far as the round shape is concerned. The emblem depicting the figure of Garuḍa, however, has no relation with the elephant emblems of the seal of Kāmarūpa kings. The seals of the Imperial Guptas exhibit the figure of Garuḍa, the emblem of the family,[28] on the upper part and sometimes as many as eight lines of writing below the emblem. The seal of king Harśavardhana (5-7/8" x 6-7/8"), has a bull emblem on the upper part and a legend containing no less than 13 lines of writing.[29] Though the seal of king Harśavardhana has a bull as royal emblem and the seal of king Bḥāskar Varman has the elephant as the royal emblem, there is much similarity in their shapes and the manner of engraving the legends below the emblems. Both king Harśavardhana and king Bhāskar Varman, who flourished in the 7th century, had friendly relations and the latter visited the kingdom of the former in the company of the Chinese pilgrim Hiuen Tsang. The round-shaped clay seals of Bhāskar Varman were also discovered at Nālandā along with the seals of king Harṣavardhana. The other two seals of the same king *i.e.*, the Doobi copper-plate seal and the Nidhānpur copper-plate seal are also cast in the same way. In the 9th century, the copper seals of the Kāmarūpa kings became oval shaped with a blunt but raised point at the top. In the 11th and the 12th centuries the points at the top of the seals of the Kāmarūpa kings became more pointed and prominent and the seal took the shape of a betel leaf. The technique of casting also, by that time, became much improved and from the a esthetic angle these were pleasing works of high class metal art. This technique of making artistic metal sculptural works became very popular by that time. The stone art style in the 12th century also became more refined and sophisticated in Assam or old Kāmarūpa as in Bengal and Bihar region. In other words, the art styles by the 12th century reached its zenith in Eastern India including Assam. In this regard, we are in full agreement with B.N. Mukherjee.[30]

The winged lion motif on the seals of the Āhom kings certainly came from the South-East Asia. Because the Āhoms (Tāis) entered the Brahmaputra Valley of Assam from Upper Burma and brought this symbol with them. It means strength or power. They also have brought many more things of their culture and introduced them in the Brahmaputra Valley in course of their rule.

Thus: (1) the seal of the Āhom kings bearing the figure of a winged lion or a dragon, which is affiliated to the great Tāi culture of South-East Asia is a new addition to the Indian art and inscription.

(2) The seals of the copper plates of the Kāmarūpa kings depicting an elephant have great significance. The same type of seals, showing elephants, which must have been found in plenty in Assam in those days[31] as today, were used by three separate pre-Āhom dynasties—the dynasty of Pushya Varman, dynasty of Śālastaṁbha and the dynasty of the Pāla rulers which is somewhat uncommon in Indian history. Considering the style of execution of the excellent pieces of the seals, they can be put on a place of pride in Indian art. In other words, the seals of the Kāmarūpa kings have no parallel in India, in so far as the a esthetic merit is concerned.[32]

Notes and References

1. M.M. Sharma. *Inscriptions of Ancient Assam*, Guwahati, *1978,* pp. 303-05.
2. *Ibid.*, pp. 10-11.
3. *Ibid.*, pp. 35-37. During my visit to the Nālandā Museum on 20th April, 1987, I could not find the seals in the showcase. In the month of February, 1996 I visited the museum again. But I failed to locate if in the museum.
4. *Ibid.*, p. 38.
5. *Ibid.*, Pls. XXII and XXIII.
6. R.D. Choudhury, *Archaeology of the Brahmaputra Valley of Assam,* Delhi, 1985, p. 231, Figs. 83, 84, 85.
7. Sharma, *op.cit.*, pp. *95-113.*
8. *Ibid.*, pp. 313-18.
9. *Ibid.*, Introduction, p. 21.
10. *Ibid.*, pp. 153-72.
11. *Ibid.*, pp. 225-40.
12. *Ibid.*, pp. 225-72.
13. Sharma, *op.cit.*, pp. 241-54.
14. *Ibid.*, pp. 193-206.
15. *Ibid.*, pp. 194-95.
16. *Ibid.*
17. *M. Neog (Ed.), Prāchya Sāsanāvali*, Guwahati, 1974.
18. *Ibid.*, Pl. 10.
19. *Ibid.*, Pl. 8.
20. *Ibid.*, Pl. 1.

21. *Epigraphia Indica*. Vol.
22. D.C. Sircar, *Indian Epigraphy,* 1965, p. 152.
23. *Ibid.*, p. 155, *E.I.,* Vol. XXIV, Pl. IIIb.
24. *Ibid.*, p. 154.
25. Fleet, *Corpus Inscription Indicaṛum* (C.I.I.), Vol. III, p. 164, Pl. XXIV.
26. Sircar, *op.cit.*, p. 151.
27. K.K. Thaplyal, *Studies in Ancient Indian Seals,* Lucknow, 1972, Pl. VI.
28. Sircar, *op.cit.,* p. 157.
29. *Ibid.*
30. B.N. Mukherji, *Eastern Indian Art Style, 1980,* p. 32.
31. See R.D. Choudhury "Asamar Sanaskritit Hātir Prabhāv," Ạsamar Cāh Mazdoor Samāj Āru Sanaskriti', Souvenir, Ed. Bipul Kumar Mahanta, Guwahati University, 1986. Also see, *Benudhar Sarma Commemoration Vol.,* Kāmarūpa Anusandhān Samiti, Guwahati, 1987, pp. 142-49.
32. I am very much thankful to Dr. D. Chutia and Mr. Atulananda Goswami, Guwahati for their suggestions and valuable help.

16

Āmbārī: An Important Workshop of Mediaeval Art

Āmbari in the heart of the city of Guwahati has presented a good number of sculptures to the art historians of the country. The Āmbari archaeological site, to the east of the Assam State Museum, has become welknown to the archaeologists and the art historians as an important art centre of the post Pālā period. In 1969 the plot of land, over which presently the excavation is going on, was aquired by the Reserve Bank of India for constructing its own building. In the same year, while digging for the foundation of the proposed Reserve Bank building quite a few stone images belonging to different Brahmanical deities were discovered along with debries. The local press gave publicity to the discovery of these images and as a result, public opinion compelled the Government of Assam to allot a different plot of land to the Reserve Bank of India and hand over the plot of land in question to the Directorate of Archaeology and Museums, Assam, in 1970. In the beginning of 1970, late Prof. H.D. Sankalia visited the Āmbari site and offered his advice to complete the excavation in a phased manner.

Towards the end of 1970, Prof M.C. Goswamī and Dr. T.C. Sarma, both of the Guwahati University, started the formal excavation at the site in collaboration with the Directorate of Museums and Archaeology, Assam. Prof. Sankalia deputed Dr. M.K. Dowlikar and Dr. Z.A. Ansari from the Decca College, Pune, to Guwahati to join the excavation camp. Both of them helped Goswamī and Sarma in the excavation work. The excavation continued up to April 1971.

During this phase of excavation a large mumber of icons were found at the site. A good number of icons representing Viṣṇu, Sūrya, Gaṅgā,

Yamunā, Śiva liṅga, etc. were found during the excavation. The images discovered in 1969 and 1970-71 can be grouped into two, according to their size. The smaller ones measure approximately 25 cms x 15 cms. The smaller ones may be taken as Series I, while the bigger ones may be taken as Series II. The images of Series I representing various deities are as follows:

Viṣṇu-4 Nos. One image is in the Anthropology Deptt., Guwahati University (*adv*. GU) and two (25 x 12 cms) are in the Assam State Museum) (*abv*. ASM)

Mahiṣamardinī-10 Nos. These images are in the Anthropology (25 x 15 cms) Deptt., G.U. while rests are in the ASM.

Sūrya-3 Nos. One image is in the ASM, while two are in the (25 x 12 cms) Anthropology Deptt. G.U.

Śiva liṅga-4 Nos. Two images are in the ASM, while two (13 cms in hight) are in the Anthropology Deptt., G.U. Two Śiva liṅgas are without *Yonipīṭha.*

In addition to these images, one broken sculpture representing the Gaja-Vyāla motif was discovered. It is excavated on a piece of black basalt. Another sadly mutilated image possibly representing Manasā is also carved on a piece of black basalt.

Series II includes the following:

Viṣṇu	-9 Nos.
Sūrya	-3 Nos.
Natarāja	-1 Nos.
Gaṅgā	-1 No.
Yamunā	-1 No.
Ṛṣi	-4 Nos.
Agni	-1 No.
Śiva liṅga	-12 Nos.
Nandī	-4 Nos.
Broken pillar	-1 No.

All the icons are in the Assam State Museum except a Śiva liṅga and a figure of Nandī which are in the Anthropology Deptt. of G.U.

In addition to these stone sculptures, one very beautiful terracotta piece representing a female figure, was discovered. It is now in the Anthropology Deptt., G.U. But this terracotta is sadly mutilated.

After 1971 no excavation was done at Āmbari till 1987. After a long gap of about 16 years, the excavation at the site was resumed under the direction of Dr. T.C. Sarma. Still the excavation is going on at the site.

In 1987-88 three trenches were dug up to the depth of 8.6". In addition to potsherds, 16 different kinds of pots, 150 varieties of earthen lamps and 133 stone images were found. The excavation has also revealed 40 miniature earthen Śiva liṅga, 44 Yonipīṭha and 2 *Gajavyāla* images. The Śiva liṅgas and Yonīpīṭhas are miniature in size and they are made of clay, while the images of Gajavyālas are depicted on stone. All other stone images numbering 133 may be grouped in Series I considering their size. The images discovered at the site represent Sūrya, Viṣṇu and Mahiṣamardinī. The number of stone Śiva liṅgas is 45. During the course of excavation, about 30 decorated or partially decorated stone blocks including a stones lab for sharpening the chisels were also found. During the excavation in winter season in 1987-88 up to 7th layer could be dug. Stone images and also other sculptural materials were found in the 5th layer.

In this season (1988-89) digging in two trenches have been completed. In these trenches a beautifully decorated disc, 20 broken terracotta figure and potsherds were found. Two miniature Śiva liṅga and also a big image of Sūrya have came to light. The stone image of Sūrya may be grouped in Series II of the Āmbari sculptures. Till now digging up to the 4th layer only has been done.

An examination of the stone sculptures found at Āmbari shows the following:

1. It is found that the icons are of the same style. One image of Sūrya is four armed, which is an uncommon feature. Above the heads of Gaṅgā and Yamunā images serpent hoods are shown. Although serpent hood is not normally found over the head of the river goddesses, in Assam some image has been discovered having this feature. An image of Indra, preserved in the A.S.M., has a hood of serpent over the head of the god.

2. All the sculptures from Āmbari bear the pre-Āhom style. It is interesting to note that not a single sculpture from the site bear Āhom, Koch or Kochārī style which flourished in the late medieval period. From the sculptures, discovered in various placed of Assam, it can be concluded that the sculptural art in Assam reached its zenith by 12th century. But

the Āmbari sculptures do not have the master pieces except the huge image of Natarāja, which is considered as one of the best stone sculptures depicting Śiva in his dancing posture. Āmbari stone sculptures are devoid of lavish ornamentation. Though the steles of the images are pointed, yet they are not fully decorated.

(1) The excavation at Āmbari shows four different cultural phases.

(a) British. (b) Mughal-Āhom period (c) Pālā period *i.e.* 10th-13th cent. and (d) pre-Pālā period (?)

(3) The images bear short inscription in characters belonging to the 13th century.

(4) All the sculptures were found lying horizontally under the earth. Although traces of some brick construction of wall have been found, no trace of temple construction has come to light. The position and the depth in which the sculptures were found lead us to think that the sculptures or the images were not stuck into the walls of the temple. They were lying in different places of the site. This shows that Āmbari must have been a workshop from where finished sculptures were dispatched to various places.

(5) The long tank (Deghalīpukhurī) near the site must have once been a channel of the Brahmaputra, which was profitably utilized by the authors or the artisans of Āmbari.

The site has not yet been completely excavated. It may take some years to complete the excavation. After completion of the excavation certainly we will be able to know many more things about the hidden past of Prāgjyotiṣapura, the ancient city of the East. No doubt Āmbari workshop will throw new light after the completion of the excavation. The paper was read in seminar on 'Early Medieval Art of India' organized by Lucknow State Museum, Lucknow from 11th to 15th January 1989. Since then more sculptural pieces have been unearthed during the excavation at the site. In 1987 excavation at the site was resumed by Dr. T.C. Sharma. It was continued for two years. Again during 1991-92, with the financial help of Directorate of Museums Assam Dr. H.K. Sarma, G.U., excavated the site. During both the excavations of the same style a large number of sculptures were found. But still it is not complete. A good number of Āmbari sculpture are on display in the Assam State Museum. In 1915 excavation at the site has been resumed under the Direction of Mr. G.N. Bhuyan and Dr. N.P. Choudhry help from the Directorate of Museums, Assam. It is to be completed.

17

Brick Temples at Na-nāth

Brick built temples belonging to pre-Āhom-Koch period in Assam are not common. From the ruins of the Da-parvatiā temple, we know that in the 6th century brick construction was known in Assam. At Mikirāti, in Nagaon District is also noticed the *garbhagṛiha* of a brick-built shrine, which may date in the same period as Da-parvatiā ruined temple. Some twenty years back, when I visited Barganġā to see the rock-cut inscription and also the standing rock-cut figures of *dvārapāla* guarding the inscription, I could see the brick built plinth of the temple. Now I learn from Dr. P. Sarma, Department of Archaeology, Assam, that no trace of the plinth of the ruined temple can be seen. Trace of brick built *garbhagṛha* at Mikirāti (Davakā) is noticed. But there is no trace of its upper portion.

Under this circumstance, the brick built small temples, which are in ruins, at Na-nāth, assume great significance. I visited the site first in 1968 and paid a second visit to this place including Rājbārī in 1988.

The ruined temples at Na-nāth are located on the southern bank of the Jogījān,[1] which is actually a dead river now. Towards little south on the bank of a dead channel of the Kapilī river is noticed another ruined brick-built temple. The ruins of this temple are located in Kenduguri which is a tribal village. One can reach Na-nāth and Kenduguri from Hozāi (Sub-Divisional headquarters). A P.W.D. road touches both the sites.

If one goes from Hozāi to Na-nāth before reaching the site of the ruined brick temples, he finds on the way first the Cāmuṇḍā temple, and then Kenduguri village and lastly, the ruined temple at Kenduguri. All of them are found on the eastern bank of the dead channel of the Kapilī river. Some years back, the stone image of Cāmuṇḍā was found alongwith other two broken stone images lying under a tree. Later the local villagers belonging to the Ḍimāsā community, brought the image to the present site and enshrined it. The image is sadly mutilated. The broken pieces, however are cemented. The other two broken stone images cannot be identified due to their mutilated condition. But it can be said that they represent some female deity. Stylistically , these two broken sculptures and the Cāmuṇḍā image mentioned above may belong to *c.* 10th century or so on stylistic consideration. The local people adore the bigger female image as Gaṅgā. The image of Cāmuṇḍā was originally kept here. During my first visit in 1968, the image of Cāmuṇḍā could be seen under a tree at this place. R.M. Nāth also noticed it.[2]

Towards a little North of the site of these two broken images, on the eastern side of the P.W.D. road, a ruined brick temple is noticed. This locality is known as Kenduguri village, inhabited by tribals. In my first visit to this place, the ruined temple was not discovered. Subsequently, the Directorate of Archaeology, Assam, exposed the ruins which consist of damaged *garbhagṛiha* and *maṇḍapa*. The superstructure has fallen down. Only lower part of the wall (about 3 to 4 feet high) of the *garbhagṛiha* and *maṇḍapa* are extant. It is a brick built temple. The image enshrined in the *garbhagṛiha* is now lost. Only the *pīṭha* of the image having a rectangular hole in the centre is *in situ*. The broken bricks are seen lying at the site. The plinth of the temple is also exposed. To the north-west of this ruined temple at a little distance a mound of bricks is noticed. Slight exposure of it will give us more information.

At a little distance to the North of the site of the ruined temple at Kenduguri, extensive ruins of brick temples can be seen. The locality is known as Na-nāth. The road to the site from Kenduguri is jeepable. Originally, there must have been nine temples or shrines, but now ruins of only seven temples can be seen. The site was visited by me in 1968 first. At that time the site was not taken over by the State Department of Archaeology. I visited the site in 1988 for the second time and saw a different picture, since the site was preserved by the Archaeology Department. The ruins of the temples were exposed and beautification programme at the site was taken up to attract the visitors.

The construction of the small temples was done very systematically in a planned way. There is a boundary wall around the temples, which are laid out in two rows facing each other. The ruins cover several acres of land. When we visited the site in 1968, the local people constructed a modern shrine at the opening of the right row. Now this temple has been shifted to the end of the same row. Visitors regularly came to this temple, though in less number.

The right row shows five temples, while the left one consists of only two temples plus the modern tinshed shrine used by the local people. The Archaeology Department has provided entrance to the site towards the south. As both rows of temples face each other, a passage has been provided for the visitors in between the rows for their convenience. It is likely that in the past also this passage exited. Though the temples were brick built, their entrance doors were of stone. Each *gabhagriha* of these temples has a Śiva liṅga, made of superior quality stone. The *Liṅgas* were carved from black basalt,while the *Yonīpīṭhas* were carved from hard granite blocks.

The first temple in the left row (from the south), like other temples at the site, has a Śiva liṅga *in situ*. The upper part of the *garbhagṛiha* is damaged. The temple consisted of only the *garbhagṛiha* and *maṇḍapa*. The *dvāraśilā* (311 cms long) at the entrance is *in situ*, while the two *śākhās* (262 cms long) are seen lying horizontally on the floor of the *maṇḍapa*. The walls of the three sides (except the front) are in good state of preservation. However, the *bhitti* inside the temple dividing the *garbhagṛiha* and the *maṇḍapa* is also standing, though the upper portion of it is lost. The measurement of the entire temple is 1602 cms x 850 cms. The height of the remaining portion of the *bhitti* is 136 cms. there are 98 *devakoṣthas* (niches) in a row on three sides (not the front) of the *bhitti* of the temple. Each *devakoṣtha* measures 27 x 27 cms. The measurement of each plaque is 24 x 26 cms. Terracotta plaques are intact only in 29 *devakoṣthas*. Rest of the terracotta plaques that were stuck into the devakoṣṭhas are either lifted by antique hunters or lost in the process of natural calamities. Some of the fallen plaques are preserved in the zonal office of the Archaeology Department at Hozāi.

The plaques depict human figures birds, animals, flower motifs, grotesques etc. Depiction of two gods Sūrya and Narasiṁha *avatāra* of Viṣṇu are also found in two plaques. A composite image showing elephant and lion is very interesting. This *gaja-Vyāla* motif is a representation of *īhāmṛigas,* the mythical figures that have been occupying an important place in Indian sculptures right from Harappa or Indus vally civilization.[3] The Indus valley seals depicting fantastic animals are nothing but the first stage of the *īhāmṛiga* figures. In the Sanchi *stupa* railing depiction of such *īhāmṛiga* figures are found in its early form. In the Gupta period this type of figure are used as ornamentation. The Da-parvatiā *dvāra,* near Tezpur belonging to the late Gupta period depicts quite a few *ihamṛiga* figures.[4]

The image of Sūrya and Narasiṁha mentioned above are in *sthānāka* postures. One plaque shows a human figure in *sthānāka* posture. The figure is flanked by two trees, which are being forcibly held by the hands of the figure possibly in an attempt to uproot them. The scene represents Krishṇa's *Arjunabhañjana* episode. Plaques showing a bull and elephant, mother and child, etc, are also found.

The four other ruined temples to the north of the first temple in the same row are also similar. The plinths of the *garbhagṛihas* of these brick temples are the only remnants. But unlike the first temple described above, these ruined temples do not bear terracotta sculptures. But all of them have each a Śiva liṅga in the *garbhagṛiha*. Above the *garbhagṛiha* in each case a thatched or tin-shed has been put up by the local committee and not by the Directorate of Archaeology. Some of these ugly and dilapidated shed have certainly reduced the beauty of the site. However, in the case of the first ruined temple such a shed is not erected. The plans of these temple are simple and identical. The northernmost of these four temples is not exposed by the Directorate of Archaeology so that the detailed plan of the temple is hidden under brick debris. The bricks fallen from the superstructure of the temple has created a small mound. The measurements of all these ruined temples are identical.

The right row shows only three temples—one modern and two old ones. The first one, like the other four ruined temples of the other row, is very simple in plan and does not bear any plaques around the wall, but the *garbhagṛiha* houses a Śiva liṅga. The size of this temple is 1080 cms x 780 cms. This is the smallest of all the temples at Na-nāth and has a tin shed above.

The next temple in the same row is very interesting. This temple is bigger than the other one but has similar plan. Like the first ruined temple of the left row, the present one also has a row of terracotta plaques around its wall, just above the *adhiṣṭhāna*. The terracotta plaques fixed in the *devakoṣṭhas* number 64. Originally all the *devakoṣṭhas* were adorned with terracotta plaques but now only 43 plaques can be seen. As in the former case, here also we find representations of divinities such as, *Varāhāvatāra*, Sūrya and Umā-Maheśvara, Kārttikeya, dancing female and other human figures, animal figures, such as, elephant, lion and horse, flower motif, *kirttimukha, kalpavṛiksha* etc. A śialiṅga is enshrined in the *garbhagṛiha*.

Directorate of Archaeology, a few years back, opened a zonal office at Hozāi and collected a number of fragmentary pieces of sculptural and architectural relics including 27 terracotta plaques from Na-nāth. All these pieces were found either lying under the earth or jungle at the site and were exposed while clearing the debris and the jungle. These pieces were originally fixed in the *devakoṣṭhas,* most probably of the first left and second right temples, which show panels of terracotta plaques, described above. These are in comparatively better state of preservation and not as weathered as some of the plaques seen fixed in the temples. These sculptures also depict animals, mythical figure, Gaṇeśa, female devotee (?) and flower motifs. A plaque also shows a fish.

An examination of these sculptures reveals that some plaques have been duplicated. A few earthen moulds of some plaques have also been found, which proves that the plaques were prepared from moulds at the site itself.

From the above description, it is clear that all the temples or shrines at Na-nāth, although brick built, used stone doorways. These *dvāras* were fixed on the entrances to the *maṇḍapa* and *garbhagṛiha* of the temples. All the temples have lost super structure. Only the *adhiṣṭhāna* and the wall portions of the temples measuring 4' to 5' high are intact. P.C. Sarma has rightly said "the smaller span but greater wall thickness of the *garbhagṛiha* proves that it was lofty temple and evidently loftier than the *maṇḍapa* attached to it. The roof of the spacious *maṇḍapa* was supported by stone columns. Some of these columns are notched lengthwise on one of its edges and the middle portion of the remaining three edges are chamferred."[5] The *dehalīs* seen lying at the site bear *kalpavṛiksha* motif which is commonly found in Assam. The *śākhās* of the *dvāras* are less decorative and so also the columns lying at the site. The columns employed to support the roof of the *garbhagṛiha* were placed on stone courses (*adhiṣṭhāna*), square in size. The *garbhagṛiha* and the *maṇḍapa* are square in size. The level of the floor of the *garbhagṛiha* is slightly higher than that of the *maṇḍapa.* We have no means to know about the other features of the temples as their upper portions are lost. However, the terracota panels that exist around the wall above the *adhiṣṭhāna* of two temples speak highly of the a esthetic taste of the artisans and patrons of the temples.

To the North at a little distance is seen the river Yogī. Across the river extensive ruins of temples can be seen at Rājbārī. Huge stone blocks, *dvāra,* and other architectural pieces prove that there must have existed some lofty temples. The ruined temples at the place were of stone. Bricks is absent here. An image of Umā-Maheśvara is still worshipped by the local people. A Śiva liṅga is seen *in situ* in the *garbhagṛiha* of the main temple which is in complete ruins. The stone image of Umā-Maheśvara, on stylistic consideration may be assigned to *c.* 10th century.

Towards west of this ruined temple site at a little distance on the north bank of the river Yogī another ruined temple can be seen. It was also a stone temple. Local people call it temple of Śaṅkhādevī. The ruins are not clearly exposed. From the style of execution, it can assigned to the period of the ruins of Rājbārī. As in Rājbārī, here *also brick* activities are absent. Across the river Yogī, opposite to the ruined temple site of Śankhadevi, another ruined temple is seen. It was a stone temple, smaller in size. The local people call it Śivabārī, as it has a Śiva liṅga. This temple was possibly contemporaneous to the other two stone temple referred to above.

On consideration of the "simplicity of the plan, type and size of the stone columns, the band of terracotta figures of the outer walls and from a few other features, such as, elevation, cella floor, theme and plasticity of some of the sculptures, it has been found that it maintains similarity with some temples of the Gupta and post-Gupta periods and particularly with the Gupta temple at Da-parvatīā,"[6] according to Sarma. It is true that some features of these temples are reminiscent of the Gupta style. The simplicity of the plan proves that they bear some Gupta traits. But the style of the terracotta sculptures seems to belong to the post Gupta-period or the 7th-8th century. The *dvāras* of these temples are not ornate and they do not bear images of Gaṅgā and Yamunā, like the *dvāra* of the Daparvatīā and temple. Thirdly, the presence to the *dvāraśilā* bearing *kalpavṛksha* motif is seen at Rājbārī ruins mentioned above.Rājbārī ruins cannot be placed in the Gupta period on stylistic consideration in any case. Daparvatīā temple also does not have *dvāraśilā* bearing *kalpavṛiksha* motif. So, considering all these aspects ruins of Na-nāth can be placed only in the 7th-8th century and not earlier.

From the ruined temples at Na-nāth we know that even after the Gupta period, the erection of brick temples was popular in North-east India, as in some other parts of the country. The brick temple at Bhitargāon constructed in the Gupta period is well known for the terracotta sculptures on its walls. Later we find at Pāhārpur and Maināmati (now in Bangladesh) brick temples bearing a good number of terracotta sculpture, which are dated in the 8th century.[7] The activities of masons, expert in the construction of brick temples and in adorning them with terracotta sculptures in Assam, is amply revealed by nine brick temples belonging to *c.* 8th century at Nanath[8] and one at Keduguri, described above.

Notes and References

1. Pradip Sarma *"Yogī Nadir Pare Pare"* Prantik *(an Assamese Magazine),* Guwahati, 16-30 Nov; 1989, p. 22.
2. R.M. Nāth,"Antiquities of the Kapil and Yamunā Valley," *Joumal of the Assam Research Society*, Vol. V, No. 1-2, 1937.
3. A.L. Srivastava, īhāmṛigas: "The Mythical and Fabolous creature in Sanchi Sculpture" *Bulletin of the Assam State Museum* No. 2, 1976, pp. 9-11.
4. R.D. Choudhury, *Archaeology of the Brahmaputra Valley of Assam,* 1985, Delhi. pp. 148-153.
5. P.C. Sarma, "The Terracotta Treasures of Na-nāth" *Sentinel*, an English daily, Guwahati, 13th April, 86.
6. *Ibid.*
7. See Robin Dev Choudhury, "Prak Āhom Yugar Śilpakalā: Yogījānar Purātāttik Sampad" *Ājir Asom* (an Assamese Daily) Guwahati, 21st April 1988 for details about the ruins of Yogījān and Na-nāth. In that article I opined that the sculptures from Na-nāth might belong to 8th/9th century A.D. But after a reexamination I would prefer to put them in *c.* 8th century A.D.

   In this article through oversight I casually mentioned that the *ihamṛiga* figures occurred in the Sāñchi *stūpa* belonging to the Maurya period. The *ihamriga* figures actually occur in the raillings of the Sāñnchi Stūpa. The railings belong to the Śunga period.
8. Sarma has dated the sculptures in 11th-12th century. We cannot support him. See, P.C. Sarma, *Architecture of Assam.* New Delhi, 1988, p. 77.

18

Some Newly Collected Images of the Assam State Museum

In the year 1977 a few important image were collected for he Assam State Museum, Guwahati. They are as follows:

(a) A bust of a female figure from Mikirātī;

(b) A *Viṣṇu* image from Khārāmedhipārā;

(c) A Manasā image from Śilghāt;

(d) A broken piece of an image from Jorpukhurī, Guwahati; and

(e) A *Lakṣmī-Nārāyaṇa* image from Kācumarī.

A bust of a female figure (25 x 18 cms)

The bust of a broken female figure possibly sculptured on piece of sand stone had been lying outside the ten-shed near the ruins of a group of small temples at Mikirātī, in the Nowgong district. The bust shows the front side of a female figure from neck to the belly only. Both the arms of the figure as the other parts of the body are sadly mutilated. However, the *hāras* worn around the neck are seen beautifying the chest of the figure. The modelling of the *hāra* and the tender and proportionate bosom recall the Gupta art tradition. This piece of art can be compared with the bust portions of the figures of *Gaṅgā* and *Yamunā* of the Da-parvatīā ruined temple *dvāra*, datable of *c.* 6th A.D.,[1] though the present piece of sculpture may date in a slightly later period than that of the Da-parvatīā sculptures. What is important is that the Gupta art style is reflected in the present piece of sculpture. Had the head, hands and the legs of this figures not been sadly mutilated, possibly at the hands of iconoclasts, it would have been a splendid art piece, and its identity would have been known to us.

Viṣṇu (27 x 14 cms)

It is a sone image of the deity collected from Khārāmedhipārā (Chaklpārā) village near Dudhnai in the district of Goālpārā. The image of the deity is sculptured on a block of sand (?) stone. As the quality of the stone is not good the minute details of the image are gone. However, it can be clearly seen that here the deity is made to stand on *samapādasthānka* attitude on *padma*. The four armed god with his right front hand is holding possibly a *padama*, while displaying the *varadamudrā*. His left front hand is made to hold a *śaṅkha*. The back right hand of the deity is seen touching the head of the *Gadādevī*, while the left one is made to touch the head of Chakrapurṣa. The *vanamālā kuṇḍala* and *hāra* worn by the deity are clear. Behind the head of the god a round *prabhā* (halo) is noticed. The figure of *Viṣṇu* including those of *Gadādevī* and *Chakrapurṣa* are in high relief. The *mukuṭa* of the god is slightly mutilated. Stylistically, it may belong to 7th century A.D. or the first half of the 8th century A.D.[2]

The present image is very important from iconographic point of view because, it is the only image of *Viṣṇu* from Assam and possible from the entire North-East India, wherein the *āyudhapuruṣas i.e., chakrapuruṣa* and *Gadādevī* are shown flanked on either side of the deity. There are a few images of *Viṣṇu* wherein *gadā* and *chakra* are represented by a male and a female figures respectively discovered in Bangladesh and in West Bengal and Bihar States of India and elsewhere.[3]

Manasā (165 x 65 cms)

This image had been kept in the compound of the bungalow of the Director of Koliabor Tea Estate, Śilghāt in Nowgong district. In the same compound several chiselled block, are also noticed. Evidently, they might belong to one temple which are now not in existence and possibly the present deity was installed in that temple. Further more, five iron cannons, one of them bearing a damaged inscription in old Assamese script and Sanskrit language dated is *Śaka* era, are also noticed in the same place. Very recently the stone image of Manasā has been acquired by the Assam State Museum, Guwahati under the registration of Antiquities and Art Treasure Act and Assam Ancient Monuments Act, 1959 and Rules, 1964. Now the image is preserved in the museum.

In this beautiful stone sculpture chiselled from a block of sand stone (?) the goddess is seen in *samapādasthānka* attitude on a *padma*. Here left hand holds a pot (?) which is not clear. The objects held in her left hand also has become equally indistinct. The body of the goddess is well ornamented and draped. Above the head of the goddess a five headed snake is seen canopying her. On either side of it are seen two nāgās (or nāginīs) in half human from with folded hands. Their tails are coming down on either side of the goddess. At the knee level of the deity are seen on either side a female figure attending upon the goddess. Above the serpent heads that canopy the head of deity, is seen the usual *krīttimukha*, sculptured just below the point of the *ślāpaṭṭa*. Below the *pīṭha* of the deity is seen an elephant in front of which a miniature female (?) figure is seen in *añjalihastamudrā* which may be identified either as the donor or a devotee. This piece of art can be placed in *c.* 12th century on stylistic consideration. The presence of the elephant vehicle under the feet of the deity in the image has made it very interesting and important. A good number of images of *Manasā*, the snake goddess, have been discovered in India, particularly in Eastern India and Bangaladesh, but not a single image of the goddess is shown with an elephant vehicle to our knowledge. It is, therefore, an image of peculiar in nature.

However, N.K. Battasali,[4] who has published a photograph of this valuable image and mentioned about the image in a footnote only, has rightly interpreted the term '*nāgendra*' as an elephant, *nāga* means ordinarily a huge snake. He has quoted a description from the *Brahmavaivarta Purāna (Śrī Kṭiṣna Janma-Khandam ch. 51.)*,[5] wherein it is said that goddess Manasā should have Nāgendra as the *vāhana*. Therefore, the sculptor of present image, by the word *nāga*, meant an elephant and not a snake. Usually the sculptor of present image, by the word nāga, meant an elephant and not a snake. Usually the sculptor, who followed the iconographical texts, used to mean a snake by the term *nāga*. But in the present case, this tradition was not continued. However, the sculptor has got the support of the icongraphical text. No doubt, the image of *Manasā* from Śilghāt is of extremely rare type and to our knowledge, this is the only image of the deity having an elephant vehicle, discovered so far in India.

A broken sculpture (Approx, 2½ x 1 cms)

This piece of sculpture is sadly mutilated making it difficult to know actually what it represents. It was found under earth opposite to S.K. Bhuyan residence, Lamb Road Guwahati. The major portion of this stone sculpture is broken and missing. The extant piece represents only the left side of the huge main missing sculpture. In this piece is seen a beautifully sculptured *makara* (crocodile) whose body portion is broken and missing with the major portion of the sculpture. The trunk of the *makara* which looks like that of an elephant, is seen rising up holding a creeper which is issued from its mouth. Just above the remnant body portion of the *makara* is seen a dwarf (or miniature) mythical creature in hybrid form of which the upper portion having two wings represents a bird, while the lower portion, having two legs, a man. This two handed figure is seen playing on a flute and in dancing pose. Above, on the border of this broken piece is noticed a beautifully sculptured figure of *Vidyādhāra*.

Now, as the major portion of this beautiful sculpture is broken and missing, it is difficult to say actually what it represents. However, looking at the *makara* and the figure playing on a flute and dancing on the *makara* (?) it may be conjectured that the sculpture represented *Gaṅgā*. This piece of sadly mutilated art, on stylistic ground should be placed in 10th century A.D.

In Assam, a few *Gaṅgā* images have already been discovered. For instance, *Gaṅgā* on the Da-parvatiā ruined temple *dvāra*,[6] *Gaṅgā* on the *dvāra* of the ruined temple at Mājagāon and *Gaṅgā* found in the Āmbārī excavation. But none of these icons of deity should have any resemblance with the present piece of sculpture. However this piece of beautiful work of art is quite interesting. The sculpture may be placed in *c.* 10th century A.D.

Lakṣmī-Nārāyaṇa (8 x 4 cms)

This image of *Lakṣmī-Nārāyaṇa* was discovered by Sri A.C. Barua, Registering Officer, Jorhat, in a village, Kāchumārī near Moran. Here the *Nārāyaṇa* or *Viṣṇu* is made to sit in *lalitāsana* posture on a lotus seat and on his left thigh seats his consorts *Lakṣmī*. *Viṣṇu* holds in his four hands clock-wise: *gadā, chakra, śaṅkha* and *padma*. The deity wears a *kīrita* (?) *mukuṭa* with three round tires at the top, the upper most one being like a round ball. The figure of *Lakṣmī* in comparison to the figure of the god looks much smaller. The object of the left hand is not clear. The lower left hand of the god and the right hand of the goddess, are embracing the bodies of each other. Below the feet of the god is seen *Garuḍa* in his usual posture.

Looking at the style of the *Kīriṭamukuṭa* the *āyudhas* and little figure of *Lakṣmī*, it can be said that the sculpture may belong to *c.* 10th century, if not later. However, this icon is very important because this is the only image of *Lakṣmī-Nārāyaṇa* discovered so far in Assam.

Now, from the broken piece of sculpture from Mikirātī. We can say that Gupta art tradition was continued and spread as far east as the Davāka kingdom representing the region around Dabakā, a place in nowgong district, which is very near to the ruined temple site at Mikirāti. Hence, the present piece of sculpture with Gupta trait has helped us in the identification of Davāka kingdom mentioned in the Allahabad pillar inscription of Samudra Gupta with the present Dabakā.[7] The image from Khārāmedhipārā, has shown the continuity of the Gupta art in Assam in the pre-Pāla or early Pāla age. The *Manasā* image with its extraordinary phenomenon, proves that the cult of *Manasā* was popular in Assam in 11th/12th century as in other parts of eastern India. The broken piece of the sculpture found near Jorpukhurī, Guwahati, depicting an uncommon theme has enhanced the beauty of the iconographic representation. The last image representing *Nārāyaṇa* and *Lakṣmī* proves that, like the image of *Umā-Mahesśwara*, the composite image of *Lakṣmī-Nārāyaṇa* was also popular in Assam in pre-Āhom period and this tradition was perhaps not continued in the Āhom period. It is to be noted that not a single image of *Lakṣmī-Nārāyaṇa* belonging to the pre-Āhom period has come to light so far. The discovery of the present sculpture bearing pre-Āhom style, proves that the image of great importance.

Notes and References

1. "Antiquity of the ruined at Da-parvatiā", by R.D. Choudhury, *Bulletin of the Assam State Museum,* No. II, pp. 51-69.
2. R.D. Choudhury, "Adhyapak Sarasvatir lagat ek saptah" (Assamese) *Prakāsh*, Guwahati, 3rd Yr., No. I, p. 44.
3. K. Desai, *Iconography of Viṣṇu*, New Delhi, 1973, Figs. 9, 10, 11 and 12. R.D. Benarji, *Eastern Indian School of Medieval Sculpture*, 1993, Pls. XIa, LXVIII, a.
4. N.K. Battasali, *Iconography of Buddhist and Brahmanical Sculptures in the Dacca Museum*, Dacca 1929, Pl. LXXIII, b.
5. *Ibid.*, pp. 223-24.
6. *Annual Report of Archaeological Survey of India,* 1924-25, pp. 98-99.
7. *'Prakas'*, Guwahati, 3rd Yr., No. I, p. 44. Also see, "Gupta influence in Kāmarūpa", by R.D. Choudhury, *Proceedings of the Indian History Congress*, Bhuvaneswar, 1977.

19

A Hoard of Metallic Images from Haharā*

Haharā, a small village near Sonāpur in Kāmarūp district is not noted for archaeological heritage, although the region, as a whole, can take pride in a number of important archaeological sites and remains. It was here that the metallic images in question, numbering altogether 15, were accidentally found in the course of digging a tank by one Tobin Basumatari some time in the month of March 1978. The images were subsequently acquired with the help of the Govt. and brought over to the Assam State Museum. Next to the Ōdālbākrā hoard, found some year back, this is the largest haul of such images made recently.

Stylistically, the images can be divided into two groups—early and late—The early group covering 10th and 11th centuries *i.e.* the Pālā style of the eastern region and the late group covering a time span ranging from 15th/16th to the 18th century A.D.

Given below is a brief description of the iconographical features of the image and their probable historical background.

Group A or Early group

1. Composite twin *Devī* images (9 cm): Of this composition, the left one sits in *lalitāsana* with a child on her lap, or rather on her left thigh to be precise, and the right hand resting on the right knee in *varadā* pose. The image on the right hand side is in *padmāsana* in *dhyāna mudrā*. Both the images are two-armed. The *prabhāvalī* has two circles right behind the

---

* The co-author of this paper is Sri S.N. Bhuyan, Director of Archaeology, Assam.

two images flanking a *Kalpa-vṛkṣa*. The pedestal has three small images at three of its corners—a bull (?) at the back left corner, a devotee with its torso and head missing at the front left corner, and a male devotee in *añjalī* pose at the front right corner. The back of the *prabhāvalī* has a few as yet undeciphered letters.

The identity of the two images cannot be determined with certainty. If the two image were to be identified as parts of a *Saptamātṛkā* complex (*Mātṛkā* images are occasionally found in groups of twos and threes), then, judging by the presence of the bull at the back left corner, the image on the left, holding a child, could well be *Māheśvarī*, while the other one could be any one of the remaining *Mātṛkās*. If, on the other hand,the image on the left is identified as Hāritī, the accompanying image still remains unidentified.

2. Hāritī (6.5 cm): The Devī sits in *lalitāsana* on a five-tiered *'padma āsana'* is two-armed and holds a child on her left thigh, while in her right hand, which rests on her right knee in *varadā* pose, she holds an indistinct object. The image is fully decorated with a *karaṇḍa-mukuṭa* and other usual jewelleries. The modelling is of perfect hand, with firm breasts and slim waist, and idiomatically similar to the one above. The aureole behind is decorated with floral motifs.

This is another fine specimen of the metallic sculptures of the medieval period.

3. Garuḍa (5 cm): This is an anthropomorphic figure of Garuḍa, shown in a kneeling position with his right knee resting on the ground. Its two hands are shown in *varadā* pose. Behind the two arms are shown the two short wings of the celestial bird. The hair-do is done at the back in a fan-like manner. The nose is aquiline.

The piece belongs to the medieval period.

4. Devī (6 cm): The Devī sits in padmāsana, is four-armed and holds in her upper right hand a lotus bud, a kartri in her upper left hand, while the two lower hands are in *abhaya* and *varadā* pose, respectively. The recombent *vāhana* shown at the pedestal is either a stylized lion or a tiger. The nature of the image could not as yet be identified. Stylistically, the image falls in the same category as the above mentioned Hāritī.

Group B or Late group

5. Tripurā-Bhairavī (7.5 cm): Seated in *padmāsana* on a corpse with its head on Devī's left, and supported by a three-tiered pedestal, the image

is four-armed and the two upper hands are in *varadā* pose, while the lower left hand has an *akṣamālā*. On her tiara is depicted the crescent moon. She wears a *muṇḍa-mālā* as garland. The radiating *prabhāvalī* has a serpent hood immediately below the *kalasa* filnial. The inner rim of the *prabhāvalī* is decorated with beaded motif. According to the *Kālikā-Purāṇa (K.P.)* (ch.74, verses 93-98 and 104-106) the Devī has in her four hands either *abhaya-mudrā, ṣraja (mālā), pustaka and varadā mudrā or pustaka, varadā-mudrā, abhya-mudrā and akṣamālā*. In this icon, the goddess has her two upper hands in *abhaya* pose, while the *varadā* pose is absent. And so is the *ṣraja*. The image, thus, can be said to be a near approximation to the details given in verses 104-106 of the *K.P.*

6. Tripurā-Bhairavī (5.5 cm): Seated in *padmāsana* on a lotus supported by a corpse with its head on Devī's left, this four-armed, three-eyed goddess has, like the previous one, a crescent on her tiara and a skull garland around her neck. Surrounding her and seated on the four corners are four females in *padmāsana* and *añjalī-mudrā*. Unlike the previous image, it has no *prabhāvalī* but a central tenon issuing right from the goddess's back. In her four arms she holds, from upper right hand onwards (clockwise), *akṣa, pustaka, abhaya-mudrā* and *varadā-mudrā* with a spherical object on the palm. This description fully tallies with verses 105-106 of ch. 74 of the *Kālikā-Purāṇa*.

7. Gajalakṣmī (.'5 cm): Four-armed, seated in *padmāsana* and surrounded on four corners by four elephants, each holding a water jar in its trunk, and each perched on a high platform supported by two tall props (the front right elephant is, however, missing), the goddess holds, in her four hands, from the upper right hand onwards (clock-wise), *padma, padma, abhaya-mudrā* and *varadā-mudrā*. The significance of the image lies in the fact that this is the first instance of a Gajalakṣmī of this type; and secondly, this is the only metallic Gajalakṣmī image so far found in this region. The goddess wears, among other things a denticled tiara and belongs stylistically to *c.* 16th century A.D., if not later.

8. Sūrya (9 cm): This is an interesting image in that the deity, flanked by two male attendants holding a *padma* each in the left hand, and with the right hand in a modified form of the *varadā* pose, is seated on the pericarp of a lotus with a fairly tall stem issuing right out of the back of the central horse below that raises the god with his two attendants far above the seven horses. The charioteer holds the reins and is seated on the back of the central horse right behind the lotus stem. The god, as

well as his two attendants, are seated in the *padmāsana* posture, the former holding a lotus in each of his two hands. Behind the image is a semi-circular band and a central cross-bar running horizontally across, with a finial at the centre of the band right over the head of the central deity.

The composition is noteworthy in that this is the only Sūrya image of this type with a long lotus stem, raising the principal deity far above the level of the chariot.

9. Mahiṣamardinī (8 cm): Ten-armed, three-eyed and standing in the conventional *āliḍha* posture with the left foot on the severed torso of the buffalo and the right foot on the back of the stylized lion of typically late medieval vintage, the Devī is flanked by a four armed Gaṇeśa on Muṣika on her right and a mono-cephallic two armed Kārtikeya on peacock on her left. The *āyudhas* on the Devī's hand are from lower right hand upwards—*triśūla, śakti, bāṇa, cakra* and *khaḍga*; and on her left hand in similar order—lock of the demon's hair, *paraśu* (?), *aṅkuśa* (?), *dhanu* and *kheṭaka.* On her head, which is adorned with a late-period *makuṭa* instead of a *jaṭā,* is the crescent moon. The rim of the *prabhāvalī* which is partly broken, is adorned with spiral motifs. The tiara-ed demon stands with his legs flexed and the right knee on the ground, holding a *khaḍga* in his two hands, and with the lion biting his right elbow. The hooded serpent of the Devī coils round the Asura's neck with its hood reared in front of his face.

10. Mahiṣamardinī (5 cm): Ten-armed and three-eyed, this image is stylistically similar to the one mentioned above, except that here Gaṇeśa. Kārtikeya and the aureole behind the Devī is absent and the demon does not sport a tiara. The *āyudhas* are, clock wise, from the lower right hand onwards—*triśūla, śakti (?), bāṇa (?), cakra, khaḍga kheṭaka, dhanu,* and indistinct object, and finally the tuft of the demon's hair.

Stylistically, it is coeval with the other Mahisamardinī image mentioned above.

11. Viṣṇu (9 cm): Standing in *samapāda* on a therio-morphic Garuḍa bird in *añjalī* pose, and flanked by Lakṣmi and Sarasvatī stand in *samapāda* on *padma* on either side, and holding respectively a *camera* and a *vīnā,* Viṣṇu here represents his *Trivikrama* aspect holding, from the upper right hand onwards (clock wise) *gāda, cakra śānka and padma.* All the images are bejewelled. Of the three garlands of Viṣṇu, the two lower ends of the *vyjayantīmālā* end up in curls. All the three images wear similar sharply denticled tiara with a central flower-bud- like projection. The eyes are wide open and slightly bulging.

The perforated *prabhāvalī* is pointed with a blooming flower topping a serpent-like decoration at the pointed end.

12. Viṣṇu (6 m): Four-armed and standing in *samapāda*, the image is similar in style and execution to the other Viṣṇu image mentioned above, the only notable difference being that while the aureole of this image is rectangular, with chamferred corners and a *kalasa* finial instead of a flower finial, and the open works limited to two oblong and paralleled slits. Secondly, while the face of the early one is roundish, that of the latter is longish. And thirdly, the latter one stands on a *padma,* and not on Garuḍa, the Garuḍa being depicted, interestingly, facing the deity in *añjalī* pose with its back to the viewer. Like the former one, this image also represents Viṣṇu in his *Trivikrama* aspect and belongs to the same period.

13. Gaṇeśa (4 cm): Four-armed and seated in *rājalīlāsana*, with the right foot resting on his *Muṣika Vāhana,* the god holds in his hands, from upper right hand onwards (clock wise),- nīlotpala, paraśu, *varadā-mudrā* and *varadā mudrā* with citrus in his palm and the proboscis resting on it. The temples of his head are abnormally bulging, over which, in the center is depicted a crescent with a star or point. His body is coiled around by a serpent, its hood raised in front of his left shoulder.

14. Gaṇeśa (3.5 cm): Seated in *rājalīlāsana* with his right foot resting on his *Muṣika*, this four-armed image has its upper right hand broken at the elbow. The other three hands hold, from the upper left hand onwards (clock wise), *aṅkuśa*, *paraśu* and citrus. Like that of the previous one, the proboscis of this image is also turned to his right and rests on the palm of the lower right hand. The image has a denticled tiara without the *jaṭā*, the latter element being depicted in the previous Gaṇeśa. The image is ill-shaped, uncouth and much inferior to the previous one in style and execution.

15. Bird (3.5 cm): The bird is a peacock standing solitary on a pedestal, with a garland- like decoration around the throat, and the feathers and the fins depicted by means of incision. Its beak is curved, the eyes somewhat bulging, and the crest fully depicted. The bird might have been a part of a Kārtikeya image. But there are no signs to confirm this, as no evidence of its being a part of a larger complex exists. It seems to be a free-standing example.

These two groups are distinguished from each other by (a) the mode of holding the *āyudhas*. While in the early group the images hold their *āyudhas* in *khatakāmukha mudrā*, in the latter group the *āyudhas* are simply held in grip, as witnessed in the sculptures of the Āhom Age; (b) the treatment of the tiara differs in both the groups. In the early group, the *mukuṭa* is a short square affair with short denticles, while that of the latter group is decorated with long denticles with a rather tall central projection; (c) the modelling or the body differs. In the early group the physique is slim and graceful, that of the latter is somewhat angular and rigid; (d) no *'bhaṅgas'* or flexions of the body is to be noticed in the late group, which is a marked feature in the early group; (e) lastly, the eyes of the image of the late group are wide open and slightly bulging, which is not the case with those of the early group.

20

Icons from Bijulībārī

Few icons were discovered in Bijulībārī near Siphjhār in the Darrang district of Assam and they were collected by the Assam State Museum authority some years back. On receipt of an information from Mr. Prem Saran, (I.A.S.), the then Deputy Commissioner of Darrang district, regarding the discovery of these objects, I paid a joint visit to the place along with Mr. Saran. Earlier about these discovery I was told by Prof. Nagen Sarma, Mangaldai, also.

The discovered objects include two stone icons, two metal icons and a few broken pots and potsherds. All these objects were kept in an open shed of the residence of Mr. Arun Chandra Das of Bijulībārī village. Mr. Das found them while digging for a tank for making fishery in a plot of land just near the National High Way. A few stone blocks are also noticed in the site *i.e.*, in the tank which was not completely dug. It appears that there must have been some small construction in the past. Some systematic excavation in the site may throw some light on the potentiality of the site.

Looking at the objects I told Mr. Saran that they should be removed to the Assam State Museum for better preservation. Subsequently, all the sculptures were removed to the Assam State Museum in a ceremony.

The first object of the group is a icon of Viṣṇu. It measures 60 cms x 33 cms. The weight of the object is 32 kg and 300 grams. The deity is made to stand in *sampādasthānaka* attitude. The four armed deity is made to hold the usual *āyudhas* (clockwise from upper left hand) *cakra, śaṅkha, padma,* and *godā*. The head of the deity is crowned with *kīriṭī mukuṭa*. The *vanamāla* and *ūpavita* and *kaṭimekhalā* worn by the deity is clearly shown. The god is flanked by his consorts. However, Sarasvatī and Lakṣmī, his consorts, are not shown as holding the usual *āyudhas*. The *śilāpaṭṭa* of the sculpture is decorated with the figure of Vidyādhāra and a *Kirtimukha* at the top. The *śilapaṭṭa* is pointed. Below the *pīṭha padamakoshas* are clearly noticed, Stylistically, this piece of sculpture belongs to 10th-11th century.[1]

The second object of our discussion is also an icon of Viṣṇu. It is a bronze sculpture measuring 12.4 cms x 6.6 cms and weighing 205 grams. Like the first image of the deity, here also the deity is shown in the usual posture *i.e.*, *sampādaṣthānaka* attitude holding the usual *āyudhas* (clock-wise) *i.e. godā, cakra, śaṅkha and padma*. The *kīriṭamukuṭa*, the *kaṭivastra* and the *vanamāla* worn by the deity are clearly seen. The god is seen flanked by his consorts. Here also the miniature figure of the goddess Sarasvatī and Lakṣmī are not shown as holding the usual *āyudhas*. If Lakṣmī's *āyudha* in her right hand can be identified as a *chowri* at all, at least Sarasvatī is not shown with usual *vīnā*. The *adhāra* is shown decorated with flame like objects behind the deity. It is pointed.

As in the first case, in the case of the second icon also the *Garuḍa*, the *vāhana* of Viṣṇu, is not shown. Both the icons are sculptured with common features and on stylistic consideration they can be dated in 11th/ 12th century.[2]

The third icon represents some female *śākta* deity. It is a stone sculpture measuring 13.7 cms x 6.7 cms and weighing 350 grams. The deity is shown as standing almost in *ālidha* attitude on a prostrate human figure. In her four hands the goddess hold clockwise: unidentified object *Kapāla, kartari and khaḍga*. The hair tuft of the goddess seems to be rising like the hood of a serpant. The *muṇḍamālā* worn by the goddess is clearly seen. The deity is pot-bellied. Below. the prostrate human figure the donor is shown. Above the head of the deity on either side of the ṭappering *śilāpaṭṭa* trace of the figure of Vidyādhāra is noticed.

From the style of standing of the deity and wearing the *muṇḍmālā*, it may be taken as an image of *śākta* deity. The details of the face of the deity is lost. Though the material used is black stone, yet it is not very hard, as it appears. The preset icon has some similarity with the Buddhist images of Māirchi from Ujani and Panditsar and images of Parnasavarī rom Naynanda and Vajrayoginī, Bangladesh illustrated by Bhattasali.[3] But the other details of our image do not tally with those images. The *āyudhas* held by these Buddhist images are quite different. Unlike our image, they do not stand on prostrate human figure. Neither Rao[4] nor Banerjea[5] has illustrated such an icon. Even Bhattacharya[6] has not illustrated an image exactly similar to our image. Gupte[7] has not noticed an icon of this type and so also Tewari.[8] The local people called it the image of Kālī. The worship of goddess Kālī is very popular in Assam amongst the *Śāktas*. Kālī is commonly worshipped in Bengal also.

But it is a matter of great surprise that not a single photograph of the Goddess Kālī has been illustrated by all these authorities. Neither they have given the detail description of an image Kālī based on texts, illustrated by all these authorities. Nor they have given the detail description of an image Kālī based on iconographic text. The reason is that it is very rare. We have not seen such image of Kālī belonging to early or medieval period. The icon of four armed Kālī with terrible look with a protruding tongue wearing a *muṇḍamālā* and keeping one leg on the chest of Śiva who lies prostrate is worshipped very commonly in eastern India to-day. The goddess is also popularly known as Shyāmā. The image of the deity is made commonly of clay.

But the image of the deity in question unlike the icon of Kālī stand on the prostrate human figure keeping her legs apart. Secondly, the present figure of the deity is pot-bellied, while the figure of Kālī is represented as slim. Unlike the commonly worshipped image of Kālī, the present deity does not have a protruding tongue.

On the other hand, the image of Māirchi, a Buddhist goddess is four faced. The figure of the deity in question is single faced. The *āyudhas* held by our image are different from that of Māirchi, illustrated by the scholars referred to above. The figures of Parṇaśavarī, illustrated by the same authorities, although pot-bellied, is four faced.

From the above discussion, it appears that the present icon cannot be identified with Buddhist deity, Māirchi or Parṇaśavarī. It is also not very similar with the image of Kālī commonly worshiped to-day. Further examination, therefore, will be necessary to arrive at conclusion with regard to the identity of this deity. During his visit to the Assam State Museum B.N. Mukherji, however, told me that the icon represented. Kāli.

The last icon is a miniature two armed female deity (7 cms x 3.4 cms, weighing 30 grams) seated cross-legged holding something with both the hands on the lap. It is a bronze sculpture. The deity is sitting on a *padmasana* in *dvibhaṅga* attitude. The identification of this figure has become difficult. The face of the deity is badly weathered. The only *āyudha* by both the hands of the deity is not clear, The *karaṇḍa-mukuṭa* worn by the deity is to some extent clear. To the left of the deity below a miniature figure, possibly representing the donor can be faced somehow. Stylistically, this piece of bronze art belong to the same period *i.e.*, 10th-11th century.

The discovery of these sculptures shows that the site belongs to the pre-Āhom or pre-Koch period. It is reported that a Viṣṇu image (stone) of about the equal size of the first image of our discussion is being worshipped near this site, which is closer to Siphjhār. There are many archaeological sites in the Darrang district which belong to the pre-Koch period. Near the site there is another site of a ruined temple on the side of the National High Way belonging to the pre-Koch period. This shows the pre-Koch Hindu culture around 10th century flourished in this part of Assam as in other parts of the Brahmaputra valley.

There were some doubts in the mind of the public of the Siphjhār region with regard to the metal of the small images discovered at the site. Some people tried to mislead the public by saying that all the images were made of gold. But the controversy was set at rest after the publication of a letter by Śrī M.C. Das, Reld. Director of Archaeology and Museum, Assam.[9]

Notes and Refrences

1. According to the *Padma-Purāṇa, Rūpamaṇḍana, Agnī-Purāṇa, Dharma-Sindhu, Vriddharahita Smṛti* and *Abhilashitartha Cintamani, it is the icon* of Trivikrama, a form of the twenty-four forms of Viṣṇu, See, T.A.G. Rao, *Elements of Hindu Iconography,* 1971, Vol. I, pt. I, pp. 220-32 and R.S. Gupte, *Iconography of Hindus, Buddhist and Jainas,* 1971, p. 95. The *Chaturvarga Chintamani,* however, calls it Adhokshaja, see, Gupta *op.cit.* p. 95.
2. According to the *Rūpamaṇḍana, Padmapurāṇa, Agniputrana, Dharma-Sindhu, Vriddharahita Smṛti* and *Abhilashitartha Cintamani* it is the icon of *Nārāyaṇa,* a form of Viṣṇu, also see, Rao *op.cit.*, pp. 229-32 and Gupta, *op.cit.,* p. 95. The *Chaturvarge Chintamani* however, calls it Hari, see Gupta, *op.cit.,* p. 95.
3. N.K. Bhattasali, *Iconography of Buddhist and Brahmanical sculptures in Decca Museum.* 1972, Pl. XIII Fig. (b) and Pl. XXIII Fig. (b).
4. Rao, *op.cit.,* see pp. 327-400 and also the plates depiction the icons of Devi.
5. J.N. Banerjea, *Development of Hindu Iconography,* 1974, see all the plates.
6. B. Bhattacharya, *The Indian Buddhist Iconography,* 1968, see all the plates.
7. Gupta, *op.cit.* see all the plates.
8. S.P. Tewari, *Hindu Iconography,* 1979, see all the plates.
9. See *Dainik Asom* (An Assamese daily published from Guwahati), 15th June, 1984, p. 2.

21

Dating of Two Images

The Assam State Museum, Guwahati, houses two important metallic images. The first is an image of Viṣṇu (?) and the other that of Mahiṣamardinī.

The standing image of Viṣṇu is made of bronze. It was discovered, according to K.N. Dikshit[1], in the ruins of an ancient temple near Dibrugarh. The image of the god is peculiar. It is shown without holding the *āyudhas* in his four hands. All the hands are shown with *tribhaṅgas* bent at the elbow and wrist joints and in *kartari-mudrā* (the attitude in which the index and little fingers point outwards and the middle and ring fingers are tucked in).[2] The god in *samapāda-sthānaka* attitude is well decked. He is crowned with a *kirīta-mukuṭa* which is less conical and it has longer outer cone. He is bejewelled with *makara kuṇḍalas* and a *hāra* with a pendant, *vāhu-kirīṭi* and *valayas*. Around the waist of the god covering the hips on the back and upper portion of the thighs a short *paridhāna* is shown as his lower drapery. His legs are shown putting on a pair of *pāduka* (sandal of wood). The figure of the divinity is cylindrical and round body-shaped, but not of a high order. The chest is little raised or projected, the belly and the waist are disproportionately small. Again, just below the waist, the hip portion is bigger in size. The *piṭha* (pedestal) upon which the god stands is of uncommon in nature. It looks like a *guru-āsana* commonly used in the *satras,* vaiṣṇava monastery of Assam. There are five steps in it; on the upper most one on which the god stands, it has four parrots in the four corners.

On either side of Viṣṇu two miniature female figures are seen in *sthānaka* attitude at lower level. The figure to the left seems to be in a dancing pose and holding a *vīnā*, the musical instrument of Sarasvatī, but the *vīnā* is not shown. The figure to the right stands erect holding a lotus bud and a *chowrie* (?). Therefore, these two figures may be taken as Lakṣmī and Sarasvatī, the consorts of the god. In the absence of any *āyudha* in the four hands of the god and the *vāhana*, it is a little difficult to identify the image with Viṣṇu. Dikshit remarks that the image, it seems likely, dates from the late-pre-Āhom period, or about the 11-12th century.[3] But on stylistic consideration, we would like to place it around 16th century and cannot support Dikshit.

The second image viz, the image of Mahiṣamardinī measures, 39 cms x 30 cms. It is made of brass. This image was discovered at Tinsukia during clearance of an old well.[3] Here the goddess is depicted with three eyes (?) ten hands without holding anything (any *āyudha*). She stands in *tribhaṅga* posture on the lion, the *vāhana*, and the *asura*, the demon with whom she fights. But here the fighting scene is not so terrific as the deity does not hold any *āyudha*, specially, the *triśūla*, which commonly she pierces through the chest of the demon. The decapitated buffalo head of the demon is lying on the ground. The head of the deity is decked with a short *mukuṭa*. Other ornaments that deck the body of a female figure are absent. The long *kaṭimekhalā* which covers her lower part bears some decorative designs. The cap worn by the demon on his head is of Moghul style, so also are the shoes worn by him and the lower garment. The lion which is attacking the demon jumping over him with the front legs is of typical late Āhom style. The museum has collected a brass sculpture of *gaja-vyāla* motif about a century old from Barpeta, of which the lion is quite comparable with the present one. The face of the goddess seems to have Mongolian feature, but her eyes are big and eye brows are prominent. Some scholars[4] have placed the image during the 12th-13th century A.D. But this date, from stylistic point of view, seems to be too early. The image in question does not bear any characteristic feature of such an early period. It bears the characteristic style of the Āhom sculpture with Moghul influence. Therefore, it belongs to the late Āhom period. We have also evidence to show that during the regime of king Rudra Siṁha, Muslim artists from Bengal were invited to Assam.[5] Therefore, we may be right in placing the image the 18th century.[6] However, both the images are important, though not from their artistic excellence, but from assimilation of different art styles. Both the images were probably installed as the main temple deities in separate temples.[7]

Notes and References

1. *Annual Report of Archaeological survey of India,* 1923-24, p. 80
2. *Ibid.*
3. *Ibid.*, p. 118.
4. B.K. Baroa, *A cultural History of Assam,* Vol. I, Guwahati 1969 p. 2111, Pl. IV, Fig. 60; P.C. Choudhuary, *A History of the Civilization of the People of Assam,* Guwahati, 1959, p. 486, P.D. Choudhuary & M.C. Das, *Ancient Treasures of Assam,* 1959, p. 34.
5. L. Gogoi, *Āhom jati, Aru Asamiya Samskriti,* Sibsagar, 1961, p. 13
6. A Mukherji, *Ciri Perdeu casting in India,* New Delhi, p. 74.
7. I am very much grateful to Dr. P.C. Choudhury for his valuable suggestions in writing this note.

22

A Newly Discovered Image of Sūrya from Bilāsīpārā

About two years or so back an image of Sūrya was discovered under the earth in a paddy field (?) in the Bilāsīpārā sub-division of Dhubri district. The image was collected by Dr. Manoranjana Datta, then E.A.C. Dhubri, and handed over to the Assam State Museum authorities for better preservation.

This stone image has been affected due to salt action. Much of the details of the sculpture has been lost. Here the deity is shown in the usual *sthānāka* attitude. He holds two lotus with his hands in the usual way. Just in front of the deity is seen the figure is Aruna, his legs hidden. The deity is flanked by two other figures. As the details of the figures have not been preserved, it has become a problem to identity these miniature figures. Since there is no trace of raised blossom in both the cases, it may not be wrong to identity them with Daṇḍa and Piṅgala. The two female miniature figure in *ālīdha* and *pratyālidha āsana* holding arrow and bow certainly can be identified with Uṣā and Pratyuṣā. The figures of Chāyā and Rañjī, the consorts of Sūrya are, however, absent in the scene. Below the figure of Aruṇa, the chariot-driver, there is depicted something the details of which have gone. Possibly one horse was depicted. On either side of this object three horses are depicted. These figures are also sadly affected. If the central indistinct figure inside the symbolic wheel of the chariot is that of a horse, it is not clear. But we can safely assume that the horse No. 7 must have been depicted here. On either side three horses are shown.

Iranian influence, which can be noticed in the style of the dress worn and boots on the feet, can be partially seen. Though the boots are not visible due to the presence of the seated figure of Aruṇa in front of the legs of the deity, yet lower garment certainly does not bear the Indian style, but rather marks of the Iranian style.

The style of the *kirīta-mukuṭa* appears to be of Gupta origin. There is a trace of the beautiful design on the upper portion (its right side) of the *mukuṭa*. But ninety per cent of the *mukuṭa* has been affected due to salt action. The *śilāpaṭṭa* of the sculpture is tapering. It is not at all pointed. Nor it has the figure of the *Kīrtimukha* at the top flanked by two *vidyādharas*. The place of the *vidyādhara* on either side of the head of the god is occupied by a flower motif. The top of the left side of the *śilapaṭṭa* has not experienced salt affect. Possibly, salt action could not attack this little portion of the sculpture due to the presence of some substance which covered this particular portion of the sculpture.[1] The flower motif to the left side of the head of the deity is not clear. But there is a trace of the motif.

Considering the style the *mukuṭa*, the presence of flower motif in place of *vidhyādhara*, the absence of the motif of *kīrtimukha* or the top of the tapering *śilāpaṭṭa,* the lower garment of the deity having Iranian influence, it can be assumed that this piece of work of art bears pre-Pālā style, which derived from the Gupta style. Hence, it can be placed safely in the 7th or 6th century A.D.

The discovery of this antiquity at Bilāsīpārā, in Dhubri district, is important. It is a stray find discovered in a paddy field (?). The find is important because of the fact in the north of the Brahmaputra in Dhubri district not a single antiquity belonging to the pre-Koch period had come to our notice prior to the discovery of this valuable sculpture under discussion. At Abhayapuri, a ruined temple belonging to the 10th-12th century was discovered, which is being preserved by the State Archaeology Department. Abayapuri is a sub-divisional headquarter in Bangaigaon district to the east of Dhubri district. The Dudhnāth temple just on the north bank of the Brahmaputra near Chāpar, in Dhubri district, has an old tradition. But the old temple does not exist now, nor could the remains of the temple be found. In the modern temple at the place a *Śiva liṅga* has been installed. This *Śiva liṅga* is said to belong to the original temple. Dudhnāth is east of Bilāsīpārā. The Mahāmāyā temple at Bagrībāri to the east of Gaurīpur, like Dudhnāth, has also an old tradition and the local Hindu population hold it in high respect.

On the south bank of the Brahmaputra, at Bhaitabarı, near Phulbārī and also at Phulbārī, opposite to Dhubri, an extensive archaeological site has been discovered. But the ruins belong to 10th-12th century A.D.[2] At Pāglātek, just on the southern bank of the Brahmaputra a temple is seen. Here a few architectural pieces are noticed. These pieces stylistically belong to c.6th century A.D., if not earlier. *Candraśālā* motifs were also noticed in the ruined temple site to the west of Pañcharatna ghāt. This type of *candraśālā* showing false *chāitya* window, can be dated in 5th-6th century A.D. Both Pāglātek and Pañcharatna ghāt are situated closely, and are just opposite to the Dudhnath temple of the northern bank of the Brahmaputra.

Considering all the factors, it is quite clear that the southern bank of the Brahmaputra of the present districts of Dhubri and Goalpara is archaeologically very potential. From this point of view, the newly discovered sculpture from Bilāsīpārā, datable to the 6th-7th century, is very important because of the fact that for the first time we have come across such an early sculpture or antiquity in the north bank of the Dhubri district. Though we have reports that there are a good number of stone sculptures on the top of the hill named Bhairab Cuḍā, no archaeologist has been able to climb up to examine them and to throw light no their age.[3] The newly discovered metallic image of Kāliyamardana, discovered in the campus of Ratnapith College near Chapar, may be dated in c 10th century.[4] Hence, we may conclude that the Sūrya image in question discovered in Dhubri district is an important find.

Notes and References

1. For the presence of the substance salt could not penetrate in this part. The nature of the substance is yet to be ascertained.
2. Archaeological Survey of India has recently discovered a number of icons of Hindu divinities belonging to the 10th/11th century at Bhāitabārī and brick structures and terracotta sculptures possibly of Buddhist deities at Śrī Sūrya Pāhār detailed to 8th 9th century.
3. This information is given by Sri Yamini Barman, Parag Das Road, Anandanagar Guwahati - 21.
4. I personally exemined the image few years back.

23

The Newly Discovered Image of Ṛiṣabhanātha at Śrī Śūrya Pāhār

It is not necessary to re-tell the scholar sand archaeologists about the importance of Śri Sūrya Pāhār and Marnoi of the Goalpara district of Assam. Scholars have published papers fand articles on the significance of the archaeological wealth of Sūrya Pāhār and neighbouring region of Mornoi. I also published some articles. In those papers and articles the existence of rock-cut icons belonging to deities of Hindu and Jaina religion and the rock-cut Buddhist votive *stūpas* were discussed.[1] It is also stated that this was the only place in Assam, where three religions met together in the past. Further, it was opined that the Buddhist votive *stūpas* could be dated in 100 A.D. or 100 B.C. The presence of these archaeological evidence already proved the importance of the site beyond doubt.

It has already been described in the published papers etc. about the natural cave caused by three huge boulders, where in two icons of Ṛiṣabanātha or Adinatha are found sculptured along with an image of Gaṇeśh. Both the figures of Adinatha or Ṛiṣabhanātha are shown in Kayotsarga posture, standing erect without wearing any cloth or body. The bigger image shows a shows a *dharma-cakdra* at the bottom, while the smaller one depicts the figure of Nandī, below the pīṭha. On stylistic consideration, these sculptures can be assigned to *c.* 8th century A.D. In this cave itself on the eastern wall (huge rock) one line of letter in Brahmi are incised. These letters bearing 8th/9th century character of Brahmi records only some names of devotees and nothing else.

Above this natural cave at a certain height on the slope of the hill there exist a small natural cave facing east caused by huge boulders. In this cave a rock-cut image of Ṛiṣabhanātha has been recently discovered. Some months back, in the last winter season, some local village noticed this sculpture while cutting jungles for fuel. Later the villagers and some members of the local Sūrya Pāhār Than Committee visited the site of the discovery of the image and by clearing the jungles an easy way was made to the site. Publicity in the local news paper was also given. Local people first taught that it was an image of Buddha. Some people however, took it to be a Jaina image. Therefore, to arrive at a conclusion, I was invited for its identification.

I paid a visit to the place on 28.2.93. and inspected the image in the company of Mr. Khanin Das, Secretary, Śrī Sūrya Pāhār Than Committee and Mr. Roy, Addl. Deputy commissioner, Goalpara by climbing the hill. This sculpture is cut on a rock in a small cave caused by huge boulders as stated above. It is facing to the east. The sculpture measures approximately 2½′ x 2½′.

The sculpture portrays a male figure seated in *dhyana sana* (cross-legged keeping the palms one over the other on the lap). The *adhāra* (frame) behind the figure is quite visible. Below the *āsana* of the deity in the centre a *Cakra* flanked by two bulls are seen clearly. To the extreme ends of the āsana two miniature figures of lion are visible. But these figures are not very clear. This portion of the image was under a thin layer of earth. After the clearance of earth and rotten tree leaves the trace of the figures of the line could be seen. Considering the presence of the bull and the Cakra, the images may be identified as Ṛiṣabhanātha or *Adinatha,* the first Jaina Tirthankara. To the right Ṛiṣabhanātha is noticed a standing male figure, which may be identified as Gomukha Yaksha. In the same way to the left of the figure of Ṛiṣabhanātha, a female figure is seen, which may be identified with Cakresvari Yakshini. The vehicle of Gomukha Yaksha, an elephant and the vehicle of Cak-resvari Yakshini, an eagle, however, could not be traced.

The quality of the rock is so bad that due to weathering effect details of the image are gone. The face of Ṛiṣabhanātha is badly affected. The figure of the Cakresvari Yakshini has also suffered a lot. The face of the Gomukha Yaksh should have the face of cow or bull. But figns of such face cannot be traced. This human face with mated hair can however, be seen. Both these attending miniature figures are in *sthānāka* attitude.

Looking at the *adhāra* and the prabhavali resembling symbolic *garbhagriha* of a temple, this rock-cut work can be assigned to *c.* 10th century. Earlier we commented that it might be dated in *c.* 8th century.[2] But our opinion has to be revised because, the development of *adhāra* is a later phenomenon, which we get in the sculpture of the Pālā period in eastern India.

The *vastra* and *alankara* worn by the figures cannot be traced at all. The chest of Ṛiṣabhanātha is wide, while waist is shown small, which is the symptom of *mahapurusa*. The adhāra style or the style of a *sikhara* in sculptures became very popular in the Pālā period in Bihar and Bengal. It also reached Assam about the same time. This design is meant to show as if the deity is installed in side a temple.

In case of other two images of Adinatha or Rishbhanatha noticed earlier, trace of *adhāra* behind the figures cannot be seen. In these cases no attending figures are noticed. The *Sthānāka* figures of the Tirthankara are seen simply standing and below the *pithas* a figure of Ṛiṣabhanātha in one case and in the other case *dharmacakra* are seen. The depiction or *dharmacakra* flanked by two bulls below the āsana are not commonly met with as the symbol of image of Ṛiṣabhanātha. Depiction of two lions at the extreme ends of the *pīṭha* is also an uncommon phenomenon. R.S. Gupta[3] has not been able to reproduce such an image of Ṛiṣabhanātha. The chart prepared by him on the basis of descriptions found in different texts also does not mention about the presence of a *dharmacakra* flanked by two bulls which are again flanked by two lion from the corners of the pithas. The figures of Adinatha or Ṛiṣabhanātha drawn by the author as per the description of the text also does not portry these symbols in one image together.[4] Though bulls, *dharmacakra* and lion as the symbol of Ṛiṣabhanātha or Adinatha, are found in an image of Adinatha or Ṛiṣabhanātha, yet the depiction of two lions, two bulls and on *dharmacakra* at a time together are rarely found. The illustrations made by R.P. Mahapatra[5] are not very clear. A close watch also did not reveal the depiction of the symbols at a time in the image of Ṛiṣabhanātha or Adinatha. From this point our recently discovered image of Ṛiṣabhanātha bears significance.

Near the archaeological site at Śrī Sūrya Pāhār towards a little east towards north-east direction, the Guwahati circle of the Archaeological Survey of India under the supervision of Mr. T. Vaidya, Deputy Superintending Archaeologist, conducted an archaeological excavation about two months ago. It has revealed a ruined brick temple. As many as eight trenches were taken by the excavator. One can very well see the portions of the burried walls or the alignment of the plinth. Some broken terracotta figures were also unearthed. The style of bricks and the terracotta sculptures lead us to assign the temple in the pre-Āhom period or in a period not later than 9th-10th century. It may also go up. Since due to rain the excavation could not be completed, in the next season, after completion of the excavation, we will be able to arrive at a conclusion in so far as the periodicity of the site of the excavation, is concerned, I paid two visits to the site of excavation.

Two years back Mr. Sarma of Archaeological Survey of India did some excavation at Bhāitbārī in the south bank of the Brahmaputra boardening Meghalaya and Assam near Indo-Bangladesh border. It is a historical site. A small archaeological mound at Budhabudhi (Medartari) just on the southern bank of the Brahmaputra is also noticed undisturbed. This should also be excavated. It is not necessary to repeat the importance of Śrī Sūrya Pāhār or Mornoi here. But it is certain that the newly discovered image of Ṛiṣabhanātha and trace of a temple have enhanced the importance of the site.

Notes and Refrences

1. R.D. Choudhury, Antiquities of Śrī Sūrya Pāhār: A source of early *History of Kāmarūpa, Sources of the History of India* Vol.II, Institute of Historical Studies, Calcutta, 1980, pp. 32-40, *Archaeology of the Brahmaputra Valley of Assam*, New Delhi, 1985, pp. 109-114., *"Assam's Earliest Archaeological Evidence at Śrī Sūrya Pāhār"*. *Facts of Indian History Culture and Archaeology*, Ed. S.P. Gupta and K.S. Ramachcndran, New Delhi, 1991, pp. 62-64. also The Assam Tribune, a Daily, Guwahati.
2. "R.D. Choudhury "Śrī Sūrya Paharat Nava Abiskrita Ṛiṣabhanāthar Murtito", *Asambani*, an Assamese weekly, Guwahati, 7th May 1993. p. 19.
3. *Iconography of the Hindus, Buddhist and Jainas*, Bombay, 1972, Pls. XXXV-XXXVI.
4. *Ibid*, pp. 163-73.
5. *Jaina Moments of Orissa*, Delhi, 1984, Fig. 8-137.

24

A Note on a Few Objects from Assam in British Museum

A few years back, Mr. W. Zwalf, Assistant Keeper, British Museum, London sent me photographs of three metal objects for identification. All these objects were collected by the British Museum authorities long back and they are being preserved there.

The first two objects are quite same and must be a pair. Both the objects are cruciform, looking like a four petalled flower. Both the objects are decorated on their obverses. The back of both the objects *i.e.*, the reverses are blank...and no sign of any decoration is noticed. In the centre of both the objects on the reverses, there is a hook in the centre. The utility of the hook is obviously to wear them by putting small loop or thread. Exactly similar objects are reported from the Central Museum of Arunachal Pradesh, Shillong.[1] These objects are identified as *Emule,* a local name given by the Ādi, a tribe of Siang District of Arunachal Pradesh, bordering Assam. These objects are worn by the Ādi tribe to cure illness. *Emule* is known as 'amulet'in English. The *Emules* from the British Museum has, thus, no relation with the cross symbol of Christianity. It is a tribal traditional object.

The second object is a bangle or bracelet. This is known as *Gām Khāru,* a prestigious ornament worn by the traditional Assamese women. Mr. Zwalf has not mentioned about the real identity of the metal. Possibly, it is made of gold or at least goldplated. There are a good number of gems fitted on the body of the object. There is an open mouth of it through which the wrist is inserted and then the mouth is closed. But the portion functions like a door is missing. An object of same type (but not like the thin and wide body of the *Gam-Khāru i.e., golā-khāru* is preserved in the Assam State Museum). It is sure that this object was also used as bangle. The ornament is studded with jems. The State Museum is also in possession of a broken object of which the central portion is like an oval shaped plate on the periphery of which four petal like object are fixed in equal distance. The petals are more or less in cruciform shape. Possibly, this piece of metal object was used for the same purpose. So, it may not be possibly wrong to identify it as a form of *Emule*.

The British Museum is in possession of a few more art objects collected from Assam in the past. Nine terracotta sculptures from Tezpur are being preserved in the Reserve Collection of the British Museum. These objects were shown to Mr. S. Gorakshakar, the then Director of Prince of Walse Museum, Bombay and me at our request. All these terracotta sculptures on stylistic consideration may be placed in the Āhom age. But their detailed study and publication are necessary.

In addition to these sculptures there are three illustrated manuscript paintings from Assam in this museum. These are—*Dharma-Purāṇa*, *Kirtan Ghośā*[2] and *Brahmavaivarta Purāṇa*. All of them are very good examples of Assamese illustrated Manuscript painting. Specially the painting of the *Brahmavaivarta Purāṇa* occupies a very high place. J.P. Lostly has rightly published, considering the merit, a coloured photograph of this manuscript on the cover of her book 'Krishṇa'[3] and again she has very rightly published an enlarged copy of the same photograph in her article in 'Mārg'.[4] This shows how the illustrated Manuscript painting of Assam has been able to attract the attention of the art historians. There may be many more objects of antiquarian value from Assam in the British Museum. There must be a good number of coins of the Āhom and Koch coins. J.P. Singh has published the photograph of a coin from the collection of this Museum.[5] He has tried to identify it as the coin of Harṣapāla. There must also be a good number of ethnographical objects from Assam. In fact, a detailed study and publication of such objects will help the scholars to a great extent.[6]

Notes and References

1. This information was supplied by Mr. Samiran Barua, Directorate of Museums, Assam, Guwahati. I am very much grateful to him.
2. "The art of the Book in India" Mārg Vol. XXXVI, No. I, pp. 18-29
3. 'Krishna' a Hindu Vision of God, London, The British Library, 1980.

4. R.D. Choudhury, *Archaeology of the Brahmaputra Valley of Assam*, Delhi, 1985, p. 203.
5. R.D. Choudhury, *op.cit.*, Fig. 45.
6. I am very much grateful to Mr. W. Zwalf, British Museum, for sending the photographs.

25

The Antiquity of the Ruined Temple at Daparvatiā

Daparvatiā, a village near Tezpur town in Assam State has already become known to the scholars, particularly to the archaeologists all over India for the beautiful carved *dvāra* of a ruined temple of the Gupta period. First, the ruin was discovered by K.N. Dikshit[1] and later R.D. Banerji[2] published a detailed account of the *dvāra*. He also noticed some terracotta sculpture while clearing the jungle at the site, datable to 6th century A.D.

The *dvāra* adorned with the elegantly standing figures of Gaṅgā and Yamunā and other decorative figure and design has been placed by Banerji in 5th/6th Century.[3]

Looking at the ruins, Banerji[4] has commented that there was a Gupta temple over which subsequently a brick temple was constructed in the Āhom period, which has been crumbled down due, probably, to the effect of earthquake. But he did not try to find out the exact plan of the temple. The present author also visited the site, but it was not possible to make out the ground plan correctly. It is for the first time, that Shri P. Sharma has made a study of the plan of the ruined temple and recently contributed a paper.[5] He said that the present ruins of the temple belonged to the one and the same temple which may be dated in 5th century A.D. in the Gupta period. He has rightly asserted that the bricks scattered about the site belonged to the Gupta period and that the stone pillears, *dvāra-śakhās, dvāraśirapaṭṭi,* the *dvāra-śilālī* and chiselled blocks of stone and the fallen bricks and the bricks of the *adhiṣtthāna* are the parts of the ruined temple. The size of the rocks as Sarma measured is 38 cm x 29 cm which is equivalent to 15" x 11½" x 2 1/4". The brick of the Āhom period is lighter, smaller and thinner than the brick of the pre-Āhom period. It may also happen that, while making such a comment Banerji took into consideration of the building or structure of the Āhom temples over the stone plinth of the pre-Āhom temples, as is evident from some other temple sites in Assam. But such a conclusion is not applicable in case of the ruined temple of Daparvatīā.

The present *dvāra* of the temple is somewhat unusually standing. In front of this *dvāra* a *Śiva liṅga* (?) is placed putting half of it into a hole that exists on a block of stone placed in the middle. The local people now worship this *Śiva liṅga* and believe that it is the original *Śiva liṅga*. But this is wrong. For, the present *liṅga* is made from a broken pillar and the size of this *liṅga* and that of the hole do not agree with each other. Had it been the original *Śiva liṅga* there must have existed a *yonī-pīṭha* too. It is highly possible that in this hole the original image of the deity of the temple was placed and that the hole was in the middle of the *garbhagṛha*. In that case, the present standing *dvāra* must have been the *dvāra* of he *garbhagṛha* facing east. Immediately west of the supposed *garbhagṛha* we do not see any trace of *sopāna*, and this leads us to take it as the *garbhagṛha* and not *mukhamaṇḍapa*. Generally, looking at the standing temple *dvāra* one likes to comment that the temple was facing west. But a close observation reveals that actually, it faces the East. In all probability, the entire temple including the *dvāra* was crumbled down in earthquake and subsequently, when the convention of constructing a Hindu temple facing East was fell into disuse and it become a customary to construct a Hindu temple facing west people arranged to keep the *dvāra* standing to face West[6]. Sarma has rightly traced the orientation of the temple and his observation that to the East of the present *dvāra* was situated the *maṇḍapa* to the further East of which was the *ardha-maṇḍapa* was perfectly correct. This *ardhamaṇḍapa* is generally mistaken as the *garbhagṛha* of the temple. So, the plan of the temple is simple. It includes *garbhagṛha, maṇḍapa* and *mukhamaṇḍapa*. Sarma has rightly contended that in so far as the plan is concerned, the temple in question bears Gupta architectural features.[7] This simplicity of the plan of this temple, which is the characteristic feature of the early Gupta temple has a good deal of similarity with the Viṣṇu temple at Doeghar, Pārvatī temple at Nachnakuthara and Śiva temple at Bhumrā, all of which are dated in 5th century A.D. *i.e.*, Gupta period, as Sarma[8] has made a comparison amongst them. The only difference is that the three temples brought for comparison are stone built, while that of ours is brick built. Sarma[9] has further contended that Daparvatīā temple should get the pride place of being the earliest brick built Gupta temple and hereby he wants to say that the temple in question should be older than the Bhitargāon brick temple. In our opinion this observation of the scholar is not sound for more than one reasons.

In the first place, the style in which the beautiful figures of Gaṅgā and Yamunā are made to stand elegantly of the lower part of the standing *śakhās* of the *dvāra* of the ruined temple at *Daparvatīā* has no parallel in perfection as far as the Gupta plastic art tradition is concerned. The master artist of this *dvāra* a rare piece of work of art, carved the figures of *Gaṅgā and Yamunā* dèpicting the gentle and flowering female beauty with calm and serenity without even slightest flaw and the upper portion of the *śakhās* and the *śirapaṭṭi* with beautiful floral and geometrical designs and other figures in details, which has already been described by Banerji.[10] On stylistic merit, Banerji has placed it in 5th-6th century A.D. and he has said that these figures represent the art tradition of Sāranāth or Benaras school of the Gupta period, as far as the modelling of these pieces of plastic art is concerned. We think that the *dvāra* in question should be placed in the later half of the 6th century A.D. on stylistic consideration. While determining the age of the Ahichchhatra Śiva temple, P.K. Agrawala[11] also remarks the full stature of the river goddess figures puts it close in time to the *Daparvatīā* example, *i.e.* in the 6th century A.D.

Banerji while commenting on the date of this *dvāra* said that it was of the time of Sāranath or Banaras school of art, as we have already mentioned, flourished in Gupta period *i.e.*, 5th-6th century.[12] He did not directly comment on the date of the object with clarity. His observation may be taken in a broad sense. If the art center flourished at Sāranath in 5th-6th century A.D., then it is reasonable to believe that the art tradition reached Daparvatīā in the ancient Kāmarūpa, the bordering Kingdom of the Gupta empire, by the end of 6th century A.D. if not a few decades earlier.

The Sāranath school of Gupta art reached its zenith by the 6th century, as the extant art pieces show.[13] By the middle of the 6th century the fall of the Gupta dynasty became well evident. Though the Gupta art tradition continued for some years, its decadence started from the 7th century A.D. due to lack of political stability at least in north India.[14] Considering, thus, the geographical and political factors, we may place the *dvāra* in question in the second half of 6th century A.D. The tradition of carving the figures of Gaṅgā and Yamunā on the *dvāras* of the temples started in the Gupta speriod. On the *dvāra* of the temple at Tigowā are seen the figures of these two river goddesses. But two figures on the *dvāra* of the temple at Tigowā, are heavy, less ornamental and not as delicate in modelling as the sculptures of the *dvāra* in question. The temple at Tigowā represents the first phase of Gupta temple architecture and is dated in 4th century A.D. *i.e.*, during the reign of Samudragupta as Smith[15] thinks. Saraswati also observes that this date may not be far off the mark.[16] Next, we find Gaṅgā and Yamunā figure on the *dvāra* of the Deogarh Viṣṇu temple. These two figures are made to stand elegantly but the heaviness and toughness in the modelling of the sculptures are noticed to some extent. Though in consideration of the style this *dvāra* can go near to ours, it seems to be more developed work of art. This temple (Viṣṇu temple at Deogarh) has been placed in early 7th century A.D. by Percy Brown.[17] Vats has also placed it in the early part of the 6th century A.D. as referred to by P.K. Agrawala.[18] Saraswati[18a] has placed it in 6th century A.D. Agrawala himself, considering the paleographical evidence puts it in 5th century or in early 6th century.[19] Hence, if this *dvāra* of the temple at Deograh is placed in the early 6th century, ours can easily be placed at the end of the 6th century A.D. on stylistic consideration.

Again, if we compare our figures of Gaṅgā and Yamunā and the *dvāra* with those of the Pārvatī temple at Nāchñakuṭhāra, we find that the *dvāra* of the temple brought for comparison is less decorated and it has only two bands (*paṭṭa*) on each of the *dvāra-śakhās*. Though the figures of Gaṅgā and Yamunā have been shown here at the bottom of the *śakhās*, yet it lacks lucidity that is evident in our sculptures.

Therefore, the most ornate *dvāra* at Daparvatīā cannot be earlier than the *dvāra* of the temple at Nāchñakuṭhāra. The *dvāra* of the Śiva temple at Bhumāra depicts the images of Gaṅgā and Yamunā. But it has only two bands on each of the *śakhās* and on stylistic consideration this *dvāra* cannot surpass the beauty of the *dvāra* from Daparvatīā. Percy Brown has assigned the temples at *Nāchñakuṭhāra* and *Bhumārā* about 500 A.D.[20] Saraswati observes, "the simplicity of design and of decoration places the Pārvatī temple at Nāchñakuṭhāra along with the early example of the first group with which it is probably co-eval in date."[21] Regarding the date of the temple at Bhumāra he says that the carving and workmanship of the temple are to be dated in first half of 6th century A.D., though R.D. Banerji was inclined to place it in the middle of the preceding century[22] . The figures of Gaṅgā and Yamunā made of clay in life size fixed at the two sides of the steps leading to the upper terrace of the Śiva temple, Ahicchatra (c.

6th century A.D.) are depicted gracefully with all the ornaments that deck their bodies in Gupta art style. But these two figures are heavier than the figure of the Daparvatiā and the *dvāra* of the Daparvatiā ruined temple is much more detailed and ornate. This point lead us to place the date of the temple in question at a later period, at least by a few years.

Now let us see whether the Bhitargāon brick temple has a *dvāra* depicting the two river goddesses as in ours. Cunningham[23] while giving the description of the temple at Bhitargāon says, another point about this temple which does not appear to be mentioned before, is that stone beams or lintels were originally placed at the front of the existing brick arch, both inside and outside of the sanctum entrance, the large cavities just above the door way on both sides prove the door frame of the missing porch was also of carved stone, similar to the door frames of the brick temples in the central provinces. It appears, before he visited the site the porch was collapsed due to the door frame having been removed.[24] On both the sides of the Bhitargāon temple Vogel did also recognize representations of Gaṅgā and Yamunā, an invariable feature of the entrance of a Gupta temple.[25] As the original *dvāra* of the temple depicting the river goddesses is missing, it has become a little difficult to know about the style of the *dvāra*. However, Cunningham, it appears, has rightly assumed that the missing stone door frame was carved in stone similar to the *dvāra* of the temples in Madhyadeśa or central province. Vogal has put the date of the temple in 4th century A.D. which seems to be too early a date. Percy Brown puts it in 5th century A.D.[26] Cunningham, Who first described it, was of the view that it could not be placed later that 7th or 8th century and might probably be older.[27] In time scale, the Bhitargāon temple could not be far removed from the Deogarh temple to which it bears some general resemblances,[28] as Sarasvatī thinks, P.K. Agrawala, however, prefers to assign it to about 500 A.D. or better a earlier.[29] Therefore, it has become almost clear that the Bhitargāon brick temple is close to the Deoghar Viṣṇu temple in general resemblance as opined by those scholars and if we place the Deoghar temple in 5th or in early 6th century A.D., the Bhitargāon temple should be dated in the some period. We have said that the Daparavatiā *dvāra* is more ornate and the figures of the river goddesses are more elegant, lucid, graceful, and more pleasing work of art in which the artist proved the perfection of his creation than any other *dvāra* and figures of the deities with which we have already made a comparison. As such, we place the *dvāra* in the later half of the 6th century, a later date than the date of the Deoghar temple or the Bhitargāon temple. Further, P.K. Agrawala comments that the Daparvatiā is closely connected with Deoghar door way in its details and it displays a step further in the elaborate scheme of carving, namely the number of bands is increased to five; behind the halo of the goddesses, now increased number of attending figures, there appear two flying geese etc.[30] This description will lead a scholar to date the Daparvatiā *dvāra* in a slightly later period than Deoghar and Agrawala has put the *dvāra* in 6th century A.D.[31]

It is also to be mentioned that R.D. Banerji[32] discovered a few terracotta sculptures from the ruins at Daparvatiā which he dated in 6th century A.D. He is supported by C.C. Das Gupta.[33] These terracotta plaques were no doubt, stuck into the temple walls. Das Gupta[33a] has made a comparative study on these pieces and is of the opinion that the Daparvatiā specimen is included in eastern Indian medieval school represented by terracotta sculptures from Sabar, Phārapur, Nālandā, Daparvatiā etc.

The next point of our consideration is the position of the figures of the river goddesses on the *dvāra*. It became a tradition to carve the figures of Gaṅgā and Yamunā in the *dvāra* of a temple of the Gupta period. It is well known that the figures of Gaṅgā and Yamunā on the *dvāra* of the Gupta temples were derived from the figures of Śālabhuñjikā shown in Sāñchi, Mathurā and Amarāvati, monuments of Suñga period. Varāhamihira in his Brhatsamhita[34] gives the detailed description of a temple *dvāra*. But he has not mentioned about the figures of the river goddesses. It may be due to the fact that in his period (latter half of the 5th century) the figures of the river goddesses were shown at the level of the *śirapaṭṭi* or even above it and not on the lower part of the *śakhās* and according to Cunningham, it is a later feature.[35] Percy Brown[36] says that in the early Gupta Hindu temple these figures are placed in the upper angle. In the later period the position of these figures came to the bottom of the *dvāra-śakhās*.

As we shall see now, in the *dvāra* of the temple at Sāñchi, though the figures of the deities are supposed to be missing, yet some blank spaces on either side above the *śirapaṭṭi* provided with, which must have meant for placing some figure, evidently of these of Gaṅgā and Yamunā. In case of Udigiri cave temple, we see *makaravahana* on either side above the *śirapaṭṭi*. The *dvāra śakhās* of Udigiri Mahāvarāha temple show the scene of descending of Gaṅgā and Yamunā in the form of rivers. However, the authropomophic forms of the goddesses are shown here occupying the upper portions of the *śakhās*. In the temples at Tegowa and Deogarh referred to above are shown the goddesses in the upper levels, Bhitargāon temple had the figure in the middle of the side walls of the entrance[37]. Ahichchhatra temple *dvāra* shows the life size figure of the two goddesses occupyıng full entrance. Nāchñakuṭhāra Pārvatī temple, it appears, has duplicate set (?) of goddesses—one in the lower part of *śakhās* and another occupying the side space over the *śirapaṭṭi* level. At Kharhod the temple shows the full six statues of the goddesses on the śākhās. In case of the Bhumārā temple we find that Gaṅgā and Yamunā are shown at the bottom of the *śakhās*, The Daparvatiā *dvāra* well depicts the figure of Gaṅgā and Yamunā with attending dwarf female figures at the bottom if the *śakhās*. From the above discussion we find that except for Bhumārā and Daparvatiā temple *dvāras*, all other temple *dvāra*s, bear more or less early features as far as the style of depicting the river goddesses is concerned. Though the temple at Bhumārā shows them at the bottom of the *dvāra-śakhās*, yet from the execution of the details, we can say that the *dvāra* in question is more developed in art style than the *dvāra* of the temple at Bhumāra, as we have already said. As such, the Daparvatiā *dvāra* should find a date in some later time. As the missing temple *dvāra* at Bhitargāon shows the image of the goddess in the middle portion of the side walls, the temple, it appears, is older than the temple at Daparvatiā.

In the third place, we should take into consideration of the sizes of the rock used in the temples. Percy Brown opines that the bigger the size of bricks the earlier the structure of the temples tends to be.[38] Sarma [39] has given the sizes of the bricks used in some of the temples quoting from P. Brown as follows:-

Temples at Ter (4th/5th Century A.D.)	17" x 9" x 3"
" " Chazarla (Do)	16" x 9" x 2¼"
" Bhitargāon (early 6th century)	17½" x 10½" x 3"
"Daparvatiā (2nd half of 6th century)	15" x 1 1½" x 2¼".

This shows that the size of brick of the Daparvatiā is smallest. The length and the thickness of the Daparvatiā bricks show that they are lesser than those of Bhitargāon, only the breadth the bricks from Daparvatiā is more than those at Bhitargāon. This type of a few pieces of bricks probably became necessary for some purpose. Hence, Daparvatiā temple, it is proved, is not older than the Bhitargāon temple.

Lastly, Daparvatiā, in ancient Kāmarūpa kingdom, was a from the mid of the Gupta dominion *i.e.*, Madhyadeśa. Kāmarūpa and Davāka are mentioned in the Allahabad pillar inscription[40] of Samudragupta dated in 4th century A.D. and it is clear from it that Kāmarūpa never formed a part of the Gupta dominion—it was a bordering kingdom. The Kāmarūpa kings acknowledged the suzerainty of the mighty emperor. Hence, a Gupta artist or architect in stead of making a venture on a new temple style *i.e.*, of bricks temple in the heart of the Gupta empire, definitely did not come to build it in Kāmarūpa, covering a great distance and tiresome journey in those days. The style of the first phase of Gupta temple architecture in stone, a new tradition, was evolved in mid India at Sāñchi, Tigowā, and Iran. So, the new style of eracting a brick temple must have started at Bhitargāon, well within the Gupta Empire.

P.K. Agrawala has made a comment by saying that there had existed other Gupta brick temples (other than Bhitargāon) at Baigram in Bengal and at Daparvatiā, which are broadly to be placed earlier than Bhitargāon example, but not much of them remains to give an idea of their superstructure.[41] It appears, his view is self contradictory, for he has assigned the Bhitargāon temple to 500 A.D.[42] As neither he nor others (Brown[43] Sarsavati[44]) have given the description and published the plan of the ruined temple at Baigram, Dinajpur district, Bengal, we find it difficult to support their views.

Sarma may be right in tracing the plan, which show the simplicity in its style. The style of the plan had led him to place the present ruined temple at a period earlier than the date of the Bhitargāon temple. It is to be considered that it took some time to reach Assam a particular style in architecture from mid India in that time. Even to-day, in days of quick communication, a style evolved in Bombay or Delhi takes at least a few years time to make itself popular in far off Assam. It also did happen in the historical period. The style of the simple plan of some early stone temple in mid-India reached Daparvatīa, in all probability, some years later and meanwhile, the style of constructing a temple with brick came to use so that the architects here preferred to construct the Daparvatiā temple with brick over the old modelled plan. However, the Daparvatiā *dvāra* is an import from North India and not local production. It was imported from the Gupta art centre of Banaras region.

Notes and References

1. *Annual Report of Archaeological Survey of India*, 1922-23, pp. 98-99.
2. *Ibid.*, 1924-25, pp. 98-99.
3. *Ibid.*
4. *Ibid.*

5. "The Antiquity of the ruined temple at Daparvatiā," *Bulletin of the Assam State Museum*, No, I, 1975, pp. 36-40.
6. *Op.cit.*, p. 40.
7. *Op.cit*, p. 38.
8. *Op.cit.*, pp. 37-58.
9. *Op.cit.*, p. 40.
10. *Op.cit*, pp. 19-99.
11. *Gupta temple Architecture*, Varanasi. 1968, p. 55.
12. *Op.cit.*, p. 99.
13. *The classical Age, Bharatiya Vidya Bhavan,* Bombay, 1962, p. 44.
14. *Ibid.*, p. 531.
15. *Indian sculpture of the Gupta period.* Also see, *The classical Age*, *Bharatiya Vidya Bhavan.* (Oz. III, 4)
16. *The classical Age, Bharatia Vidya Bhavan*, Bombay, 1962, p. 504.
17. *Indian Architecture*, (Buddhist and Hindu), Bombay, 1956, p. 60.
18. *Op.cit.*, p. 38.
18a. *Op.cit.*, p. 517.
19. *Ibid.*
20. *Op.cit.*, p. 60.
21. *Op.cit.*, p. 507.
22. *Ibid.*, p. 511.
23. A.S.R., XI, p. 142. P1. XV.
24. Vogel, *Annual Report of Archaeological Survey of India*, 1608-9, p. 14.
25. *Ibid.*
26. *Op.cit.*, p. 41.
27. *The classical Age, Bharatiya Vidya Bhavan,* Bombay, 1962, p. 517.
28. *Ibid.*
29. *Op.cit.*, p. 47. Further he has contended that the life size Varaha incarnation of Viṣṇu from a niche of the Bhitar Gaon temple bear striking similarity with Varaha image at Udayagiri cave datable to 4th century A.D. Inspite of the difference in medium, treatment and modelling of the two figures they are so alike that there could not be the remoteness of more than a generation between the two". *Ibid.*, p. 73.
30. *Ibid.*, p. 46.
31. *Ibid.*, p. 55.
32. *Annual Report of Archaeological Survey of India*, 1924-25, pp. 98-99.
33. *Origin and Development of Indian Clay sculpture*, 1944, p. 228.

33a. *Ibid.*
34. *Brhat Samthita*, 56. Also see, Agrawala, *op.cit.*, p. 66.
35. Agrawala, *op.cit.*, p. 66.
36. *Op.cit.*, p. 59.
37. Agrawala, *op.cit.*, p. 91.
38. *Op.cit.*, p. 50.
39. *Op.cit.*, p. 39.
40. *Corpus Inscriptions Indicarum*, Vol. III p. 11.
41. *Op.cit.*, p. 44.
42. *Ibid.*
43. *Op.cit.*, pp. 50-51.
44. *Op.cit*, p. 507.

26

Gold Objects from Śingimārī in Gāro Hills District

In the year 1976 a few gold objects were discovered at Śingimārī, about 27 km off from Phulbārī in Gāro Hills district of Meghalaya. The findspot of the object is on the side of Phulbārī—Gārobāndhā road. The objects were discovered on the land of Sri Bisa Sha of Śingimārī village during spade work for cultivation by a labourer. Sri Sha brought those things and kept with him for a few days. But the Śingimārī police station took charge of the objects and sent them to the D.C. Gāro Hills district from whom the Chief Secretary of Meghalaya brought them to Shillong.

According to the report published in the Dainik Assam, 21st June 1976, Sri Sivananda Sarma, the then their President of the Goālpārā Anusandhān Samiti, visited the site and examined the objects. He was of the opinion that one of the objects, a gold plate, showed a figure of 18 handed Mahiṣamardinī. Further, he commented that the find spot of the object was near the Mahāmāyā temple of the 10th Century A.D. He told me this personally.

I was keen to examine the objects. I visited Meghalaya State Museum on 1st Sep; 1977 with that intention. But I was surprised to know that such objects were not kept in that Museum. However, on further enquiry I could located them in the Central Library, Meghalaya. I requested the authorities to preserve these valuable objects in the Meghalaya State Museum in the interest of the scholars.

The objects include a gold locket bearing an image of Mahiṣamardinī, two beads of gold, a mutilated circular object of gold with decoration, a worn-out copper (?) plate with an iron plate and a few (three or four) broken pieces of gold. Evidently, the broken pieces of gold are from the circular decorated object. As I was in a hurry, I could not spend more time for examination of the objects.

1. The God Locket: It is a square box type hollow object measuring 7 x 7 cms. It is about I cm thick. On the upper side of it two small rings are attached, evidently, for hanging purposes. The obverse of the object shows an image of Mahiṣamardinī. The goddess is 16 armed and her hands hold the *āyudhas* clock wise: *triśūla (?), chakra*, object not shown, object not shown, object not shown, object not shown, object not shown, holding the hair of the *asura*, object not shown, object not shown, object not shown, object not shown, *khaḍaga* and *damaru*. The chest portion, the left leg, the body of the *asura*, the face of the lion are mutilated or torn. Through these torn portions of the object can be seen inside and one can be sure that the object is hollow. The right leg is on the back of the lion. The exact position of the left leg is not clear because of its mutilated condition as is stated above. But the fighting scene of the goddess with mahiṣāsura, whose decapitated head is lying below, is clearly shown. The lower garments cannot be seen due to the damaged portion of the image. On the head of the deity is seen a short *mukuṭa*. Just below the *mukuṭa* on the deity a crack has developed.

Behind the deity a *prābhāvalī* in semi-circular shape is arranged. Outside the *prabhā* on the upper two corners of the object foliage decorations are noticed. Similar decorations are also noticed on the lower two corners of this square object. The reverse of the object is plain. Possibly, the figures of Mahiṣamardinī and other designs which are on relief were embossed separately and later joined with the plain reverse. The presence of two small rings attached to the upper side of the object leads us to postulate that it is a locket of a necklace.

2. Two beads: These two objects also appear to be of gold. The first one is bigger and it has some grooves on the body. The holes of the bead are prominent. The other bead is like a round turban. The holes of this bead are also prominent and on either side of the holes a short pipe is joined, evidently, to be inserted into the hole of the other bead for better fitting purpose.

3. A round golden object: It is a circular gold object about 42 cm in circumference. Some portions of the border of it are broken. In the center of the object on the obverse a red jem is fixed on it. Around this object is shown some creeper design having long leaves. The execution of the object is quite good and the decoration is in relief. The reverse of the object shows nothing.

4. A broken thin copper plate (?) with an iron pin: The fourth object is a wornout copper (?) plate. It is very thin and most of the portions are broken and missing. Only the middle portion is remnant. On this a iron nail is fixed. It is not possible to say exactly for what purpose it was used.

However, looking at the fixed nail on the center of the broken thin plain copper (?) plate it can be assumed that this plate must have been fixed on the back side of the round decorated gold object so that it could be fixed on the headgear of some lady as ornament.

Such type of gold objects are not commonly found. It appears that all the objects represent some ornaments. The gold locket and the beads must have been from some necklace of which the other beads are missing. The round gold object must have been fixed on the hair knot (hair pin) of some lady as ornament. This round object is very much like a round halo of an image of medieval period.

At the present state of our knowledge, it is difficult to say anything about the antiquity of these pieces of gold objects. However, we can say that such types of ornaments are not used by any community in Assam. The style of execution of Mahiṣamardinī on the locket and the decorated round object, it appears, does not have any affinity with the Āhom style or Āhom style with Mughol traits. Some women of rich families of Nepalese community wear ornaments heavily and Nepalese are mostly śāktas. But it is certain, these represent ornaments were used by ladies of some royal family or some rich family of the past. Further investigation will be necessary to determine their antiquity.

27

Temple Ruins at Mājgāon

Ruins of two temples have been noticed at Ghorporā-cuburī of the village Majgāon, within the Tezpur town area, Assam. The site is a little west of the State Transport workshop. The actual site of the ruins is now included in a cemetery and just near to the east stands a bamboo garden. Till recently the ruins were covered with jungles. Now they have been cleared off by the local people. Many new residential buildings have been constructed near the site.

From the ruins scattered in the place it can be guessed that there were two temples, wihch might have fallen down in the wake of an earth-quake. About a century ago somebody dug the place, removed some parts of the temple structures and, most probably, the images of the deities. Even now the actual location disturbed with heaps and ditches are seen. It appears from the existing evidences that the *maṇḍapa* of the temples was at a higher level than that of the *garbhagṛhas*. There must have been *sopānas* (flight of steps in between the *garbhagṛhas* and the *maṇḍpas*). This type of *garbhagrāha* was quite common in temples of medieval period in Assam. Both the temples were standing parallel at a distance of about hundred yards with their *garbhagṛhas* to the east of the *maṇḍapas*.

In this area twenty four pieces of stone, sculptured, decorated or undecorated, of different sizes are lying scattered. Of these twelve pieces are more or less in a group and hence, these must have belonged to the first temple situated to the north of the other. The other twelve pieces of stone are lying scattered to the south forming another group. Evidently they belong to the second temple. There are also some stone pieces under the earth, which are slightly visible and slight digging will expose them. The pieces of a stone lying on earth that are worth mentioning are as follows:

1 A. *śirapaṭṭi*: It is 230 cm in length and 77 cm in breadth. In the upper part of this *śirapaṭṭi*, there is a row of miniature *śikhara*. In side each of the *śikhara* a seated *yogī* is shown. Below this row in the middle an image of Gaṇesha is sculptured in *āsana* attitude. This *śirapaṭṭi* must have been employed in the *dvāra* of the first temple.

2. *śīlālī* or *Dehalī* (door sill): It is 232 cm long and 77 cm broad. This huge *śīlālī* does not bear the usual two figures of retreating lion and those of an elephant pair and vase. Here only a decorative design resembling a small tree evedently *kalpavṛksha* motif is carved in the middle. This type of *śilāli* is not commonly met with in the ruins of the temple belonging to the pre-Āhom period in Assam. However, a piece of *śīlālī* depicting such design is noticed lying on the road side on the Hemachandra Goswami road in Uzanbazar, Guwahati and we have this motif in the ruins elsewhere in Assam.

In addition to these two pieces, a broken piece of *amalaka* and some pieces of chiselled stone of half circular shape, which were definitely used in the *adhisṭhāna* of the *garbhagṛha* are lying there. The pieces of stone which were employed in the second temple are also of similar nature. These pieces are as follows:

1. A. *śirapaṭṭi*: It measures 187 x 77 cm. This is almost similar to the *śirapaṭṭi* of the first temple. The upper part of this *śirapaṭṭi* shows a line of miniature *śikharas*. But inside the *śikharas* the seated figures of yogīs are not shown in this case.

2. A. *śīlālī*: It measures 247 x 77 cm. This *śīlālī* of the *dvāra* of the second temple is strikingly similar to that of the first temple. A broken piece of the *amalaka* and some other pieces of stone are also lying here as in the first case.

The *dvāra-śākhās* of both the temples are in the temple site. One *śākhā* is noticed at little a distance, in the bamboo garden. This *śākhā*, undoubtedly, was brought from the ruined temple site. Another two *dvāra-śākhās* of the same type is seen in the *nāmghar* (modern shrine preserved and owned by late Mrs. Prafulla Bala Barua), quite near to the ruined temple site. The upper part of each of these *śākhās* shows, decorative floral and creeper designs in two *paṭṭas* (bend). In the lower parts of the lone *śākhā* and one of the *śākhās* kept in the *nāmghar* figures of Gaṅgā, Nandī and Dvārapāla are seen in *sthānaka* attitude. Here the figure of *Nandī* is shown in anthropomorphic form. But the face of the figure looks like the face of a bull. The other *śākhā* preserved in the *dvāra* of the same *nāmghar* in its lower part carries the figures of Yamunā, Nandī and Davarapāla. Some more pieces of chiselled stone are lying near this *nāmghar*. All these pieces were evidently removed, along with the *śākhās*, from the ruined temple site. Now, of these two *dvāras* from the ruined temples one *śākhā* is not noticed. Most probably this *śākhā* is under the earth. From the size of the *dvāraśākhās*, *śirapaṭṭis* and śilālī, it is clear that both the temples were of big size.

It may be recalled that the figures of Gaṅgā and Yamunā were sculptured on temple *dvāra* first in the Gupta period. The standing *dvāra* of a ruined temple at Daparbatīā was noticed by R.D. Benerji.[1] This *dvāra* bears two beautiful figures of Gaṅgā and Yamunā in elegant posture at the bottom. This *dvāra*, which still stands in the original site of the temple, must have been dedicated to *Śiva* and is about two miles away from ruined temples at Majgāon, as the crow flies. The Daparvatīā *dvāra* on stylistic ground may be placed in *c*. 6th century A.D. if not earlier. But the Majgāon temples, on stylistic consideration, may be placed in *c*. 9th century A.D.[2] Though these two ruined temples were built nearly three centuries after the Daparbatīā temple, yet the tradition of carving the figures of Gaṅgā and Yamunā was continued. From this it is quite clear that the Daparbatīā *dvāra* was influenced by the Gupta characteristic feature prevalent at that time in North Indian temples and that the Majgāon continued to maintain the Gupta tradition, though in a slightly different way. It shows that at least as late as 9th century Gupta art tradition was prevalent in the Brahmaputra valley, quite far from the Gupta dominion. This is further proved by the Tezpur Rock-cut inscription of Harjjar Varman, a king of Kāmarūpa in 9th century A.D. whose capital was at Hārupeśvar, modern Tezpur. This inscription is dated in Gupta Era 510-829-30 A.D.[3]

It is interesting to note that the figure of Nandī is depicted in anthropomorphic form holding a *daṇḍa* along with the figures of the Dvārapāla, Gaṅgā and Yamunā.

Not a single image had been noticed in the ruined temple site. But taking into consideration the presence of the figure of Gaṅgā, Yamunā and Nandī on the *dvāra-śākhās* and the figure of Gaṇeśa in the *śirapaṭṭis*, it can be inferred that both the temples were dedicated to Śiva, who was the worshipping deity of the kings of Kāmarūpa at that time.

The Harjjarpukhurī, a very big tank, which still exits at Tezpur was excavated in the regime of Harjjarvarman. Therefore, it may be quite possible that the ruined temples in question were also built at the same time.

Nutes and Rofefence

1. *Annual Report, Archaeological survey of India*, 1923-24, pp. 22f.
2. P.C. Sharma has placed in late 8th century. See, *Architecture of Assam*,1988, p. 43. I visited the site as early as 1969. Later also I visited it.
3. P. Bhattacharya, *Kāmarūpa Sasanavali*, 1931, pp. 185-92.

Select Bibliography

Agrawala, V.S. : "A catalogue of the Brahmanical images in Mathura Art", *J.U.P.H.S.,* XXII, pp. 102-10, XXIII, pp. 35-147.

Gupta Art, Lucknow, 1948.

Siva Mahadeva, the Great God, Varanasi, 1966.

"A Note on Mediaeval Temple Architecture", *J.U.P.H.S.,* XVI, pp. 113f.

Studies in Indian Art, Varanasi, 1965.

Agrawala, R.C. : "Some Interesting Early Mediaeval Sculpture in the Jhalwar Museum", *J.I.M.* XI, Bombay, pp. 21-22.

Banerji, R.D. : *The Age of the Imperial Guptas,* Benares, 1933.

The Mediaeval School of Eastern Indian Sculpture, Delhi, 1933.

Nepalese Art, Department of Archaeology, Nepal, 1966.

History of Orissa, Vol. 2, Calcutta, 1930.

Banerjea, J.N. : *Development of Hindu Iconography,* Calcutta, 1956.

"Hindu Iconography", *J.I.S.O.A.,* Vol. XXXI, pp. 55-129; Vol. XIV, pp. 1-74.

"Sūrya, Adityas and the Navagrahas", *J.I.S.O.A.,* Vol. XVI, pp. 47-102.

Biswas, S.S. *et al.* : *Terracotta Temples of Bengal,* Delhi, 1995.

Bandopadhaya, B. : *Metal Sculptures of Eastern India,* Delhi, 1981.

Bhattacharya, P.K. : *Iconography of Sculptures*, North Bengal University, 1983.

Barua, B.K. : *A Cultural History of Assam,* Vol. 1, Nowgaon, 1951.

Early Geography of Assam, 1952.

Barua, B.K. : "Iconographical Representations of some Sākta Goddesses in the Kālikāpurāṇa," *P.K. Gode Commemoration Vol*, 1960, pt. III, pp. 1-18, Poona.

Barua B.K. and H.V.S. Murthy : *Temple & Legends of Assam,* Bombay, 1965.

Barua, K.L. : *Early History of Kāmarūpa,* Shillong, 1933.

Beal, S. : (tr.) *Life of Hiuen Tsiang,* London, 1888, 1914.

Bhattacharya, B. : *Indian Buddhist Iconography,* 1924.

Bhattacharyee, A. : *Sculptures and Icons of Mediaeval Assam,* Calcutta, 1978.

Bhattasali, N.K. : *Iconography of the Buddhist and Brahmanical Sculpture in the Decca Museum,* Decca, 1929.

Brown, P. : *Indian Architecture* (Buddhist and Hindu), Bombay, Vol. 1, 1959.

Butler, J. (Captain) : *Administrative Report of the Nagā Hills,* Calcutta, 1870-71.

Butler, J. (Major) : *Travels and Adventures in the Province of Assam,* London, 1855.

A Sketch of Assam, London, 1847.

Chatterji, S.K. : *The Place of Assam in the History and Civilization of India,* Guwahati University, 1955.

"Brahmi—the Mother of Indian Script", Indian System of Writing, Publication Division, Govt. of India, 1966, New Delhi.

Kirāta Jana Kṛti, 1951.

Indo-Aryan and Hindi, 1942.

Chakladar, H.C. : *Aryanisation of Eastern Indian,* Calcutta, 1962.

Choudhury, P.C. : *The History of Civilization of the People of Assam upto the 12th Century A.D.,* Guwahati, 1966.

"Archaeological Finds at Narakasur Hill", *J.A.R.S.,* XVI, pp. 60-63.

Choudhury, P.C. : "Guwahati: an Ancient City of the East", *Kāmarūpa* (Souvenir, All India Science Teachers Conference, Guwahati, 1967) pp. 4-10.

Choudhury, P.D. : *Archaeology in Assam* (a brochure), Guwahati.

Choudhury, P.D. and M.C. Das : *Ancient Treasures of Assam*, Guwahati, 1959.

Choudhury, R.D. : *Archaeology of the Brahmaputra Valley of Assam,* Delhi, 1985.

Sculpture of Assam, Guwahati, 1987.

Choudhury, R.D. : *Cataloque of Metal Sculptures in the Assam State Museum,* Guwahati, 1988

Asamat Purātatta Carcar Agragati (Assamese) Guwahati, 1992.

Choudhury, N.D. : *Historical Archaeology of Central Assam from the Earlist Period to A.D. 12th Century*, New Delhi, 1985.

Coomaraswamy, A.K. : *A History of Indian and Indonesian Art,* London, 1927.

The Yakshas, 1931.

The Boston Museum of Fine Arts Bulletin, Boston, 18, No. 106, April, 1920.

Portfolio of Indian Art, Bombay, 1923.

Dasgupta, C.C. : *Origin and Evolution of Indian Clay Sculpture,* University of Calcutta, 1961.

Dasgupta, K.K. : *Wood Carvings of Eastern India,* Calcutta, 1990.

Datta, Manoranjan : *Sculpture of Assam,* Delhi, 1990.

Deva, Krishna : (ed.) *Journal of the Indian Society of Oriental Art,* Vol. XX & XXI.

"The Temple of Khajurāho in Central India" *A.I.,* No. 15, pp. 43-65.

Temples of North India, Delhi, 1969.

Dhaky, M.A. : "Mattavāranam in Vāstuśāstras" *J.O.I.B.,* XVI, No.1.

"The old temple at Lamba and Kameśvara temple at Auwa", *J.A.S.B.* Vol, VIII, No. 3, 1966.

"Western India Art", *J.I.S.O.A., Special No. 19.*

"Brahmanasvami temple at Varman", *J.O.I.,* Baroda XIV, No. 3-4.

Diskalakar, D.B. : "Some Brahmanical Sculptures in the Mathura Museum", *J.U.P.H.S.,* Lucknow Vol. V, Pt. 1 pp. 18-57.

Donald : *Ivory Carving in Assam,* 1900.

Fergusson, J. : *History of Indian and Eastern Architecture,* Vol. 2, London, 1910.

Foucher, A. : *The Beginnings of Buddhist Art,* London, 1918.

Fouchet, M.P. : *The Erotic Sculpture of India,* London, 1959.

Gait, E.A. : *A History of Assam,* Calcutta, 1926.

Report on the progress of Historical Research in Assam, Shillong, 1897.

List of Archaeological Remains in the Province of Assam, Shillong, 1897.

Getty, A. : *Gaṇeśa,* Oxford, 1936.
Guha, U.C. : *History of Cachar.*
Gupte, R.S. and B.D. Mahajan : *Ajanta and Ellora,* Bombay, 1962.
Havell, E.B. : *Ancient and Mediaeval Architecture of India,* London, 1915.
Indian Sculpture and Painting, London, 1908.
Hunter, W.W. : *A Statistical Account of Assam,* 1-2, Calcutta, 1879.
Hutton, J.H. : *The Sema Nagas,* London, 1921.
The Angami Nagas, London, 1921.
Jayaswal, K.P. : *An Imperial History of India,* 1934.
Johnstone, J. : *My Experience in Manipur and the Naga Hills, London,* 1896.
Khandalavala, K. : "Some Nepalese and Tibetan Bronzes in the Collection of Mr. R.S. Sethna of Bombay", *Marg,* Vol. IV. I., pp.21-40.
Kramrisch, Stella : *Indian Sculpture,* Calcutta, 1933.
The Hindu Temple, 2 Vols., Calcutta, 1946.
"The Pala and Sena Art of Bengal", *Rupam,* No. 37.
"The image of Mahadeva in the cave temple of Elephant Island", *A.I.* No. 2 pp.4-8.
The Art of India, London, 1955.
The Art of Nepal, New York, 1964.
Lal, B.B. : "An Examiation of Some Metal Images from Nālandā", *A.I.,* No. 12, pp.53-57.
Mahtab, H.K. : *The History of Orissa,* Cuttack, 1949.
Majumdar, R.C. : *History of Bengal,* Dacca University, 1943.
Mankodi, K.L. : *The Hindu Iconography of the South Deccan,* (an unpublished thesis, Deccan College, Poona University), 1966.
Martin, M. : *Eastern India,* London, 1838.
Misra, B. : *Orissa under the Bhauma Kings,* Calcutta, 1934.
Mitra, R.L. : *The Antiquities of Orissa,* Calcutta I, 1964.
Monahan, E.J. : *Early History of Bengal,* Oxford, 1925.
Mookerji, R.K. : *Hindu Civilization,* London, 1936.
Mukherjee, B.N. : *Eastern Indian Art Style,* Calcutta, 1980.
Nath, R.M. : *The Cultural Background of Assam*, Shillong, 1948.
Naik, A.V. : *Archaeology of the Deccan,* (an unpublished thesis), Deccan College, Poona University 1947.

Nautiyal, K.P. : *The Archaeology of Kumaon Region,* Varanasi, 1969.

Nagar, M.M. : "A Vishnu Image from Aligarh", *J.U.P.H.S.*, Lucknow, XVIII, pp.98-100.

Neog, M., (Ed.) and H.K. Barpujari : *Professor Surya Kumar Bhuyan Commemoration Volume,* Guwahati 1966.

Neog, M. : *Studies in the History and Culture of Assam,* Guwahati, 1973.

Nigam, M.L. : (Ed.) *Decorative Arts of India,* Hyderabad, 1987.

Panigrahi, K.C. : "Sculptural Representations of Lakuliśa and other Pasupata Teacher", *J.I.H.*, Trivandrum, XXXVIII, III, pp. 635-43.

Archaeological Remains at Bhubaneswar, Calcutta, 1961.

Panikkar, K.M. : *Sri Harsa of Kanauj,* Bombay, 1922.

Rajkhowa, B. : *A short account of Assam,* 1915.

Historical sketch of old Assam, 1917.

Rao, T.A.G. : *Elements of Hindu Iconography,* Vol. 2, Madras, 1914.

Ravetry, H.G., (tr.) : *Tavaqāt-i-Nāsirī,* London, 1881.

Rowland, B. : *The Art and Architecture of India—Buddhist, Hindu and Jaina,* London, 1953.

Ray, N.R., *et al.* : *Eastern Indian Bronzes,* Delhi, 1986.

Sankalia, H.D. : *The Archaeology of Gujarat,* Bombay, 1941.

The University of Nālandā, Madras, 1934.

Studies in the Historical and Cultural Geography and Ethnography of Gujarat, Poona, 1949.

"Six Different Types of Gaṇeśa Figures", *J.I.H,* Vol. XVIII, Pt.II, pp.188-94.

"Rare Figures of Vishṇu from Gujarat", *J.U.B.*, VII, IV, pp.3-7.

"Socio-Economic and Geographical Background of Khājurāho", *J.I.H.*, XLIV, pp.29-44.

Sarasvati, S.K. : *A Survey of Indian Sculpture,* Calcutta, 1957.

Early Sculptures of Bengal, Calcutta, 1962.

Shakespeare, L.W. : *History of Upper Assam, Upper Burma and N.E. Frontier,* London, 1914.

Sharma, B.N. : "Hindu Deities of Nepal," *Dr. R.K. Mookerjee Commemoration Volume,* Lucknow, 1974.

"Unpublished Pāla and Sena Sculptures in the National Museum, New Delhi", *East and West,* Rome, 23, 1-2.

Sharma, B.N. : "Assam in Prehistoric Times", *Kāmarūpa,* (a souvenir, A.S.S.) 1967, pp. 83-89.

Sharma, P.R. : *The Archaeology of Nepal.* (Unpublished thesis Deccan College), Poona, 1963.

Sarma, P.C. : *A Study of the Temple Architecture of Assam from Gupta period to the End of the Ahom Rule,* (Unpublished Ph.D. thesis 1981, Guwahati University.

Shukla, D.N. : *Vāstu Śāstra,* Vol. 2, Lucknow, 1960.

Sivaramamurti, C. : *Indian Sculpture,* New Delhi, 1961.

Indian Bronzes, 1963.

Srivastava, *et al.* : (Ed.) *Kalā: Journal of Indian Art History Congress,* Guwahati, Vol. I & II.

Some Aspects of Indian Culture, New Delhi, 1969.

Smith, V.A. : *Fine Arts in India and Ceylon,* Oxford, 1930.

Thapar, D.R. : *Icons in Bronze,* Asia Publication House, 1961.

Tripathi, L.K. : "The Erotic Scenes of Khajurāho and Explanation", *Bharati,* No. 3, (1959-60) pp.82-104.

Vats, M.S. : "The Gupta temple at Deogarh", *M.A.S.I.,* No. 70, Delhi, 1952.

Wade, J.P. : *Geographical Sketch of Assam*, 1927, Sibsaga.

Waddell, L.A. : *The Buddhism of Tibet,* London, 1895.

Watters, T., (tr.) : *On Yuan Chwang's Travels in India,* London, 1904.

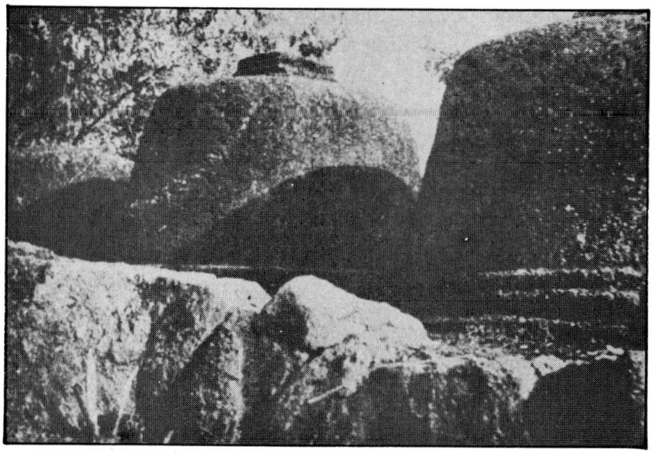

Pl. 3.1 Rock-Cut Votive Stūpa at Śrī Sūrya Pāhār

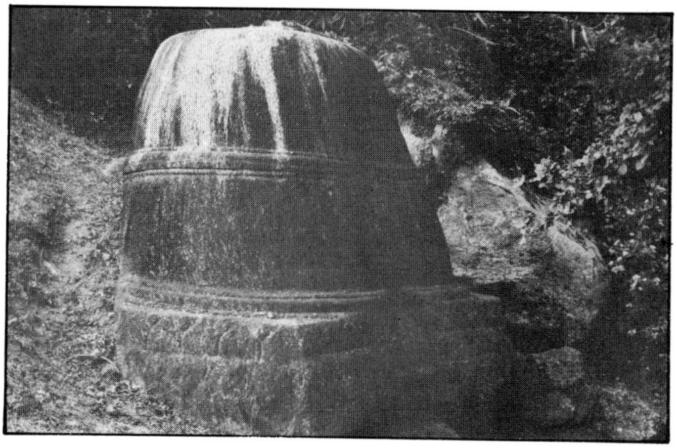

Pl. 3.2 Rock-Cut Votive Stūpa

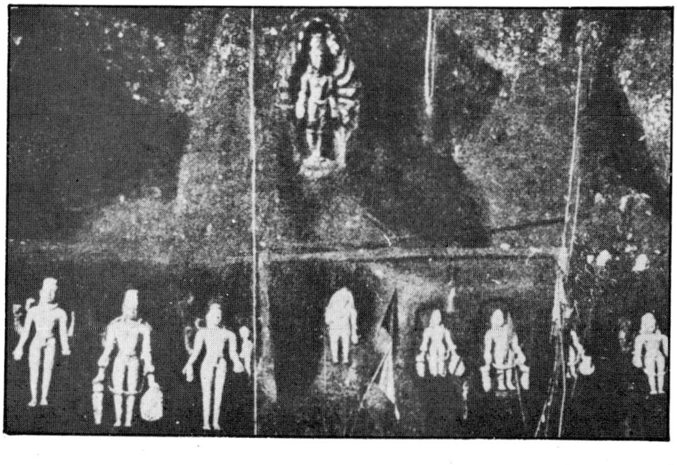

Pl. 3.3 Rock-Cut Votive Stūpa at Śrī Sūrya Pāhār

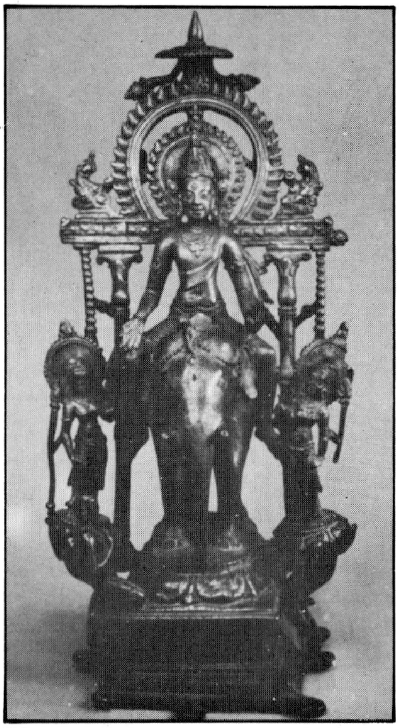

Pl. 5.1 Indra, Bronze, Kāhilipārā, Guwahati

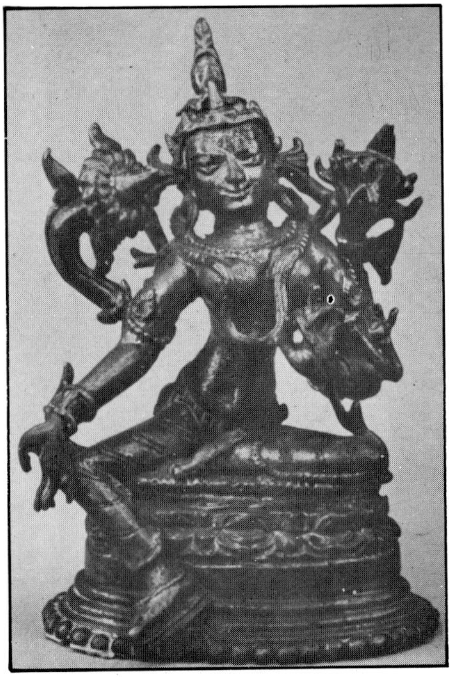

Pl. 5.2 Tara, Kāhilipārā, Guwahati

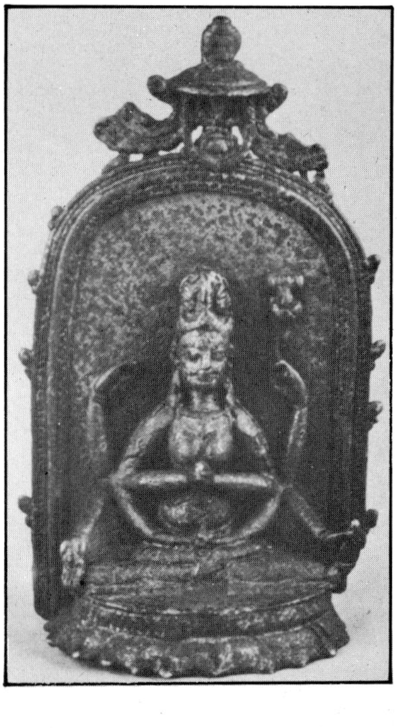

Pl. 5.3 Chuṇḍā, Kāhilipārā, Guwahati

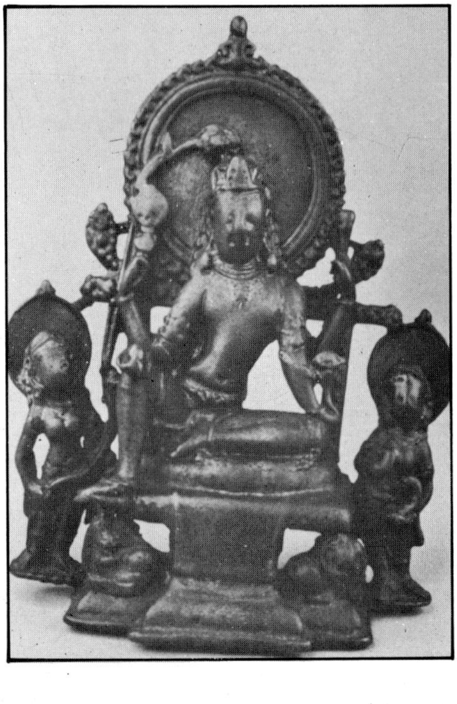

Pl. 5.4 Vishṇu, Kāhilipārā, Guwahati

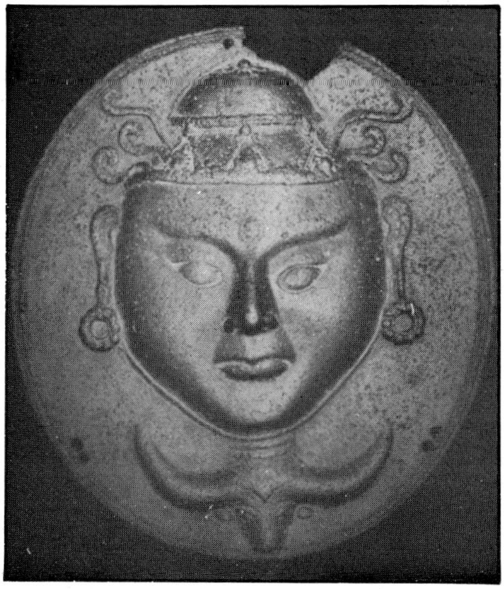

Pl. 5.5 Durga, Kāhilipārā, Guwahati

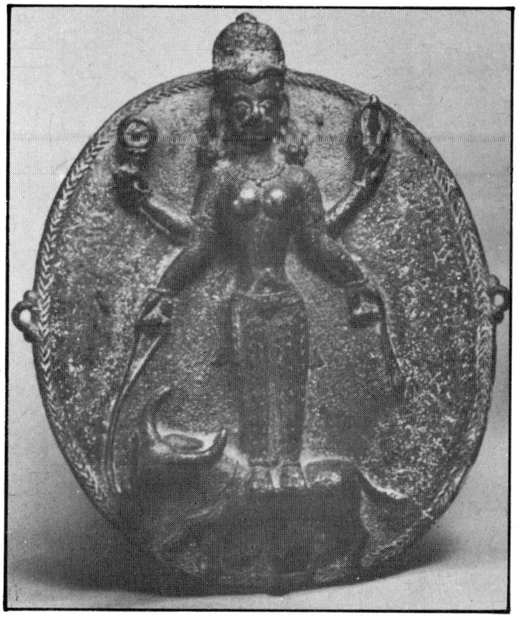

Pl. 5.6 Female Deity, Kāhilipārā, Guwahati

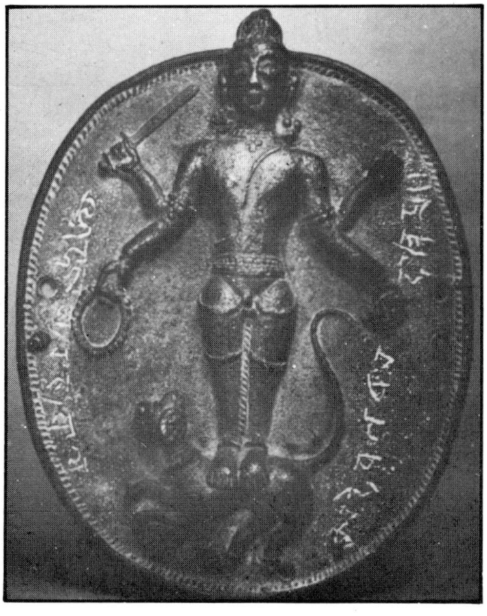

Pl. 5.7 Male Deity, Kāhilipārā, Guwahati

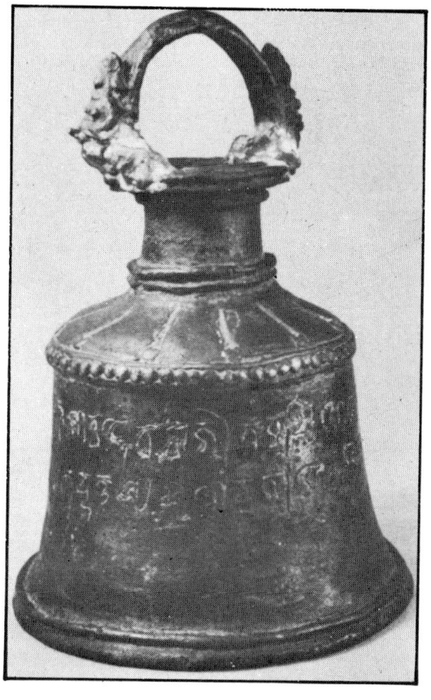

Pl. 5.8 Metallic-Bell, Kāhilipārā, Guwahati

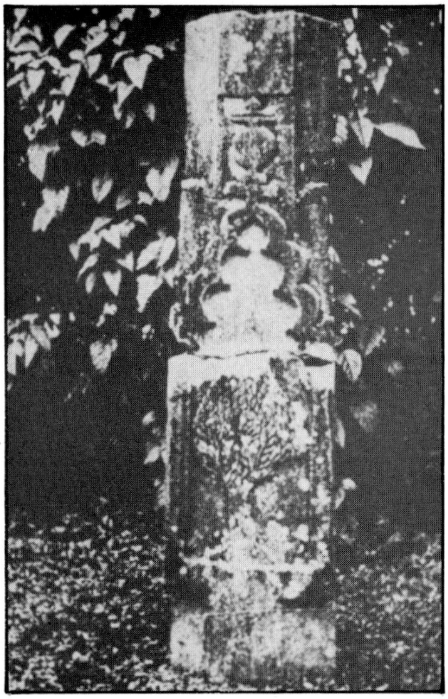

Pl. 6.1 Sculpture, Representing a Tree, Bargāng T.E.

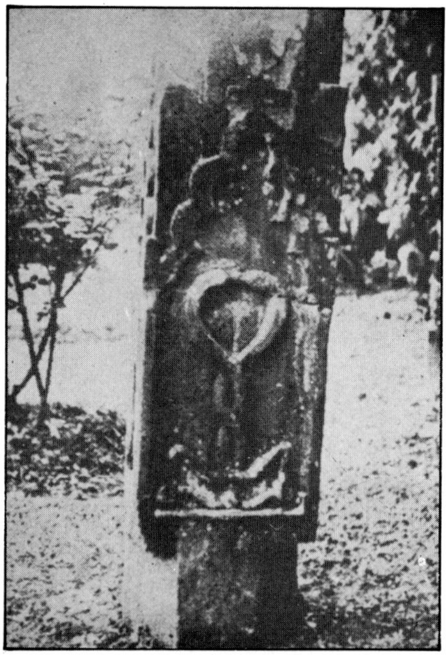

Pl. 6.2 Sculpture Representing Two Snakes, Bargāng T.E.

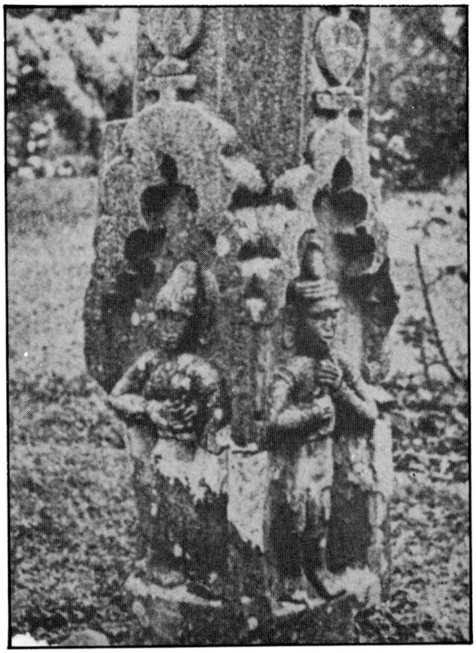

Pl. 6.3 Sculpture Representing a Male & a Female Figure, Bargāng T.E.

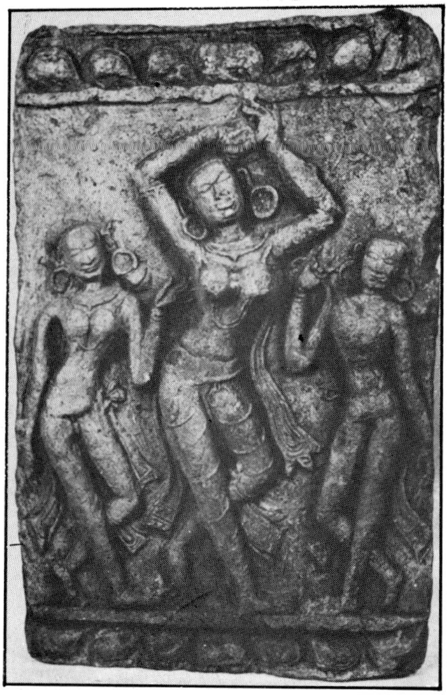

Pl. 8.1 A Female Figure Cheni-kuthi, Guwahati

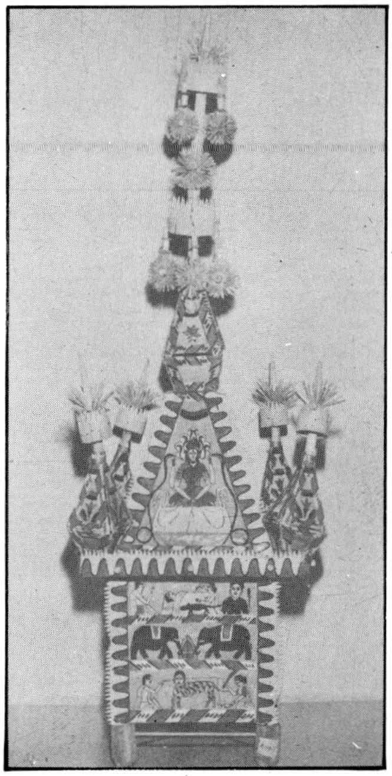

Pl. 9.1 An Alter or *Maju,* Object of the Rābhā Tribe

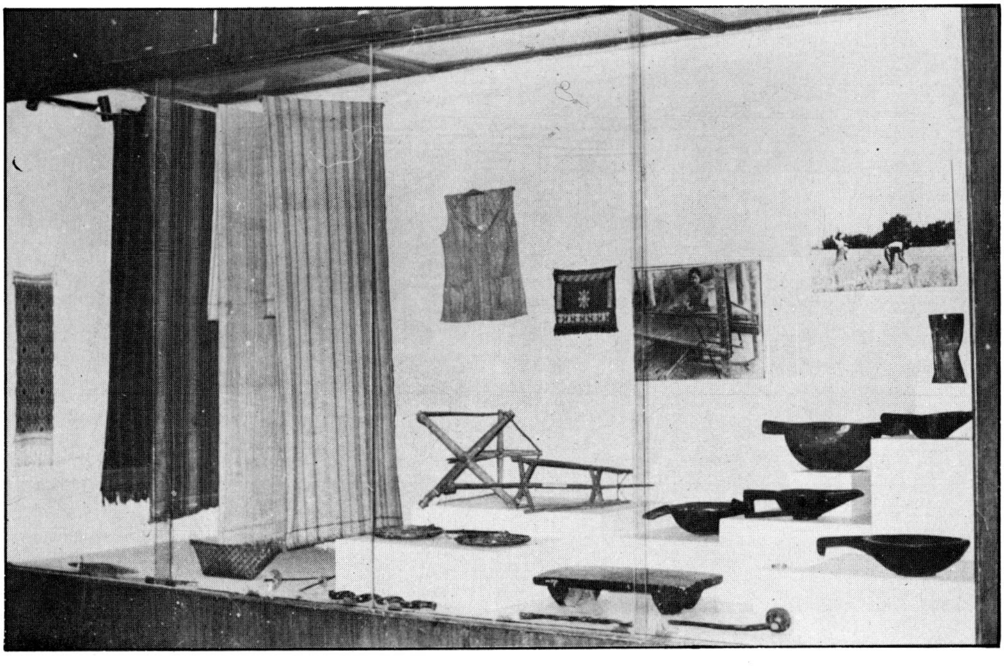

Pl. 9.2 Objects of the Bodo Tribe

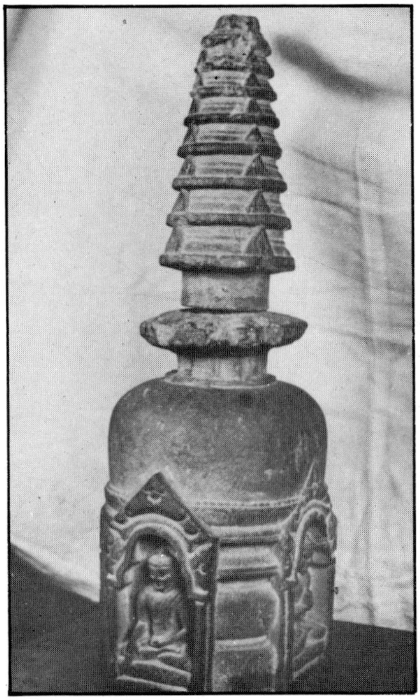

Pl. 11.1 Votive Stūpa, Bihar, preserved in the Assam State Museum

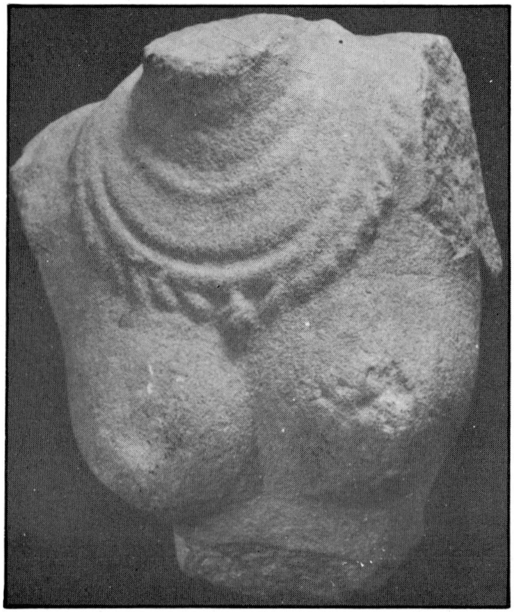

Pl. 18.1 Bust of a Female Figure Mikirāti, Nagaon District

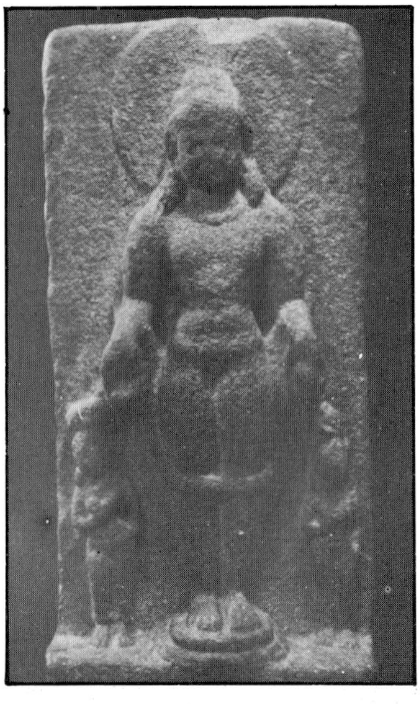

Pl. 18.2 Vishṇu—Khārāsākāl Pāra Dudhuoi, Goalpara District

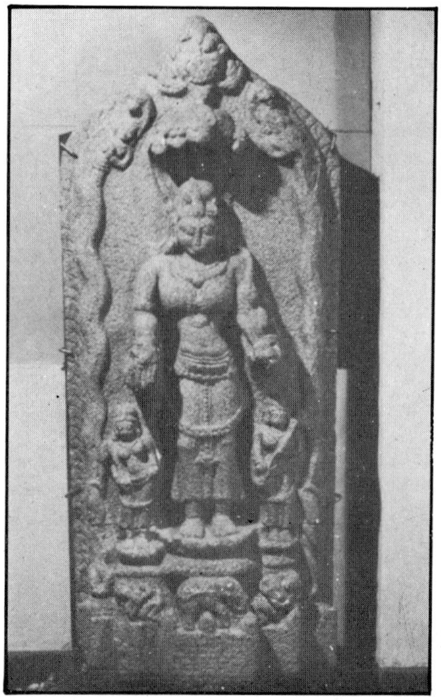

Pl. 18.3 Manasā-Kaliabor, Nagaon District

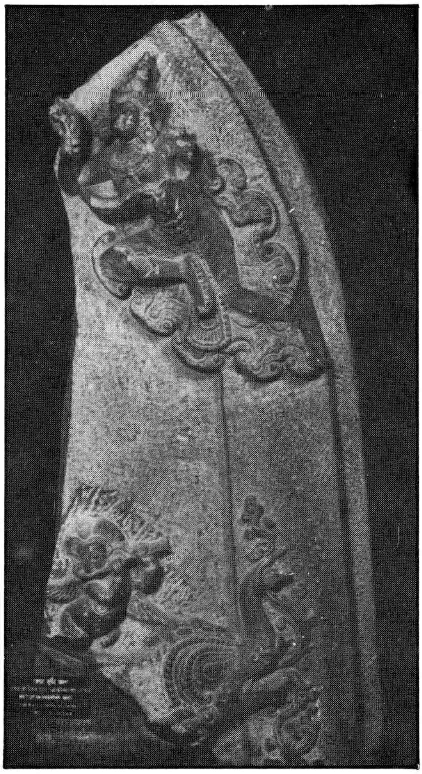

Pl. 18.4 Part of an Image of an Unknown Deity, Uzanbājār, Guwahti

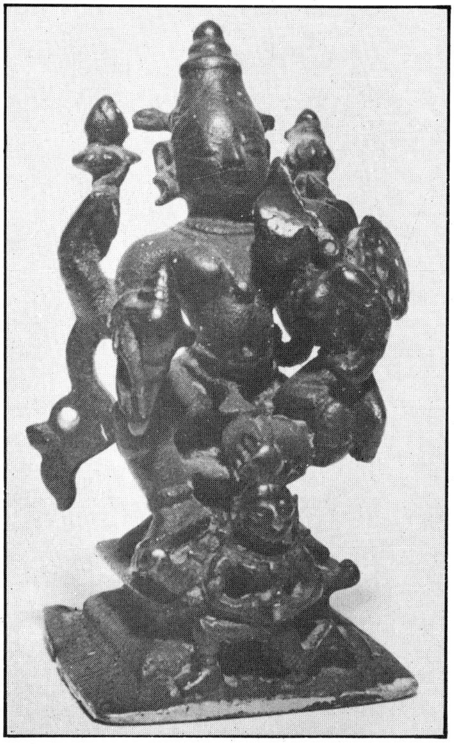

Pl. 18.5 Lakshmī-Nārāyaṇa, Kachumārī, Sibsagar District

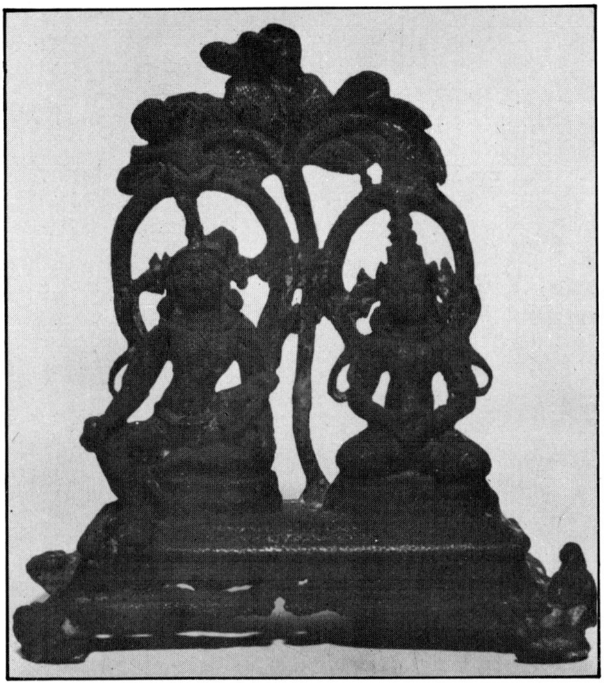

Pl. 19.1 Pārvātī-Lakshmī, Hahārā, Kāmarūpā District

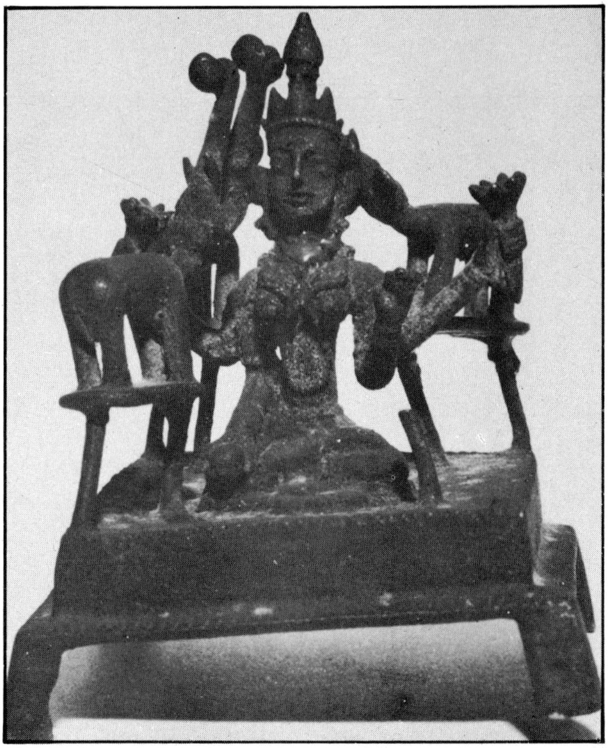

Pl. 19.2 Gaja-Lakshmī, Hahārā, Kāmarūpā District

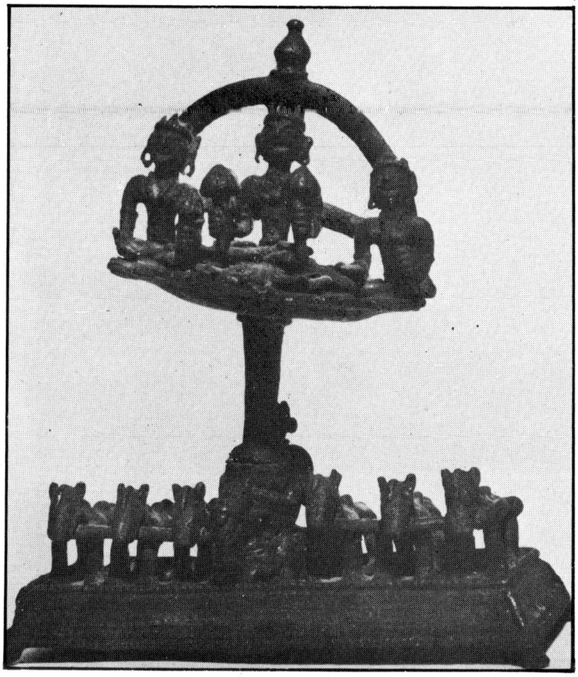

Pl. 19.3 Sūrya, Hāhāra, Kāmarūpa

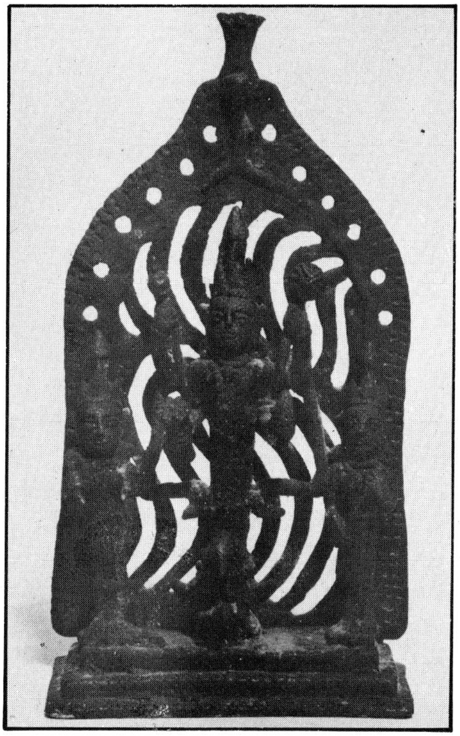

Pl. 19.4 Vishṇu, Hāhāra, Kāmarūp District

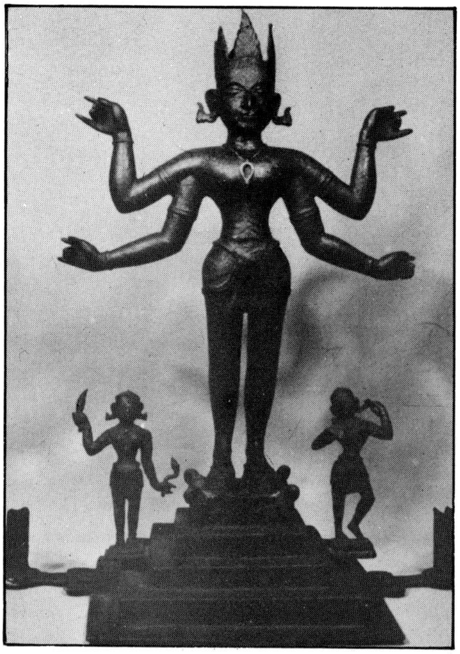

Pl. 21.1 Vishṇu, Lāruā Mouza

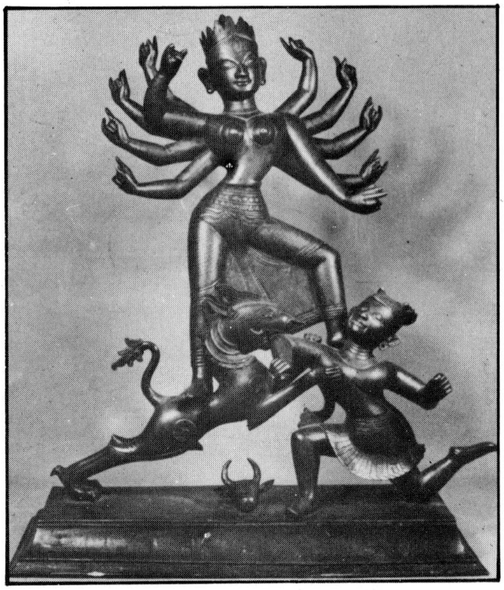

Pl. 21.2 Mahiṣamardinī—Tṛbhaṅga

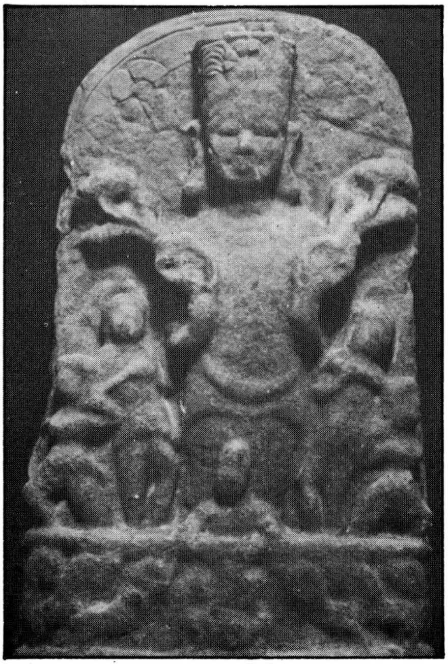

Pl. 22.1 Sūrya (Stone), Bilāsipārā,
Dhubri District

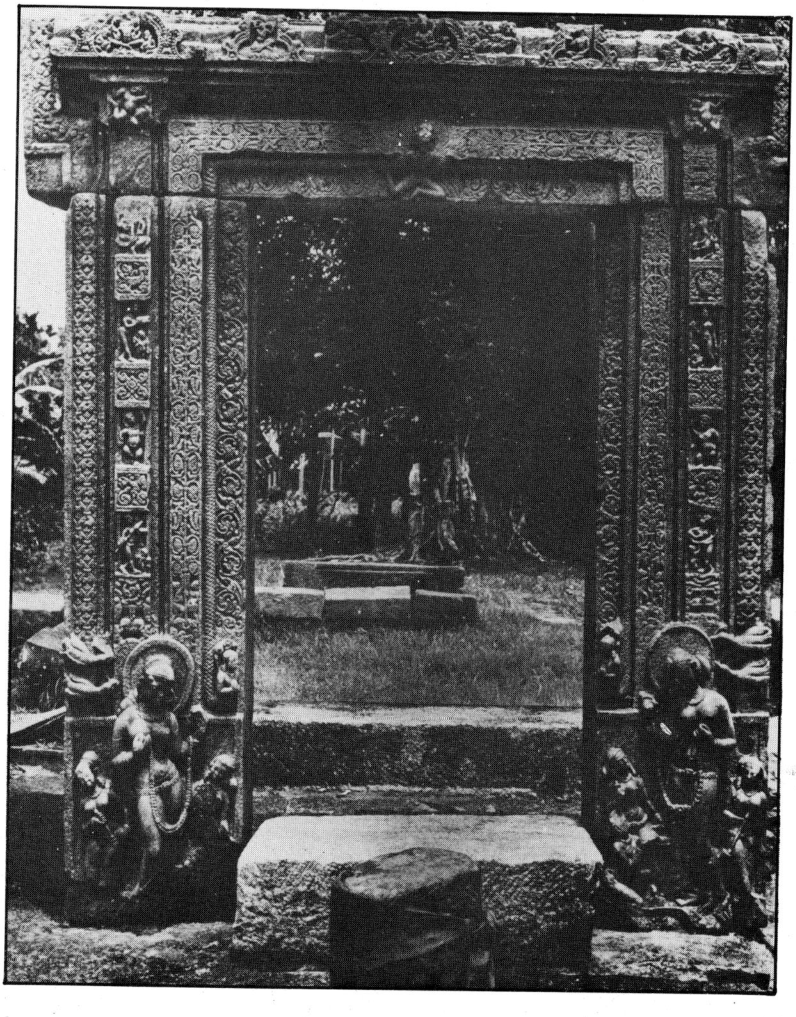

Pl. 25.1 Stone Door Frame

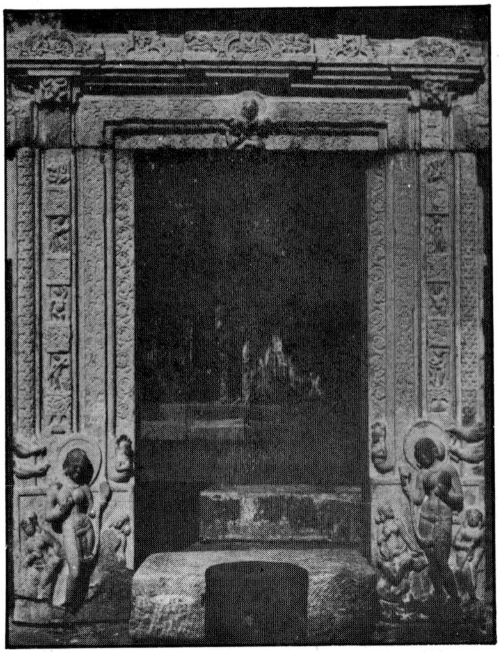

Pl. 25.2 Stone Door Frame

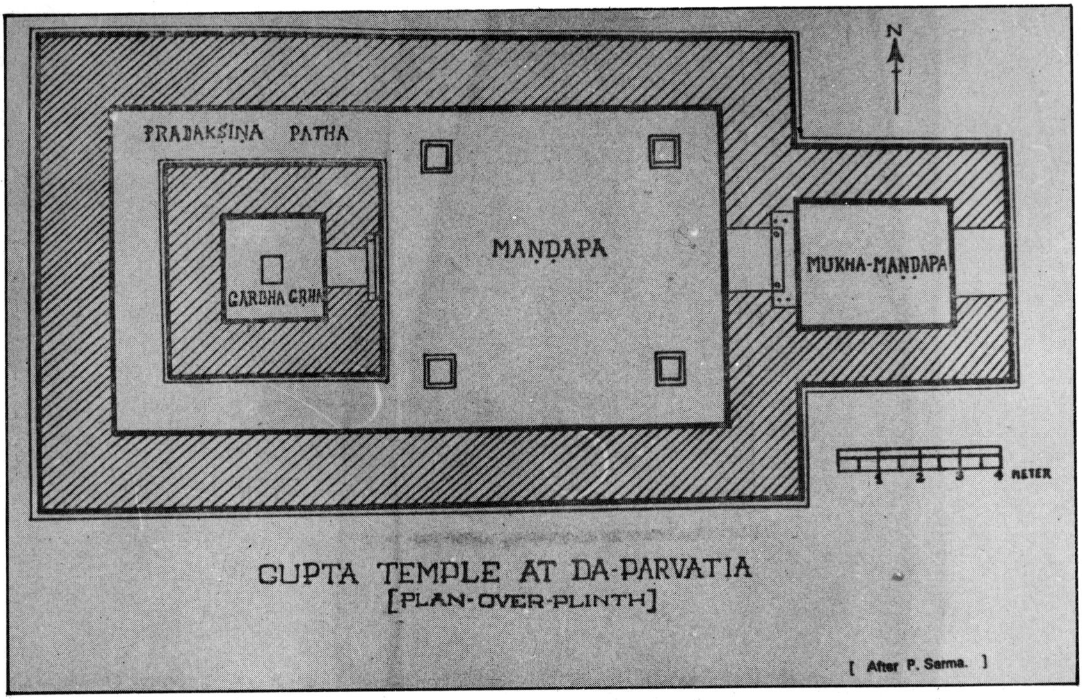

Pl. 25.3 Gupta Temple at Daparvatīā